PATERNOSTER THEOLOGICAL MONOGRAPHS

An American Augustinian

Sin and Salvation in the Dogmatic Theology of
William G. T. Shedd

PATERNOSTER THEOLOGICAL MONOGRAPHS

A full listing of titles in this series
appears at the end of this book

PATERNOSTER THEOLOGICAL MONOGRAPHS

An American Augustinian

Sin and Salvation in the Dogmatic Theology of William G. T. Shedd

Oliver D. Crisp

WIPF & STOCK · Eugene, Oregon

Wipf and Stock Publishers
199 W 8th Ave, Suite 3
Eugene, OR 97401

An American Augustinian
Sin and Salvation in the Dogmatic Theology of William G. T. Shedd
By Crisp, Oliver D.
Copyright©2007 Paternoster
ISBN 13: 978-1-55635-658-2
ISBN 10: 1-55635-658-7
Publication date 10/29/2007
Previously published by Paternoster, 2007

This Edition Published by Wipf and Stock Publishers
by arrangement with Paternoster

Paternoster
9 Holdom Avenue
Bletchley
Milton Keyes, MK1 1QR
Great Britain

PATERNOSTER THEOLOGICAL MONOGRAPHS

Series Preface

In the West the churches may be declining, but theology—serious, academic (mostly doctoral level) and mainstream orthodox in evaluative commitment—shows no sign of withering on the vine. This series of *Paternoster Theological Monographs* extends the expertise of the Press especially to first-time authors whose work stands broadly within the parameters created by fidelity to Scripture and has satisfied the critical scrutiny of respected assessors in the academy. Such theology may come in several distinct intellectual disciplines—historical, dogmatic, pastoral, apologetic, missional, aesthetic and no doubt others also. The series will be particularly hospitable to promising constructive theology within an evangelical frame, for it is of this that the church's need seems to be greatest. Quality writing will be published across the confessions—Anabaptist, Episcopalian, Reformed, Arminian and Orthodox—across the ages—patristic, medieval, reformation, modern and counter-modern—and across the continents. The aim of the series is theology written in the twofold conviction that the church needs theology and theology needs the church—which in reality means theology done for the glory of God.

Series Editors

David F. Wright, Emeritus Professor of Patristic and Reformed Christianity, University of Edinburgh, Scotland, UK

Trevor A. Hart, Head of School and Principal of St Mary's College School of Divinity, University of St Andrews, Scotland, UK

Anthony N.S. Lane, Professor of Historical Theology and Director of Research, London School of Theology, UK

Anthony C. Thiselton, Emeritus Professor of Christian Theology, University of Nottingham, Research Professor in Christian Theology, University College Chester, and Canon Theologian of Leicester Cathedral and Southwell Minster, UK

Kevin J. Vanhoozer, Research Professor of Systematic Theology, Trinity Evangelical Divinity School, Deerfield, Illinois, USA

For my parents

Contents

Acknowledgements	xiii
Abbreviations	xv
Introduction	1
A Biographical Sketch	1
Problems Facing the Modern Reader of Shedd	4
Overview of the Book	7
Concluding Remarks	10
Chapter 1	
In Defence of Traducianism	12
Shedd's Traducian-Realism	14
Creationisim and the Problem of Imputed Sin	16
Soul-Fission	17
Shedd on Human Nature	22
Critique of Shedd's Position	24
Shedd on Human Nature Once Again	24
Are Souls Fissiparous?	25
Creationism and Imputed Sin	33
Conclusions	35
Chapter 2	
Augustinian Realism and the Imputation of Sin	37
Some Terms of Reference	38
Augustinian Realism in Shedd and Strong	42
Charles Hodge's Idiosyncratic Federalism	49
Conclusions	54

Chapter 3
The Theanthropic Person of Christ — 56
Shedd*ing* the Classical Doctrine of the Person of Christ — 57
Traducianism, Realism and Christ's Human Nature — 66
Conclusions — 73

Chapter 4
The Impeccability of Christ — 75
The Argument from Scripture and the Person of Christ — 75
How an Impeccable Christ can be Tempted — 80
Three Problems for Shedd's Account — 87
Can Christ's Human Nature *be Peccable?* — 87
Can Christ's Human Nature be Peccable? — 88
The Paradox of Innocent Temptation — 95
Conclusions — 96

Chapter 5
Sin, Atonement and Representationalism — 98
Dogmatic Preamble — 98
Situating William Shedd's Views on these Matters — 102
Shedd*ing* Light on the Atonement — 103
Shedd's Historico-Theological Argument Against Consistent
Representationalism — 104
Shedd on the 'Two Unions' — 106
Shedd and Consistent Realism — 111

Chapter 6
The Nature of the Atonement — 115
An Outline of Shedd's Doctrine of Atonement — 116
Brümmer's Critique of Penal Substitution — 127
Conclusion — 136

Chapter 7
The Extent of the Atonement — 138
Shedd's Argument in *Dogmatic Theology* — 139
Clearing up Some Terminological Problems — 139
Unlimited Atonement, Particular Redemption — 140

Three Alternatives to Shedd's Position   142
The Extent of the Atonement and the 'Larger Hope' in *Calvinism:*
Pure and Mixed   146
The Number of those who are Saved   146
Reasons for Holding to the 'Larger Hope'   156
Objections to Shedd's Account   160

Conclusion: An Augustinian Vision of Sin and Salvation   **166**

Bibliography   **171**

Index   **179**

ACKNOWLEDGEMENTS

I am grateful to the following friends and colleagues who have helped me at various stages in the production of this volume: Claire Crisp, James Gibson, Alan Gomes, Paul Helm (who has read almost all the manuscript at least once), Mark Herzer, Daniel Hill, Steve Holmes, Mark Noll, Robin Parry, Michael Rea, Ethan Schrum, John Webster (who suggested I write this book), Maartin Wisse, Mark Wynn and Garry Williams.

Earlier versions of several chapters, or parts thereof, have been published previously, some of which have been considerably revised for the present volume. These include: 'Scholastic Theology, Augustinian Realism and Original Guilt' in the *European Journal of Theology* 13 (2004): 17-28; 'Federalism vs. Realism: Charles Hodge, Augustus Strong and William Shedd on The Imputation of Sin' in *International Journal of Systematic Theology* 8 (2006): 1-17; 'Shedding the Theanthropic Person of Christ' in *Scottish Journal of Theology* 59 (2006): 327-350; 'William Shedd on Christ's Impeccability' forthcoming in *Philosophia Christi* vol. 9 (2007); 'Sin, atonement and representationalism: Why William Shedd was not a consistent realist' in *Scottish Bulletin of Evangelical Theology* 24.2 (2006): 155-175; and 'Pulling traducianism out of the Shedd' *Ars Disputandi* 6 (2006), located at <http://www.arsdisputandi.org>. I am grateful to the editors and publishers of these journals for allowing this material, or parts of it, to be reproduced here.

Early drafts of the two chapters on the theanthropic person of Christ and the impeccability of Christ were written at the University of Notre Dame, USA, during a research fellowship in the academic year 2004-2005. I am grateful to the Director and fellows of the Center for Philosophy of Religion for their help and stimulation. The latter parts of the book were written on returning to the UK, and to academic life in another community, the Department of Theology and Religious Studies at Bristol University. I should like to thank my colleagues in the department for being so supportive in the period of transition and writing up, and especially to Gavin D'Costa, as Head of Department.

This book is dedicated to my parents, Christopher John Crisp and Julia Margaret Crisp, with love and gratitude.

ABBREVIATIONS

William Shedd wrote a number of works of theology, as well as works on literary criticism and history. There is no standard or critical edition of Shedd's works, although there is now a useful edition of Shedd's *Dogmatic Theology*. I have tried to work with editions of Shedd's works that are currently available, where that has been possible. Shedd reproduced a number of essays that appeared in his *Discourses and Essays* in *Theological Essays*, with minor alterations. I have used both collections in the present work. The following abbreviations are used throughout this volume, the bibliographical details of which are given at the end of the book:

CPM	*Calvinism, Pure and Mixed*
CR	*A Critical and Doctrinal Commentary on the Epistle of St. Paul to The Romans*
DE	*Discourses and Essays*
DT	*Dogmatic Theology, Third Edition*
HCD1	*A History of Christian Doctrine Vol. 1*
HCD2	*A History of Christian Doctrine Vol. 2*
LE	*Literary Essays*
OH	*Orthodoxy and Heterodoxy*
SNM	*Sermons to the Natural Man*
TE	*Theological Essays*

Introduction

William Greenough Thayer Shedd (1820-1894) is not a thinker on the lips of most theologians today, nor, I imagine, on their minds. Yet Shedd has been hailed as one of the most important systematic theologians America has produced.[1] This study is an attempt to stimulate greater interest in this nineteenth century dogmatician, by considering what he had to say about the nature of sin and salvation, two central aspects of the Christian faith that he thought about with considerable care. Shedd was a theologian in the Reformed tradition, and this marked his approach to each area of theology in a profound way. But he was not an uncritical Calvinist. Although what he has to say about these two dogmatic *loci* is very much of a piece with the western, Augustinian, theological tradition, he is at pains to distinguish what he has to say about sin and salvation in several important respects from many of those who would be natural theological bedfellows within his own theological tradition. In particular, Shedd distances himself from what he sees as 'later Calvinism' on the question of the origin of the soul, and the related matter of the propagation of original sin from Adam to his progeny.

A Biographical Sketch

Shedd's life is interesting, not least because his career spanned the Church and the Academy.[2] He was a minister in both Congregational and Presbyterian

---

[1] For example, 'the three greatest theologians which the American Church has yet produced are Jonathan Edwards, W. G. T. Shedd, and R. L. Dabney, and the careful student of the writings of these great masters in philosophy and theology can discern the kinship which exists between their imperial intellects and saintly hearts.' Thornton Whaling, 'Review of Shedd's Dogmatic Theology' in *Presbyterian Quarterly* 9 (1895): 323. In modern times Monica Grecu has said of Shedd's *Dogmatic Theology* that it ranks, 'second only to the work of Jonathan Edwards'. See 'William Shedd' in *American Literary Critics and Scholars, 1850-1880*, Monica M. Grecu and John W. Rathbun (eds.) (Detroit, MI.: Gale, 1988), p. 217. Both authors are cited by Alan Gomes in his editor's introduction to Shedd's *Dogmatic Theology, Third Edition* (Phillipsburg, NJ.: Presbyterian & Reformed, 2003), p. 33, n. 70, who concurs with Grecu in her assessment of Shedd. All citations from Shedd's *Dogmatic Theology* will be from this edition, which supersedes previous editions of the same work. I shall refer to it in footnotes as DT, followed by page number.

[2] There is at present no standard biography of Shedd. What biographical resources there are, are rather piecemeal. See, for instance 'Shedd, William Greenough Thayer' in *Notable Americans, A Biographical Dictionary*, ed. Rossiter Johnson, Vol. IX (Boston, MA: The Biographical Society, 1904) – sadly, not entirely accurate on points of detail.

polities, and held an appointment as a professor of English Literature (publishing a major critical edition of the works of Samuel Taylor Coleridge in seven volumes [1853]) as well as several quite different theological appointments, covering homiletics and practical theology, church history, what today would be called biblical criticism, and systematic theology.

Shedd was a son of the manse. His father, Marshall Shedd, was a Congregationalist minister, who had married Eliza Thayer, the daughter of a wealthy Bostonian merchant. William was born in Acton, Massachusetts on June 21st, 1820. He matriculated to, and, four years later, successfully graduated from the University of Vermont with his bachelor's degree in 1839. Shedd's later work was marked by the influence of his mentor at Vermont, the philosopher James Marsh, whose interest in Romanticism and Coleridge, as well as the philosophical thought of the Cambridge Platonists, made a lasting impression on Shedd and is reflected in Shedd's emphasis on the importance of the historical spirit in the development of ideas.[3]

After graduation, he moved to New York City, where he taught in a grammar (high) school for a year. During this period he professed Christian faith whilst attending a Presbyterian church. This led Shedd to follow in his father's footsteps, and leave school teaching to take up ordained ministry. To this end, he entered Andover Theological Seminary, from where he graduated in 1843. Andover was one of the principle centres for ministerial training in the US at this period, alongside Yale Divinity School, and Shedd was trained by some of the most able theological minds of the time. Of particular importance

---

See also Robert T. Handy, 'Shedd, William Greenough, Thayer' in *American National Biography,* eds. John A. Garraty and Mark C. Carnes (New York: Oxford University Press, 1999). This is a more reliable guide to the outline of Shedd's life. Similar material is presented by Monica M. Grecu in her essay 'William G. T. Shedd', in *American Literary Critics and Scholars, 1850-1880*. There is also relevant biographical material to be found in two works on the history of Union Theological Seminary, in New York City, one of which was published fairly recently. See Robert Handy, *A History of Union Theological Seminary In New York* (New York: Columbia University Press, 1987) and George L. Prentiss, *The Union Theological Seminary* (n.p.: 1899). The most accessible recent treatment is Alan Gomes' biographical sketch that prefaces his edition of Shedd's *Dogmatic Theology*. See Gomes, 'A Historical and Theological Introduction to W. G. T. Shedd and His Dogmatic Theology' in DT: 16-36. Another useful source is Cushing Strout, 'Faith and History: The Mind of William G. T. Shedd' in *Journal of the History of Ideas 15* (1954): 153-162.

[3] This has been noted by Cushing Strout in 'Faith and History: The Mind of William G. T. Shedd', and more recently by Ethan Schrum in an unpublished paper, 'Evolutionary Metaphysics, Presuppositional Methodology and "Old Calvinist" Theology: The Unusual Blend of William G. T. Shedd's Philosophy of History in the Intellectual Tempests of Nineteenth-Century America'. For the importance of James Marsh, see for example Bruce Kuklick, *Churchmen and Philosophers, From Jonathan Edwards to John Dewey* (New Haven, CN: Yale University Press, 1985), ch. 10 and Louis Menand, *The Metaphysical Club* (London: Harpercollins, 2002), ch. 10.

for Shedd's theological development was the influence of Leonard Woods, who was a defender of Old School Presbyterianism at Andover when it was a seminary renowned for its connection to the New England tradition of Edwardsian revivalist theology. Shedd remained committed to a conservative, but progressively more idiosyncratic brand of Calvinistic theology that was deeply influenced by traditional Presbyterian theology, even when it made matters rather difficult in controversies with other members of faculty at Union Theological Seminary later in his life. He was ordained on January 4th 1844 and moved from the Boston area to become the Congregationalist pastor in Brandon, Vermont, for two years.

Shedd married Lucy Ann Myers of Whitehall, New York, on October 7th, 1845, the same year in which he moved from the pastorate to his first academic appointment, as professor of English Literature at his *alma mater*, the University of Vermont. The study of English Literature was then a relatively new branch of the humanities, Shedd's appointment being one of the first in the subject in North America. His marriage to Lucy yielded four children.

He remained at Vermont for seven years, before making another change of career, to his first theological appointment as Professor of Sacred Rhetoric and Pastoral Theology at Auburn Theological Seminary. He stayed there for only two years (1852-1854), before moving to his old theological school, Andover Seminary, where he was made Brown Professor of Ecclesiastical History and Pastoral Theology, a position he occupied for eight years. During this period he laid the theological foundations for much of his later work, particularly his *History of Christian Doctrine* and his *Dogmatic Theology*, both of which display his mastery of much of the patristic, medieval and reformation theological traditions. It is worth noting that as Shedd was instilling traditional Reformed thinking into his students that would not have been out of place at the Princeton Theological Seminary of Charles Hodge or Benjamin Warfield, Edwards Amasa Park was initiating students at Andover in the New Haven tradition of New England theology.[4] Shedd and Park remained theologically at variance during their time teaching together at Andover. Shedd was firmly Old School in his Calvinism – although not at this time, Presbyterian in his polity. By contrast, Park was in the 'Edwardean' tradition of New England Congregationalism. This was a matter that divided them in a number of important areas of theology, particularly the doctrine of original sin and the nature and scope of the atonement. Yet both men retained good collegial relations with one another.

Nevertheless, in 1862, Shedd moved from Andover to act as assistant

---

[4] See, for example, Park's highly regarded anthology on New England theology, *The Atonement* (Boston, MA.: Congregational Board of Publication, 1859). Judicious selections from Park's contribution to New England theology can be found in *The New England Theology, From Jonathan Edwards to Edwards Amasa Park*, eds. Douglas A. Sweeney and Alan C. Guelzo (Grand Rapids, MI: Baker Academic, 2006), Part 8.

minister in a Presbyterian congregation at Brick Presbyterian Church in New York City, alongside Dr Gardiner Spring. The move was precipitated by Shedd's increasing dissatisfaction with what he perceived to be the theological latitudinarian tendencies of New England Congregationalism, represented on the faculty of Andover (including, one presumes, that of Park). As well as a change of tack in his career, this involved an ecclesiological shift, from the Congregationalist polity he had grown up in, to a Presbyterian one. He remained committed to Presbyterianism for the rest of his life.[5]

He stayed at Brick Presbyterian Church for about a year – a short ministerial sojourn – before returning to academic theology, this time as the first Baldwin Professor of Biblical Literature at Union Theological Seminary in New York City. He was to remain at Union for the remainder of his academic career, moving into the Roosevelt Chair of Systematic Theology in 1874. Auburn Theological Seminary honoured Shedd with the Doctor of Divinity degree (DD), in 1857, and in 1876 the University of the City of New York conferred upon him the Doctor of Laws degree (LLD). He was made an emeritus professor at Union in 1890, but continued to teach there for a further three years, whilst the Seminary sought to appoint his successor. However, his health eventually failed and he retired from active teaching responsibilities. During his retirement he defended the Westminster Confession of Faith in several polemical works, directed against the revisionist tendencies within his own Presbyterian denomination.[6] He died in New York City on November 17th, 1894, aged 74 years, just a few months after completing the somewhat miscellaneous supplemental volume to the two earlier volumes of his *Dogmatic Theology* of 1888.

Problems Facing the Modern Reader of Shedd

Contemporary reflection on the work of an historical figure is fraught with difficulties. To what extent do the social and cultural assumptions of nineteenth century America impinge upon, or affect, what Shedd has to say? To what extent is Shedd an heir of a particular theological tradition? Who are his principle interlocutors? Are there important ways in which his thinking on a given topic is a response to a particular historical situation? These

---

[5] Gomes cites John DeWitt observing that Shedd 'felt entirely at home in the Presbyterian Church. Not only was he a high and pronounced Calvinist; but he believed that a Church should be organized by and committed to a system of religious truth; and that in its organization it should prove adequate means to secure the fidelity of its teachers to the system.' DT: 18, citing John DeWitt, 'William Greenough Thayer Shedd, D.D., LL.D.', in *Presbyterian and Reformed Review* 5 (1895): 310.

[6] See William G. T. Shedd, *Calvinism; Pure and Mixed* (New York: Schribner and Sons, 1893, reprinted by the Banner of Truth, 1988) and *Proposed Revisions of the Westminster Standards*, (New York: Schribner and Sons, 1890).

historiographical questions are important, but not ones that form a large part of this volume.

Instead, we shall focus on the dogmatic, or theological content of some of the central strands of Shedd's theology (for present purposes, I shall use the terms 'dogmatic' and 'theological' interchangeably). That is, we shall concentrate on the arguments Shedd puts forth in defence of what he sees as the defining contours of a coherent and orthodox theological understanding of the nature of sin and the atonement. I have endeavoured to pursue this project bearing in mind the distance that separates Shedd from the modern reader, his particular nineteenth century sensibilities and the theological influences upon him. Theology, for better or worse, is intimately bound up with a tradition (although its concerns are not only historical). It is in many ways a conversation with theologians of the past in the pursuit of new ways of presenting the gospel for the present.[7] As the twentieth century Swiss theologian Karl Barth put it,

> To study theology means not so much to examine exhaustively the work of earlier students of theology as to become their fellow student. It means to become and to remain receptive, for they still speak, even though they may have died long ago.[8]

This book is such a conversation, with one particular interlocutor. Our concern will be to interrogate Shedd: Why do you think this? What does this mean? Does it make sense? Of what continuing relevance is this? And I think this sort of inquiry is particularly appropriate for the work of a theologian like Shedd who was deeply concerned with doing theology in a way that was steeped in the tradition. He was nothing if not an interrogator of the past, rooting out those theological ideas he found conducive to his own theological concerns, even if it meant standing against the tide of theological opinion amongst his theological peers.

It certainly cannot be said of Shedd that his work was fideistic or theologically positivist. To put the same thought another way, he assumed theology must be done in the broader context of other intellectual disciplines, all of which are pursued to the glory of God. He did not think that theology is the only intellectual discipline which speaks truthfully about God, and that all other subjects are only worthwhile to the extent they reflect this theological

---

[7] At least, that is how it seems to me, although I concede that not everyone will agree. I owe this way of thinking about the nature of dogmatics to Steve Holmes, although he will be the first to admit, he is not the only person to have said sometime like this – I recall Machiavelli saying something similar about his own work in relation to history in *The Prince*. For examination of this 'listening to the past' motif, see Stephen R. Holmes, *Listening to The Past, The Place of Tradition in Theology* (Carlisle: Paternoster Press, 2003), particularly the first and last chapters.
[8] Karl Barth, *Evangelical Theology: An Introduction*, trans. Grover Foley (London: Fontana, 1965), p. 161.

commitment (just as the logical positivists of mid-twentieth century philosophy thought that only philosophy pursued in a particular, empiricist tradition carried any intellectual weight). His conversation partners included a wider group of thinkers than many theologians do today. So, for instance, it is not uncommon to find him citing Shakespeare or Milton or Coleridge in the same breath as Augustine or Odo of Tournai or Turretin, treating literary and theological, as well as philosophical ideas with equal seriousness. This catholicity of sources matches an overall catholicity in his thinking. Shedd is not afraid of embracing the mainstream of the Christian tradition. His is a properly Augustinian theology in the full-blooded sense of that term (although he would have preferred the somewhat anachronistic term 'elder Calvinistic theology'). Despite the fact that he is an heir of Reformed theology and, in particular, the theology of Reformed Scholasticism, he does not write as a schoolman. His prose has a pellucidity that is rare in much systematic theology. He has the directness of a Calvin and the philosophical thoroughness of an Anselm, but without the method of, say, an Aquinas or a Scotus (which is not to say the scholastic method is not a useful way of conducting theological discourse). But he manages to retain a philosophical acuity in the way he presents his arguments even though he avoids the more philosophical method of scholastic theology.

He was, undoubtedly, a philosophical theologian, much of whose early career had been spent immersed in Coleridgean idealism, to which he remained committed in later life.[9] (He was not, in this respect, like other theologically conservative Calvinistic theologians of the time, many of whom advocated Scottish common sense realism.[10]) But this should not be taken to mean that Shedd was a thinker whose only interest in Scripture was to make it fit his own procrustean bed of philosophical ideas. Of course, no systematic theology is without its blind spots, and there is much to disagree with in Shedd as with any

---

[9] Shedd edited an edition of Coleridge's works whilst on faculty at Vermont. The abiding influence of the idealism he imbibed from Coleridge and his teacher James Marsh, can be seen in several later pieces of work, such as his essay 'The Nature, and Influence, of The Historic Spirit' in his *Theological Essays* (Eugene, OR.: Wipf and Stock, 2001 [1877]), and a number of articles in the collection *Literary Essays* (Eugene, OR.: Wipf and Stock, 1999 [1878]), including 'Coleridge as a Philosopher and Theologian'.

[10] The common sense realism that reigned at Princeton is well known and documented. See, for example Bruce Kuklick's essay in *Charles Hodge Revisited: A Critical Appraisal of His Life and Work* eds. John W. Stewart and James H. Moorhead (Grand Rapids, MI: Eerdmans, 2002) and his earlier work in Kuklick, *Churchmen and Philosophers*, ch. 5. The contours of Shedd's idealism and his debt to Coleridgean romanticism is treated with great thoroughness in Mark A. Herzer's unpublished 2003 Westminster Theological Seminary PhD thesis, entitled 'The Influence of Romantic Idealism in the Writings of William Greenough Thayer Shedd'. The bibliographical information on editions of Shedd's works in Herzer's thesis is also invaluable.

other theologian. But Shedd was very much a biblical as well as systematic thinker (we have already noted that he was a professor of New Testament literature at one point in his career, before he became a dogmatic theologian). And this is reflected in the way he approaches particular theological problems. So, for instance, when he deals with the person of Christ, say, or the doctrine of original sin, or eschatological problems with everlasting punishment in hell, he is always concerned with what Scripture says. What bearing does the biblical witness have upon this matter? What theological and metaphysical resources can we bring to bear upon the whole council of God in order to unpack what it teaches? Whether or not we are convinced by what Shedd has to say, it is clear that this was his intention, even if, on occasion, he goes well beyond the letter (if not the spirit) of Scripture.

Overview of the Book

Shedd is unequivocally a defender of traducianism. This is the idea that the soul is somehow transmitted from one generation to the next just as genetic material is passed on from parents to their children. He also held to a version of Augustinian realism, which is roughly the idea that Adam's progeny are somehow metaphysically united with Adam so that God is perfectly just in treating Adam's offspring as punishable for Adam's sin. These two metaphysical notions, both espoused by Augustine and many of his theological heirs, have not always been popular amongst Reformed theologians, who, for the most part, (but with some notable exceptions) moved away from the explicitly realist language of Augustinianism, tending to speak instead of the imputation of Adam's sin and of Adam's role as representative of the human race. Shedd argues that the earlier Reformed thinkers were more Augustinian on both of these matters than later Reformed divines. He also argues that there are good theological reasons for preferring a broadly Augustinian way of thinking about the origin of the soul and the transmission of original sin, than its (later) Reformed alternative. We shall consider Shedd's defence of traducianism in the first chapter of this volume. His arguments for Augustinian realism form the basis of the second chapter, using two other nineteenth century theologians, the Prinetonian Charles Hodge and the Baptist Augustus Strong, as foils for the development of Shedd's particular brand of this realist doctrine.

What is interesting about Shedd's defence of these two interrelated notions is the way in which he embraces the consequences they have for other aspects of his dogmatic theology, particularly what he has to say about the nature of salvation. So, for example, Shedd is unafraid to trace traducianism into his Christology, and deals head-on with the problem it poses for his doctrine of the theanthropic (God-Man) person of Christ. The problem is this: Christ is said to have a human nature which is, at least in part, derived from the substance of the Virgin Mary. Yet, according to a traducian way of thinking, this means Christ inherits not only the physical characteristics of the Virgin's DNA, but also some 'psychical' or 'soulish' aspect too. But then, Christ has a soul that is tainted with original sin, just as the soul of the Virgin was and the souls of all her ancestors going back to Adam. As he sets out his account of the theanthropic person of Christ Shedd has an ingenious argument that circumvents this difficulty for his own position, a matter that we shall come to in chapter three.

But Shedd's theological acumen extends beyond his defence of traducianism and Augustinian realism. He also offers an interesting argument in favour of the traditional theological idea that Christ was not merely without sin, but incapable of sinning. This is in keeping with the biblical idea that Christ was like us in every way, 'sin excepted'.[11] There are problems with his argument, but even if his reasoning is not deemed to be entirely convincing, it represents a careful and forthright defence of the impeccability of Christ, which also makes a real effort to deal with the humanity and peccability of Christ's human nature. This Christological problem has an obvious bearing on the relationship between sin and salvation. If Christ is not impeccable, that is, incapable of sinning, how can he be divine? Yet if he is not capable of sinning, how can he be truly human? To put this last point somewhat differently, if Christ cannot feel the 'gravitational pull' of temptation, he cannot truly know what it is to be like us in every way, sin excepted. But, for Christ to be the saviour, it is not sufficient that he remained sinless although he could have sinned. For then, according to Shedd and the Augustinian tradition of which he was a part, Christ was capable of behaving in ways that a divine person is not. For God, according to classical theology *cannot*, not merely *may not*, sin.[12] Such matters are taken up in chapter four.

The relationship between the atonement and original sin is the subject of chapter five. In Romans 5: 12-19, the Apostle Paul famously compared the work of Adam and Christ and the effect each had upon the human race. This comparison has been the subject of considerable theological discussion.[13] Many Reformed theologians have taken the view that Adam's role as the representative of the human race is mirrored by Christ's role as the representative of those he has come to save. As Adam represents his progeny, who suffer as a result of his primal sin, so Christ represents those human beings he comes to save (usually, in Reformed theology, some number less than the totality of humankind – the elect). Shedd's defence of Augustinian realism

---

[11] 'For we do not have a High Priest who cannot sympathize with our weaknesses, but was in all points tempted as we are, yet without sin.' Hebrews 4:15. Cf. Hebrews 2:18.

[12] For biblical references traditionally thought to support this doctrine see, Habakkuk 1: 13, 2 Cor 5: 21, I John 1: 5 and 1 John 3: 9.

[13] Shedd offers an exegetical argument for this Augustinian reading of Romans 5 in his commentary on Romans, entitled *A Critical and Doctrinal Commentary on the Epistle of St. Paul to The Romans* (Eugene, OR.: Wipf and Stock, 2001 [1879]), pp. 110-144.

means he does not think that Adam acts as a mere representative of the human race. But he does think Christ acts in a representative role in the atonement. This raises an interesting theological question: Why does Shedd not go further and endorse a consistently 'realist' way of thinking about the 'two Adams'? Although Shedd offers a number of reasons for thinking that realism cannot apply to the atonement as he thinks it does to the imputation of Adam's sin, and although the idea of a 'consistent realist' alternative to Shedd's position does have to overcome a number of serious theological obstacles, there may be more to this view than is often thought. I shall suggest that there may be reason to think a consistent realism worthy of more serious consideration than Shedd devoted to it.

Shedd's discussion of the nature of the atonement is also worthy of attention. He cashes out his representationalist understanding of the atonement in a version of the penal substitution doctrine. This is the view that Christ atones for sin by becoming a substitute for those he came to save, taking upon himself the punishment due for the sins of fallen human beings (which Shedd, understood to mean some number less than the totality of humanity). In setting forth some of the central aspects of Shedd's version of penal substitution, we shall tackle the question of whether Shedd's thinking on this matter has any ongoing significance, by bringing what Shedd says into dialogue with the work of one recent critic of penal substitution, the Utrecht philosophical theologian, Vincent Brümmer. I argue that, although Shedd's version of penal substitution is not without difficulties, his account represents a robust version of the doctrine that is able to withstand almost all the criticisms Brümmer raises for the penal subsitutionary theory of atonement. This comprises chapter six.

A final chapter considers Shedd's understanding of the extent of the atonement and its relationship to the so-called 'larger hope'. This is the belief, touted by several prominent nineteenth century Calvinists including Shedd, that the number of the elect will greatly exceed the number of reprobate. Shedd maintains that the atonement is unlimited, or universal in scope, but restricted in application - a characteristically idiosyncratic way of construing the principle, going back to the great medieval theologian, Peter Lombard, which states *the atonement was sufficient for all but efficient only for some*.[14] Taken together these claims in Shedd's thinking are cashed out in surprising ways. He thinks that all infants that die in immaturity are amongst the elect; that a large number of those who have no knowledge of the person and work of Christ will be amongst the elect; and that this comports with biblical prophecy about the

---

[14] Peter Lombard, *IV Libri Sententiarum*, ed. Ignatius Brady OFM, 2 Vols. *Spicilegium Bonaventurianum 4-5*. (*Grottaferrata: Editions Collegii S. Bonaventurae Ad Claras Aquas*, 1971-1981), *3. 20. 3*. There he says, 'Christus ergo est sacerdos, idemque et hostia pretium nostrae reconciliationis; qui se in ara crucis non diabolo, sed Trinitati obtulit pro omnibus, quantum ad pretii sufficientiam; sed pro electis tantum quantum ad efficaciam, quia praedestinatis tantum salutem efficit.'

culmination of world history - again, in common with a number of Reformed theologians who have taken an optimistic view of biblical prophecy in these matters. Thus, for Shedd, commitment to an Augustinian notion of particular election and reprobation need not mean that divine grace is restricted to some small remnant of humanity. It is consistent with a much more hopeful way of thinking about the nature of salvation that includes far more of humanity than is excluded. And this is tied into the nature of Christ's atoning act: it is inconceivable for Shedd that such a glorious event should have less than stupendous consequences for the number of human beings reconciled to God.

Our consideration of Shedd's thinking on sin and salvation closes with some reflections upon the nature and success of his theological project, in the conclusion. I argue that although Shedd's consideration of these two doctrinal *loci* is not without difficulties – indeed, serious problems in some instances – his contribution to theological science is an important one that should not be overlooked. Though he came to conclusions that many will find unusual or theologically unpalatable, what he says about these matters forces those who read his work to think though their own theological assumptions with greater care than they might have done previously. And in a number of different areas, such as his doctrine of the nature and scope of the atonement, or his doctrine of Christ's impeccability, what he has to say has continuing merit as a positive contribution to theology. Even where his ideas seem a little strange or outdated to modern ears, his conclusions are invariably supported by careful thinking about the issues under consideration.

Concluding Remarks

Some years ago, Robert Jenson wrote a book in which he laid out the theology of Jonathan Edwards in short compass. It was, as the title suggested, 'A Recommendation' of, 'America's Theologian'.[15] Edwards was undoubtedly one of the towering intellects of the western theological tradition. But Shedd was also a thinker worth contending with, who was like Edwards in several respects. Both men possessed minds schooled in philosophical as well as theological ideas; both moved from Congregationalist backgrounds to Presbyterianism late in life; both held a number of different appointments in the Church and Academy; and both were theologically independent thinkers, preferring unfashionable ways of thinking to the mainstream of their own theological tradition. Today, there is a growing academic industry devoted to

---

[15] See Robert W. Jenson, *America's Theologian: A Recommendation of Jonathan Edwards* (New York: Oxford University Press, 1988).

the explication and application of Edwards' theological legacy.¹⁶ There is no comparable literature on Shedd.¹⁷ Of course, Shedd is not Edwards, just as Colin Gunton is not Karl Barth. But among the 'great cloud of witnesses' Shedd's voice should be heard; what he has to say is important and worthy of consideration. It is hoped that this volume may go some way to stimulating interest in Shedd's work, which is helped by the new edition of Shedd's *Dogmatics*, edited by Prof. Alan Gomes, that has made access to his *magnum opus* much easier for the current generation of theological students. If, as a result of the writing of this volume more theologians turn to Shedd when considering a particular issue, as they currently turn to Karl Barth, John Calvin, Martin Luther, Thomas Aquinas, John of Damascus or Augustine, then the main objective in composing this work will have been achieved.

---

[16] An interesting review article of recent work on Edwards has been written by Kenneth P. Minkema, and is entitled, 'Jonathan Edwards in the Twentieth Century' in *Journal of the Evangelical Theological Society* 47 (2004): 659-687.

[17] I mean there is no comparable industry devoted to Shedd's work. There are scattered references to Shedd in the literature, and one or two articles on aspects of his thinking or theology. There are also one or two unpublished PhD dissertations which treat Shedd's work in detail, but very little else.

CHAPTER 1

In Defence of Traducianism

One of the most important contributions that William Shedd made to systematic theology was his vigorous defence of a version of traducianism. This is the notion that the souls of human beings are not created individually and *ex nihilo* by divine fiat, but rather, are propagated from one generation to the next, just as the physical part of a human being is propagated from one generation to the next.[1] The alternative view, that God creates the soul of each individual out of nothing at the moment that individual begins to exist, is called creationism.[2] There are several ways this could be understood depending on when it is thought human life begins. It might be that individual human beings begin to exist from conception, when ensoulment (i.e. the possession by a soul of a body) occurs. But it might be thought that the human zygote begins to exist and is only ensouled at some later time *in utero*. Both of these views have been taken in the tradition, and both could be construed along creationist lines (although they need not be).[3] What makes a particular view of the origin of the soul creationist, rather than traducian,[4] is the idea that God creates the soul out of nothing at the first moment the individual human begins to exist. Whether this moment is at conception, or some later time is a separate, though related

---

[1] Unless otherwise stated, in what follows the noun 'soul' refers to human souls only.

[2] Lynne Rudder Baker states that in the early church there were three competing views of the soul: creationism, traducianism, and pre-existence – the doctrine that God has a 'stock of souls from eternity and allocates them as needed'. We shall not consider pre-existence as a theory of the origin of the soul, because it is not a view that is supported by Scripture, and is usually thought to be unorthodox. See Baker, 'Death and the Afterlife' in William J. Wainwright (ed.), *The Oxford Handbook of Philosophy of Religion* (Oxford: Oxford University Press, 2005), p. 370 ff. Shedd considers and rejects pre-existence in several places. See Shedd, *A History of Christian Doctrine, Vol. II* (Eugene, OR.: Wipf & Stock, 1999 [1864]), pp. 3-10 and Shedd, DT: 430-431.

[3] The theologian most often associated with a 'delayed ensoulment' version of creationism in the tradition is Thomas Aquinas. For discussion of this issue, see David Albert Jones, *The Soul of The Embryo* (London: Continuum, 2004).

[4] It might also be worth pointing out that the creationism in view here is not to be confused with the 'creationism' that has to do with a particular view of the origin of the world and the creation narratives of Genesis 1-3.

issue, and one that we shall ignore.[5]

Famously, theologians have been divided on the question of the origin of the soul, and some, like Augustine, were unable to decide which view of this matter is the correct one.[6] What makes Shedd's contribution important is the clarity and rigour of his defence of traducianism, rather than any particular originality in his argument. (Shedd is quick to admit at various points in his argument, his own debt to earlier Reformed theologians such as Jonathan Edwards, John Owen and Francis Turretin.)

In this chapter I propose to give a critical account of several aspects of Shedd's doctrine with particular reference to his treatment of the subject in his *Dogmatic Theology*,[7] the mature statement of his theological views. We shall not consider everything he has to say on the subject in detail. Our focus is on the way in which Shedd attempts to overcome philosophical-theological problems for traducianism presented by creationists on the one hand and what he calls 'representationalists' on the other.[8] In this context, representationalism is the doctrine that Adam is somehow the representative or 'federal head' of humanity, and that his primal sin is imputed to his progeny, whom he represents in this action.[9] Shedd argues that representationalism is false, and

---

[5] Although, for the record, it is clear Shedd maintained that human foetuses are ensouled from the moment of conception. See DT: 471.

[6] For discussion, see Herman Bavinck, *Reformed Dogmatics Vol. II, God and Creation*, trans. John Vriend, ed. John Bolt (Grand Rapids, MI: Baker Academic, 2004), pp. 580 ff.; Gerrit Berkouwer, *Man: The Image of God*, trans. Dirk W. Jellema (Grand Rapids, MI: Eerdmans, 1962), ch. 8; Heinrich Heppe, *Reformed Dogmatics*, trans. G. T. Thomson (London: Collins, 1950), ch. XI; Jones, *The Soul of The Embryo*, chapter 7; and Francis Turretin, *Institutes of Elenctic Theology Vol I*, trans. George Musgrave Giger, ed. James T. Dennison, Jr. (Phillipsburg, NJ: Presbyterian and Reformed, 2002), pp. 477-482. As Bavinck points out, 'the argument between traducianism and creationism remained undecided in Christian theology'. Moreover, 'in the strength of their arguments traducianism and creationism are almost equal' (pp. 580-581).

[7] Shedd deals with traducianism elsewhere and we shall refer to his other work in this area where it is pertinent. See, his essay, 'The Doctrine of Original Sin' in *Discourses and Essays, Revised Edition* (Andover, MA.: Warren F. Draper, 1870 [1856]) reprinted by The University of Michigan University Library in the *Michigan Historical Reprint Series*, n.d., pp. 259 ff. Shedd's HCD2 offers a much more sustained treatment of the issues, that complements what he has to say in DT. There is also relevant material in Shedd, CR: 119-142, where he exegetes Romans 5: 12-19.

[8] In DT Shedd's presentation of traducianism is divided into three areas. These comprise biblical, theological and physiological arguments. The focus of this chapter is on his theological arguments in particular, although the section on physiological arguments will be touched upon, where it has a bearing upon the theological.

[9] Representationalism also applies to the doctrine of the atonement, as Shedd points out elsewhere in DT: 461 ff. An atonement theory is representationalist where Christ is thought to act as my representative, taking upon himself the penal consequences of my sin, which is a central theme of the penal substitutionary understanding of the

that Adam's sin is really my sin. Hence, he links commitment to traducianism (souls and bodies are passed down mediately from our first parents) with commitment to a particular theological account of the imputation of original sin, known as Augustinian realism. This, very roughly, is the view that Adam's sin is (somehow) my sin because we are both parts of one metaphysical whole, created by God. Of course, there is conceptual overlap between traducianism and Augustinian realism, and most often theologians who are committed to one of these doctrines are also committed to the other (although, as Shedd points out, there are exceptions to this, such as Francis Turretin. See DT: 458). It may be that some doctrines about the manner in which sin is transmitted imply traducianism. But not all versions of Augustinian realism require traducianism. Nevertheless, Shedd defends both of these doctrines. In a similar fashion, theologians who defend representationalism usually also hold to creationism (viz. the origin of the soul), although it is possible to be both representationalist and traducian. In this chapter, we shall be concerned with Shedd's traducianism rather than his Augustinian realism, *per se*, which is the subject of the succeeding chapter. However, where the latter is informative for Shedd's account of the former, we shall have to deal with it as well.

We shall proceed in two stages. In the first, Shedd's version of what we might call traducian-realism is set out. In the process, we shall consider his arguments against what I shall dub creationist-representationalism – the main alternative to his own position that he deals with.[10] In a second section, I shall offer some critical comments on Shedd's defence of traducianism.

Shedd's Traducian-Realism

Shedd thinks that humanity is a species that originates with Adam and Eve:

> Traducianism applies the idea of species to both body and soul. Upon the sixth day, God created two human individuals, one male and one female, and in them also created the specific psychico-physical nature from which all the subsequent individuals of the human family are procreated both psychically and physically. (DT: 431)

---

atonement, a doctrine Shedd defends. So, in one respect, Shedd himself is a representationalist in the matter of the atonement, but not in the matter of the imputation of Adam's sin. We will consider this aspect of Shedd's thinking in the fifth chapter.

[10] This is not the only logically possible alternative, of course, but it is the alternative that Shedd spends his time dealing with. We shall see that it is possible for a theologian to be both a creationist and an Augustinian realist.

Our first parents contained, as it were, the whole of human nature that is propagated to subsequent generations of human beings. And, as it is propagated, human nature is dispersed, or divided as each new individual human being is generated. So, each new human being has his or her own particular individual nature. But each individual human being is also one part of a much larger entity, namely, humanity. To make this clear, consider the example of a lump of clay and a piece of stoneware made from the lump (an image Shedd himself uses at one point in DT: 470). The lump of clay is rather like the human nature that is had by Adam and Eve. As the first human pair, they have the whole of human nature, just as the lump of clay is a whole lump of clay – no clay has yet been removed from the lump to form individual pieces of pottery. But consider what happens when the potter does remove a small piece of the lump of clay to make a stoneware cup. He gouges out the smaller lump from the larger lump, and forms it on his wheel into a cup, which he then fires and sells. The cup is still a part of the original lump of clay, or what was a part of the original lump. It is also the particular receptacle into which the potter has formed it. We might say that the cup is a small part of the greater whole, that is, the original lump of clay. But it is also a particular thing, the individual cup. And the more cups are made from the original lump, the more the original lump is divided up into the different receptacles into which the clay is formed.

In a similar way, Shedd claims that Adam and Eve 'contain' the whole of human nature. But as they begin to procreate, that human nature is propagated. Cain, Abel, Seth and every other human being is like the cup formed from the original lump. Like the cup, the progeny of the first human pair are individual entities in their own right, but also 'contain' a small part of the human nature their parents had as a whole. And, as each new generation is formed, so each parental pair passes on both genetic and, to use Shedd's phrase, 'psychical' material to their progeny. Moreover, like the lump of clay, the 'lump' of Adam's nature out of which individual humans are formed is diminished with each division. Thus Shedd:

All the individuals of a race can be propagated only from the first two individuals. Should an individual pair be taken at the middle of the series it would be impossible to derive as much population from them as from Adam and Eve. And the reason is that they do not contain the whole specific nature, but only a portion of it.... There is a constant diminution of the primitive nonindividualized human nature when once its division and individualization begins at conception. (DT: 490)[11]

---

[11] Shedd thinks of a species as a generic nature that is created by God and exemplified by different individuals of the species. Human nature is had by Adam an Eve *in toto*, and 'spread' by propagation to individuals, in whom 'fractions' of this nature are

Creationists and traducians share in common the idea that the physical parts of a human being are passed on through procreation from parent to child. My body is formed from the fusion of the gametes of my parents, producing a genetically unique individual.

The difference between the two views lies in the question of the generation of the soul. Assuming human beings are composed of a body and soul, is the soul also passed from parent to child as the traducians claim? Or does God create each new soul for each new individual? Shedd presents several theological reasons for thinking that the traducian view (or a version of the traducian view) is correct.[12]

Creationism and the Problem of Imputed Sin

The first of these is that traducianism, when coupled with Augustinian realism, yields a coherent picture of the transmission of original sin from one generation to the next whereas a creationist-plus-representationalist view of the same problem, does not. In his *Dogmatics*, Shedd returns to this problem again in the context of his anthropology and his Christology. But in his discussion of traducianism proper (in DT: 429-493), Shedd argues that the problem with the creationist-representationalist view is that it cannot account for the transmission of that which is essentially 'mental' (which I think we can charitably take to be a euphemism for the soul). He says,

> If each individual soul never had any other than an individual existence and were created *ex nihilo* in every instance, nothing mental could pass from Adam to his posterity. There could be the transmission of only bodily and physical traits. There would be a chasm of six thousand years [sic] between an individual soul of this generation and the individual soul of Adam, across which "original sin" or moral corruption could not go "by natural generation". (DT: 446)

Shedd thinks that some creationist-representationalists, like the Genevan Reformed Orthodox theologian Francis Turretin, realise that their own view leaves them without a satisfactory solution to the problem of the transmission of sin, and introduce elements of a traducian-realist view into their own thinking in order to augment the creationist-representationalism they start out with. 'Hence', says Shedd, 'the creationist partially adopts traducianism' (DT:

---

individualized. Compare the following: 'A species or a specific nature is that primitive invisible substance or plastic principle which God creates from nonentity, as the rudimental matter of which all the individuals of a species are to be composed.' (DT: 465) It is not entirely clear whether Shedd thinks this sort of metaphysical arrangement is restricted to human beings, as bearers of the divine image, or includes other created species as well.

[12] He also presents a biblical case for traducianism, in DT: 438-444, citing passages like Ps. 139, Acts 17: 26 and Heb. 7: 10 in favour of the traducian position.

447). But this cannot work, because 'natural union [viz. Augustinian realism] logically excludes representation, and representation logically excludes natural union. Either theory by itself is consistent; but the two in combination are incongruous.' (DT: 449)

The problem seems to be this. Creationism posits the creation of each new soul by God for each individual human being. But, Shedd says, this means that only the physical part of a human being is passed from one generation to the next through procreation. How then can we explain the transmission of original sin from one generation to the next? Not according to creationism, says Shedd, because on the creationist view, original sin cannot be transmitted from one soul to the next in the same way as genes are passed from one generation to the next. The soul of each individual is created *ex nihilo*; the parents of each individual do not transmit it. But then, Adam's fall has no bearing on my own sinfulness because his sin and my sin are distinct (presuming, as it seems Shedd does, that original sin is a property of the soul, not the body). In fact, as Shedd points out, on the creationist view it appears that each soul apostatises from God by itself. 'Upon the theory of creationism, the withdrawal of the Holy Spirit from the newly created soul is an arbitrary, not a judicial act.' What is more the 'so-called guilt of obligation to penalty (*reatus poenae*), on the ground of which the withdrawment of grace rests [in classical theology], is putative and fictitious, not real. It is constructive guilt – the product of an act of sovereign will which decides that an innocent person shall be liable to penal suffering because of another's sin.' (DT: 456-457)

The creationist-representationalist view means that Adam's progeny are punishable for a sin that they are not culpable for. Their souls are not passed down from the first human pair, so they cannot partake of the guilt of Adam's sin. Hence, on Shedd's way of thinking, they cannot be culpable for Adam's sin. But, says Shedd, this is intolerable – liability to punishment *presumes* culpability. Christ, unlike the sinner, may be said to be punishable for my sin although he is not culpable for my sin. But this is no counter-example according to Shedd, because Christ, unlike the sinner, volunteers to act in this manner. The sinner has no choice in the matter of inheriting original sin (DT: 457).

But traducian-realism does not suffer from this problem with the transmission of sin. According to traducianism, the soul is somehow transmitted from one generation to the next as the physical parts of a human are. This, coupled with a realist explanation of original sin means that my sin really is Adam's sin because my human nature, that is, my human body and soul, are generated from the same human nature that originated with Adam and Eve, our first parents.

Soul-Fission

But this raises a second issue, to do with the nature of the souls traducianism posits. This has to do with how an immaterial substance, a soul, can be transmitted from one generation to the next in the same way that my genetic material was passed to me at the moment the gametes of my parents fused. Are souls entities that are fissiparous? If so, are individual souls generated when they 'split off' from the soul of the parent(s)?[13] Shedd would appear to be committed to both of these claims. He thinks that the soul and body of a child is derived simultaneously 'out of the common human nature' (DT: 478). Return to the analogy of the clay. Adam has the complete human nature (the large lump of clay). Subsequent generations of human beings are literally 'chips off the old block', or 'bits of the old lump (of clay)'. It is rather like thinking that each son of Adam was a lump of clay and their offspring were bits of clay removed from them, and so on for each generation. All human beings are composed of a human nature – a body and soul – that is a small part of the original human nature had by Adam and Eve.[14]

Now, on the question of the propagation of souls from the first human pair, Shedd says that traducians need not claim either (a) that the soul is originated by propagation, or (b) that the soul is transmitted by physical propagation (DT: 478-479). On the first of these matters, the soul of a given individual is, says Shedd, a 'fraction' of the original soul given to Adam by divine fiat. So each individual soul is not originated in the act of propagation, but is a fraction of the first soul, generated by God for Adam that is somehow individualised in the moment of procreation. This would appear to mean that souls are indeed fissiparous.

This account needs to be distinguished from another similar view that is not consistent with Shedd's position. For instance, it would appear to be consistent with much of what Shedd affirms (though not all) to say that every human being has a 'part' of one indivisible human soul held in common by the species. This would be rather like saying the one Holy Spirit is participated in, or possessed, by many different believers. Just as one entity (the Holy Spirit) indwells many other entities (Christians), so the one human species soul

---

[13] An earlier, and cruder, argument similar to this in some respects is given by Tertullian. See Tertullian, *On The Soul*, § 25 in *Latin Christianity: Its Founder, Tertullian, Ante-Nicene Fathers Vol. III*, trans. P. Holmes, eds. A. Roberts and J. Donaldson (Grand Rapids, MI: Eerdmans, 1981 [1885]).

[14] Elsewhere, in a brief discussion of traducianism in his essay 'The Doctrine of Original Sin' in DE, Shedd has this to say: 'If, however, the distinction between creation and development be clearly conceived and rigorously observed, it will be seen that there is no danger of materialism in the doctrine of the soul's propagation. For development cannot change the essence of that which is being developed. It must unfold that, and only that, which is given in creation. Now, granting the creation of the generic man in his totality of soul and body [viz. Adam], it is plain that his mere individualization by propagation must leave both his physical and spiritual natures as it found them, so far as this distinction between mind and matter is concerned. For matter cannot be converted into mind my mere expansion, and neither can mind be changed into matter by it.' (p. 259, footnote.)

'indwells' or 'possesses' many different human bodies. If this way of thinking about Shedd were correct (which it is not), then his view would not require souls to be fissile, since there would be only one species-soul shared between different human beings. But, since this would conflict with other things Shedd says concerning species and species-natures – matters which we have already touched upon - I think we can exclude such a reading of Shedd's account. In any case, it would surely be unorthodox to say that all human beings have only one species-soul in which every human being has a share, or part thereof. And Shedd was certainly a stickler for theological orthodoxy.

We come to the second matter. Shedd denies that the soul is propagated by the physical act of procreation. This, it would seem, is an attempt to stave off criticism that traducianism makes the soul into some property of the body, what today would be called property-dualism, or double-aspect theory. But if this motivates his denial, it would appear to be wide of the mark. It could be that human gametes are 'carriers' of soul-stuff as well as DNA, which, when symgamy takes place, generates a new immaterial, as well as material, substance.[15]

Shedd also objects to the hylomorphist view[16] propounded by Odo of Tournai (DT: 484).[17] Odo's view is complicated, not least because it is embedded in a thoroughly medieval account of different species of souls and their propagation, which seems rather arcane to the modern reader. For instance, in the third book of his treatise *On Original Sin*, Odo says this:

---

[15] Something like this view is advocated by J. P. Moreland and Scott B. Rae in *Body and Soul, Human Nature and The Crisis in Ethics* (Downers Grove, IL: IVP, 2000), p. 221. Is this clearly a case of traducianism? Not necessarily. It might be that human gametes *generate* soul-stuff that they then 'carry', and which, if fused with another human gamete, will yield a genetically new individual with an embryonic soul that is formed from the soul-stuff carried by the gametes in some way analogous to the fusing of genetic material in syngamy. Such a position would be a version of emergent dualism that was creationist, rather than traducian. Nevertheless, the Moreland-Rae proposal could be taken along traducian lines, and it is this sort of reasoning that Shedd overlooks.

[16] This is the Aristotelian view of the relation between body and soul, which states that the soul is the form of the body. That is, the soul organizes the body into which it is integrated, rather like the lump of clay has to be 'organised' into the shape of a cup, or plate, by the potter. On a hylomorphist way of thinking, the lump of clay is 'matter', whereas the vessel into which it is shaped, is the 'form' that organises the clay/matter. In a similar way, the soul gives form to the matter of the body, according to hylomorphist accounts of the soul-body relationship. It is not clear that Shedd rejects hylomorphism as such, although he objects to Odo's hylomorphism.

[17] Odo of Tournai presents a sophisticated account of the origin of the soul, which is now more widely available in translation. See Odo of Tournai, *On Original Sin and A Disputation With The Jew, Leo, Concerning The Advent of Christ, The Son of God, Two Theological Treatises,* trans. Irven M. Resnick (Philadelphia, PA: University of Pennsylvania Press, 1994).

> A soul comes from a soul through a seed [*semen*], just as its body is propagated by its seed from a body, or a tree from a tree. Thus [they say that] the seed power is in the soul, just as in the body.

Odo's point here seems to be that souls are self-propagating as bodies are, and that like bodies, souls are generated from some sort of 'seed'. He elaborates on this point later in the same passage, where he seems to suggest that the soul's seed nourishes the seed of the body into its particular form (as per hylomorphism):

> Therefore, the body's seed draws with itself the seed of the soul, namely the power of growth, which power nourishes the corporeal seed into a human form, the power growing with it into a rational soul. As a result, just as a particle which is not a human body flows from the human body in sowing the seed, so a particle which is not a human soul flows from a human soul like the seed.[18]

Shedd cites this passage, and glosses Odo as follows:

> The merely material and physical semen is rationalized and spiritualized by the mental life which ejects it, so that the human embryo becomes both psychical and physical, animal and rational, while the brute embryo remains only physical and animal. (DT: 485, n. 4. 1. 2)

But if Shedd denies this particular traducian account of the propagation of human souls – which, aside from the medieval language, presents an interesting argument for traducianism - what does he propose to replace it with? It is not clear. He does say that 'it is no valid objection to the doctrine of existence in Adam and in foregoing ancestors that it is impossible to explain the mode' (DT: 481). The fact is, says Shedd, the mode of the transmission of souls from one generation to the next is mysterious. This does not mean that traducianism, or Augustinian realism, is false.

But will this do? There are aspects of many Christian doctrines, the origin of the soul included, that are mysterious, and Shedd is right to point this out. After all, it is very difficult to make sense of matters pertaining to objects that are essentially immaterial. We have no means by which to ascertain many of the properties of such entities, unless they are revealed to us (by God), because they are literally nowhere, or at no place where we can examine them – they have no physical extension.[19] And, notoriously, there is very little in Scripture

---

[18] Odo, *On Original Sin*, pp. 70 and 71 respectively.

[19] *Pace* Thomas, who believed the soul is 'located' where the body whose form it is, is located. See Eleonore Stump, 'Non-Cartesian Substance Dualism and Materialism without Reductionism' in *Faith and Philosophy* 12 (1995): 512, and, amongst moderns, William Hasker, who thinks the soul is located somewhere in the central nervous system (see *The Emergent Self* [Ithaca: Cornell University Press, 1999]). Roderick Chisholm even postulated that the soul is a very small entity somewhere in the brain! See Philip L.

about the manner in which souls are propagated.[20] So Shedd's appeal to mystery at this point in his argument might not be an unprincipled one, although it is rather frustrating that he draws a veil over this particular aspect of his position when he has felt free to speculate about other issues in the neighbourhood of the question of the soul's origin. And, in particular, it is frustrating that he makes this move without offering some account of how such immaterial objects might be fissile.

Indeed, we might want to enquire on what principled basis Shedd *can* reject Odo's account of the mode of the soul's propagation, if we cannot know how souls are disseminated because such matters are mysterious. I suppose it could be argued that one can reject an obviously false option without pretending to know what the content of the right option might be (although Shedd does not make this move).[21] But, although he seems unhappy with Odo's position, Shedd does not explain why Odo's view is to be rejected. And it certainly does not seem to be obviously false. He does comment that Odo's introduction of the notion that material seed is made 'psychical' by the action of an individual soul upon it in the act of propagation is 'not an improvement' but 'introduces difficulties' that do not obtain with Augustine's version of the doctrine – whose view he finds more conducive to his own traducianism (DT: 484). But that is all he really says on the matter.[22] And this seems inadequate. For all Shedd knows, Odo's answer to this question is the right one. At least, Shedd offers no argument against Odo's view beyond these piecemeal comments, which makes it difficult to see why Shedd thinks Odo's account is so wrong about the mechanism for traducianism. In any case, Odo's solution does have this virtue: it offers a carefully plotted explanation of the mode of the soul's transmission from one generation to the next, that avoids the crass caricatures that often pass for traducianism, thanks to the likes of Tertullian.[23]

Quinn, 'Tiny Selves: Chisholm on the Simplicity of the Soul' in Lewis Hahn, (ed.), *The Philosophy of Roderick Chisholm* (LaSalle, IL: Open Court, 1997), pp. 55-67.

[20] There is material relevant to whether souls are propagated, which Shedd picks up in his section on the biblical material that supports his traducianism in DT: 438-444. But this is a different matter from the manner or mode of that propagation. It is on this matter that Scripture is (arguably) silent – or, at least, metaphysically underdetermined.

[21] Example: An extra-terrestrial life form is discovered frozen in the artic permafrost in a spacecraft that crashed on the planet many years ago. Where did the creature originate? We do not know, but we do know (through various experiments on its physical structure, what the craft is composed of, and so on) that it did not originate on earth.

[22] Mark Wynn has suggested to me that Shedd's rejection of Odo's view might be more to do with his fear that Odo says too much about the nature of traducianism, whereas Augustine recognises that traducianism is inherently mysterious and wisely refrains from elaborating the doctrine.

[23] This raises the following question, How can Christ have a sinless human nature if his human soul and body are derived from the sinful human body and soul of his mother (assuming her body and soul were sinful)? Shedd offers a brief answer in DT: 475. He

But even if it is thought that Odo's account is unworkable (perhaps because his scholastic metaphysics are outmoded, or unpalatable), there may be other, similar ways of construing the mode of the soul's propagation that offer useful ways of thinking about this matter. And, for all we know, one such explanation, if coherent, might also be the truth of the matter.[24] Shedd may be right that the mode of the soul's transmission is mysterious, but I do not see how this particular aspect of the cluster of issues pertaining to the origin of the soul is any more mysterious, or any less speculative, than other aspects of the problem that Shedd feels perfectly happy to pronounce upon. Shedd's comments here do seem rather *ad hoc*. But perhaps we can fill in the conceptual gap Shedd wants to leave in his account of traducianism with something like Odo's view of the mode of the soul's transmission, or some alternative story that yields an unequivocally traducianism conclusion on this matter that does not seem incoherent.[25]

Shedd on Human Nature

A third issue in Shedd's account of traducianism has to do with what human nature consists in, and, therefore, what it is that is passed on from one generation to the next. I will deal with this more briefly than the previous points, because I have covered this material in more detail elsewhere.[26]

Shedd denies that human nature is a property of a substance – a view that he imputes to Charles Hodge (DT: 469). Instead it is, he thinks, a substance in its own right. In fact, human nature consists in a human body and soul, which, as Shedd makes clear, each human being consists of, from the earliest stage of human development. 'Man at every point in his history, embryonic as well as fetal, is a union of soul and body, or mind and matter.' (DT: 471). And, of course, it is a condition for most versions of traducianism – though not a necessary condition of traducianism as such - that human beings have a soul

---

takes it up again in his discussion of Christology. We shall come to this matter in a later chapter. In brief, Shedd's argument is that the Holy Spirit sanctifies Christ's human body and soul at the very moment of miraculous conception.

[24] I have already sketched one such possibility: human gametes are carriers of soul-stuff, which, at the moment of syngamy, generates a new soul as the complement of the new genetic individual thereby generated. This soul-stuff is a 'part' of the soul of the parent, just as the DNA transmitted with the gamete is a physical 'part' of the human parent. Thus, as the human parent passes on one half of the genetic code for a new human individual, so also, each gamete carries one half of a psychical 'imprint', or 'pattern', which, when fused with the 'pattern' of another gamete in the moment of symgamy, generates a new soul, just as the new body is generated.

[25] For instance, the view, given in the previous note, or, alternatively something like the traducianism offered by J. P. Moreland and Scott Rae in *Body and Soul,* ch. 6.

[26] See, Oliver D. Crisp, *Divinity and Humanity: The Incarnation Reconsidered* (Cambridge: Cambridge University Press, 2007), ch. 2.

and body.[27] Not all Christian thinkers agree that human beings are composed of a body and soul. Accordingly, those Christians who are materialists will not be sympathetic to Shedd's characterisation of human nature, nor, I presume, to the notion of traducianism. (Unless, the materialist wants to defend the view – often falsely attributed to traducianists – that the soul is a material entity, or a composite part of a material entity, which is, I take it, not a biblical view of the soul.[28]) For if human beings have no soul, then no immaterial substance exists that can be passed down from one generation to the next.

However, a Christian materialist could claim that souls are the epiphenomena of certain sorts of material organisation, which cease to exist when that matter degrades, or the organism that is constituted by this matter dies. Or, the Christian materialist might believe the mind is some immaterial aspect of the human being, or some property of the brain, but not a distinct substance conjoined with the physical body of a human being. It might be possible to construct some version of traducianism that is satisfied by such materialist accounts of the soul/mind. But this would not satisfy Shedd, who is, I think, quite clearly a substance dualist.

Those who think of natures and individual essences as properties or sets of properties, will find Shedd's account of human nature, like that of the medievals whom he seems to follow in this matter, baffling. How can a human nature be a concrete particular rather than a property, or set of properties?[29] Perhaps it is possible to make sense of this property-account of human nature along traducian lines, if it makes sense to think that certain properties can be 'transferred' from one entity to another. To give an example, we might think that a length of wiring that has an electrical current running through it, and a

---

[27] Idealists might also be either creationists or traducians about the nature of the soul, if they think of minds as souls, or soul-like. Perhaps an idealist of a Berkeleyan persuasion might be inclined to say that God creates different human minds and the ideas such minds have, out of nothing. Or, perhaps a traducian-Berkeleyan might think that God creates the first human minds, which (somehow) generate later human minds. The point here is that traducianism and creationism are theories about the origin of the soul, not about the constitution of human beings, as such.

[28] For a defence of the view that the Bible presents a consistent case for souls being immaterial entities, see John Cooper, *Body, Soul and Life Everlasting* (Grand Rapids, MI: Eerdmans, 2000 [1989]).

[29] One of the most illuminating discussions of the difference between a medieaval ontology and contemporary, essentialist ontology, can be found in Nicholas Wolterstorff's 'Divine Simplicity' in James E. Tomberlin (ed.), *Philosophical Perspectives 5: Philosophy of Religion* (Atascadero, CA: Ridgeview Press, 1991), pp. 531-552. Wolterstorff characterises the medieval ontology as a constituent ontology (entities are constituted by certain things, including a nature – seen by the medievals as a concrete particular). Contemporary (essentialist) ontology he speaks of as relational ontology – entities exemplify certain properties in relation to other things, e.g. 'being referred to by Wolterstoff'.

light bulb that has an element lit by that same current, being fed into it by the length of wire, both have the property, 'being the conduit through which this electrical current is flowing'. But the light bulb only has this property when the light switch is thrown and the current travels from the wire to the bulb.

In a similar way, it might be the case that human nature is a property that an entity has, just in case that entity has passed to it a certain material and soulish organisation from two parents. But this does sound rather more like Shedd's account than the property-account of human nature. For this sounds as if human nature is a concrete particular that exemplifies certain properties, rather than a property that is exemplified by certain entities. In any case, Shedd's view is that human nature is fundamentally a substance that exemplifies certain properties, not merely a property, and that 'soul-stuff' (my word, not Shedds') is passed from one generation to the next.[30]

Critique of Shedd's Position

We are now in a position to offer some criticism of Shedd's version of traducianism. I shall take the three different strands of his argument dealt with in the previous section, in reverse order.

Shedd on Human Nature Once Again

First then, on human nature: here I have very little to say, since I am largely in agreement with Shedd about what human natures are.

However, I am less happy with his characterisation of what I shall call a species-nature, that is, the notion (with which we began our exposition of Shedd) that you and I are all carriers of a nature held in common with Adam. My objection to Shedd's understanding of this is not directed towards the idea of a species-nature as such. I suppose each human being has an individual nature, or essence, and that the class or set of human natures can be characterised as a species-nature. My objection is to Shedd's way of thinking about this species-nature. The idea that the first human pair have the whole of this species-nature, and that this nature is subsequently differentiated in instances of human nature exemplified by different human beings via the propagation and individuation of this species nature in the particular progeny of Adam, is, it seems to me, a rather baroque way of thinking about such metaphysical matters.

This, by itself, is hardly an overpowering objection to Shedd's way of thinking about species-natures. It is not obviously incoherent to think of a species scattered through spacetime, with each individual of the given species

---

[30] The distinction between these two views of human nature (or two sorts of view), is developed more fully in chapter two of Crisp, *Divinity and Humanity*.

exemplifying this species-nature. But I am not sympathetic to the idea that a species-nature is a concrete particular, as Shedd seems to be.[31] Although I share Shedd's view that particular instances of human nature are concrete particulars, I do not think that species-natures are also concrete particulars. Species natures are, it seems to me, more like properties: abstract objects that may or may not be instantiated in the actual world. (In the language introduced into Christology by Thomas Morris, a species-nature is a kind essence: that property or properties necessary for belonging to a particular natural kind.[32])

Are Souls Fissiparous?

More needs to be said about the second issue in Shedd's traducian-realism: whether souls are capable of generating other souls.[33] Here we run into

---

[31] Recall Shedd's words, quoted earlier: 'A species or a specific nature is that primitive invisible substance or plastic principle which God created from nonentity, as the rudumental matter of which all the individuals of the species are to be composed.' DT: 465. This is from the section concerning physiological arguments for traducianism. In the previous section on the theological arguments for traducianism, he says something similar: 'natural union [realism] when examine will be found to be race-union; and race-union must be total not partial, psychical as well as physical, in order to be of any use in justifying the imputation of Adam's sin.' DT: 457. See also DT: 473, where he distinguishes between the 'general term' nature, and person, and states that, 'the general term *nature* denotes an objective entity or substance, as much as the general term *person*.'

[32] Thomas Morris, in his work on Christology, speaks of individual essences and kind essences. My use of individual nature is different from Morris's individual essence in that, like Shedd, I think individual natures are fundamentally concrete particulars, not merely abstract objects (properties, or sets, or bundles of properties). However, my use of the term species-nature is, as far as I can see, just a different way of speaking about the same metaphysical thing Morris does, when he says that, in addition to individual essences there are kind-essences, or natures. Like Morris, I think that kind-essences, or, as I have expressed it, species-natures, are abstract objects, whereas Shedd seems to think of both individual natures and species-natures as concrete particulars. I use the language I do, rather than the language Morris and others have adopted, because it better approximates Shedd's idiolect, and to avoid the reader confusing my view of the distinction between individual natures and species-natures with the language deployed in recent philosophical theology by Morris and others. See Thomas V. Morris, *The Logic of God Incarnate* (Ithaca, NY: Cornell University Press, 1986). Cf. Alvin Plantinga, *The Nature of Necessity* (Oxford: Oxford University Press, 1974), ch. V.

[33] I am not sure there is sufficient evidence to show whether Shedd was a Thomist, or Cartesian, or some other species of substance dualist, see, for instance, his comments in DT: 471. The literature on substance dualism is growing. Representative examples of contemporary Cartesianism include John Foster, *The Immaterial Self: A Defence of the Cartesian Dualist Conception of The Mind* (London: Routledge, 1991), Richard Swinburne, *The Evolution of the Soul* (Oxford: Oxford University Press, 1986) and

difficulties in interpreting Shedd's views. For one thing, is ambiguous whether his substance dualism is Cartesian (souls are persons that happen to be 'attached' to a certain hunk of matter), or hylomorphist (souls are the form of the body, which they give shape to and organise), or, indeed, some other alternative, e.g. emergentism: the soul supervenes on the body; at a certain stage of bodily complexity the soul comes to be. (The reader is directed to DT: 471 ff. where Shedd deals with the relationship between bodies and souls.) For this reason, our assessment of his claim that souls are fissiparous will have to include an analysis of several different ways in which Shedd's view could be construed.

But before attempting this, another objection to Shedd's view needs to be addressed: that souls are simple substances, and therefore cannot be fissiparous, as traducianism requires. By a simple substance I mean a substance that is not a compound of other substances and is not composed of some more basic 'stuff'. Souls are essentially incorporeal simple substances. This means souls are quite different from material substances, which are composed of more basic elements, such as sub-atomic particles. If souls are simple, they are not composed of an immaterial equivalent to sub-atomic particles (e.g. 'soul-stuff').[34] But this means that souls have no parts. It also means that a soul is incapable of fission because an entity that has no parts is incapable of splitting. In which case, Shedd's contention about soul-fission cannot get off the ground.

Similar reasoning applies, *mutatis mutandis,* to parturition. I take it that parturition denotes a reproductive act, where some part of a parent – its seed - generates or gives rise to, an offspring. Such a process need not involve fission. When a human reproduces after its kind it does not split into two. We might say humans are constitutionally parturient but not fissile. Similarly, soul-fission and soul-parturition is not the same thing. But if a soul is simple, it is incapable of parturition because it has no seed-like parts that may give rise to, or generate, a second soul. From this it should be clear that if souls are simple substances, they are incapable of soul-fission in the way Shedd envisages (even if Shedd has in mind something more like parturition than soul-fission).

Sometimes, creationists have argued that a soul, unlike a body, has no physical extension; so it is not susceptible to being divided in the same way that physical objects are. Let us call this *the indivisibility objection to traducianism,*

Charles Taliaferro, *Consciousness and The Mind of God* (Cambridge: Cambridge University Press, 1994). A defence of a Thomist account is given in David Braine, *The Human Person: Animal and Spirit* (Notre Dame, IN: University of Notre Dame Press, 1992). Criticism of these traditional dualisms and an emergent-dualist alternative, are given in Hasker, *The Emergent Self.*

[34] Roderick Chisholm uses this terminology for souls in his 'On the Simplicity of the Soul' in James E. Tomberlin, (ed.) *Philosophical Perspectives 1: Philosophy of Religion, 1991* (Atarscadero, CA: Ridgeview Press, 1991), p. 167 ff.

or *the indivisibility objection* for short. One contemporary exponent of this view is Richard Swinburne:

> Of any chunk of matter, however, small, it is always logically, if not physically, possible that it be divided into two. Yet it is because matter is extended, that one can always make sense of it being divided.... But that kind of consideration has no application to immaterial stuff. There is no reason why there should not be a kind of immaterial stuff which necessarily is indivisible.[35]

And Swinburne thinks soul-stuff does have the property of being indivisible. His suggestion that 'there is no reason' why an immaterial entity such as a soul should not be indivisible is trivially true *if* souls are simple substances. But the traducian will not concede this.[36] Since Shedd's claim that souls are fissile is false if souls are simple substances, let us pursue the possibility that Shedd believes souls are complex substances made up of something more basic – some 'soul-stuff' (whatever that might be).

If the soul is a complex substance, then the indivisibility objection has no purchase. For no traducian worth his salt would object to the suggestion that souls cannot be *physically* divided as bodies are. But the fact that souls cannot be divided as physical objects can, does not imply that souls are indivisible. In other words, an objection to traducianism based solely on an analogy between the divisibility of bodies and indivisibility of souls falls foul of the fallacy of equivocation. In order for the objection to go through some reason would have to be given for thinking that immaterial objects like souls are *constitutionally* incapable of division. Such a reason is not provided by the indivisibility objection alone, without the assumption that souls are simple – which is just what the traducianism cannot allow.

Of course, most creationists do not rest their whole case against traducianism on the indivisibility objection. There are, in fact, several different ways in which the creationist could supply the reason required for the objection against Shedd's notion that souls are fissiparous to go through without begging the question about the simplicity of the soul. One reason that can be found in traditional creationist objections to traducianism has to do with the idea that souls are incorruptible.[37] If souls are incorruptible, so such theologians claim,

---

[35] Richard Swinburne, 'Personal Identity: The Dualist Theory' in Michael J. Loux, ed., *Metaphysics: Contemporary Readings* (London: Routledge, 2001), p. 439.

[36] At least two contemporary traducians have suggested that souls are complex entities. See the discussion of souls as 'complex entities' in Moreland and Rae, *Body and Soul*, p. 69.

[37] There is also the persistent criticism from classical theologians who are creationists that traducianism is somehow an incipient materialism. The idea seems to be that if souls are propagated through natural generation, they must be passed through the gametes, and therefore must be a part of the gametes in some sense. But I take it that this is not a serious objection against traducianism. For one thing, it simply does not follow

then they cannot be divisible. Thus, for example, in his discussion of the origin of the soul, the post-Reformation Reformed theologian Francis Turretin observes, 'all modes of propagation are pressed by the most serious difficulties; nor can they be admitted without overthrowing the spirituality of the rational soul'. Later in the same passage he goes on to say,

> that spiritual substance [i.e. the soul] is made either from the whole soul of the father or from a part only. Not from the whole because thus the soul of the father would be divisible into parts, and because that substance is corruptible and perishes in the very instant the soul is produced. But then it will no longer be a spiritual or incorruptible substance.[38]

Turretin's comments could be taken to mean (a) souls are incorruptible, and (b) things that are incorruptible cannot suffer division, because division itself is an instance of corruption, or entails the corruption of that which is divided. One way of trying to flesh out this sort of claim (not one that Turretin offers, but one a defender of this construal of the incorruptibility claim might make) is analogous to the argument for the necessity of divine perfection one finds in perfect being theology. A perfect being theologian, following in the footsteps of Anselm of Canterbury, could say that God cannot cease to be perfect without ceasing to be divine: his perfection is a necessary condition of his being divine.[39] In a similar fashion, one might claim that it is in the nature of a soul to be incorruptible, so that it is not possible for a soul to be corrupted without the loss or diminishment of the soul concerned. Division of a soul is an instance of such corruption, or entails such corruption - the diminishment or destruction of the soul. So, if a soul is incorruptible, it is indivisible too. Let us call this the *incorruptibility objection.*

One could press the point in a slightly different way, without recourse to the notion of incorruptibility, using the principle that the division of an entity entails the destruction of that entity and/or the generation of a new entity or entities. Here the idea is that if a particular thing is divided, then the product of such division, or any component part thereof, cannot be the same as the original entity prior to the moment it was divided. This seems to be a plausible principle when applied to material objects that are composed of fundamental particles,

---

that if a soul is propagated through natural generation that the soul itself must be some physical part of the gamete, as I have already made clear.

[38] Turretin, *Inst. Vol I*, p. 480. Turretin also argues that if both parents are the source of a propagated soul, it is difficult to see how this can be the case without either (a) conceding that the whole of each parental soul is transmitted (and mixed?) in the act of propagation, leaving the parents soul-less, or (b) conceding that souls have some sort of 'seed', which is he not willing to grant (on the grounds, one presumes, that souls are indivisible). But these are not the only options if souls are fissile.

[39] See Anselm, *Proslogion,* in *Anselm of Canterbury, The Major Works*, (eds.) Brian Davies and Gillian Evans (Oxford: Oxford University Press, 1998).

such as protons, electrons and so forth. Given this principle, the division of a loaf of bread, or a lump of clay entails the destruction of the original whole object (the whole loaf; the whole lump) and the generation of several new objects: two pieces of bread; two smaller lumps of clay. There are, of course, well-known objections to this way of thinking. If the bread is divided into two, it could be argued that there still exists an object composed of the parts of the loaf. The fact that those parts no longer occupy contiguous space does not mean they are not parts of a whole object. But, even on this rather non-commonsensical way of counting things that includes mereological sums of objects that may be spatially scattered, the action of dividing the bread does have this important consequence (that may be thought to tell against the scattered-object view): before the bread was divided there was one whole object existing in a particular space. After the moment of division, this is no longer the case.

This line of thinking could be construed in one of several ways. The first version involves the claim that entities cannot lose any parts *whatsoever* without ceasing to exist. This metaphysical idea is often called *mereological essentialism* – a doctrine some will find too high a price to pay for the dividends it promises.[40] Given mereological essentialism, we could reason as follows: all objects, including immaterial objects like souls, are mereological wholes that are incapable of losing any parts whatsoever, without being destroyed. If a soul is fissile, then it is capable of losing parts. But this is metaphysically impossible because no object can lose parts. So souls are not fissile. Notice on this way of thinking, that the property 'being fissile' is not a property any object, souls included, possess. By ruling out fissiparousness *tout court*, this mereological essentialist objection does offer a way of countering Shedd's soul-fission. But such reasoning will not commend itself to most readers as sound.

One could opt for a weaker version of this sort of objection, which stipulates only that entities cannot lose any essential properties or parts without ceasing to exist and that one of the properties essential to souls is 'being indivisible'. But this more metaphysically modest way of construing the mereological objection is patently question begging. Hence, it is quite useless against Shedd's notion of soul-fission.[41] Without the claim that souls are simple entities, the argument from the indivisibility of the soul, taken along the lines I have suggested, is

---

[40] There are well-known problems with mereological essentialism. A trivial example: each time I have a haircut, are we to suppose that the entity that existed before the haircut – call it Longhair – ceases to exist once my hair has been cut, only to be replaced by a different entity, that we might call Shorthair? This seems deeply implausible. For discussion of mereological essentialism, see Roderick Chisholm, *Person and Objection* (London: Allen and Unwin, 1975).

[41] It is question begging because it relies on the premise that indivisibility is an essential property of souls. But this is precisely the point at issue!

either at least as contentious as traducianism (in the mereologically essentialist form) or question begging.

Thankfully, there are other potential drawbacks to Shedd's 'soul-fission' in the neighbourhood. Here is one that uses aspects of a modified Cartesian substance dualism and problems familiar from the literature on diachronic personal identity. The modification is that this objection does not include the claim that souls are simple, which Cartesians normally do. Call it the *modified Cartesian diachronic personal identity objection*. It could be argued that it is metaphysically impossible for a person to divide, and souls are (normally speaking) persons.[42] This reasoning need not depend on persons being simple substances. It could just be that persons are indivisible mereological wholes, in which case persons might be simple substances, or persons might be complex substances that have all of their parts essentially.[43] If persons are souls that are mereological wholes of some sort, it is impossible for souls to divide, since the division of souls would mean the destruction of a person.[44] This reasoning presumes, like Descartes, that human persons are essentially souls that are contingently related to certain hunks of matter: the human body that 'houses' them in this life. In fact, this is no more than the extrapolation of Cartesian substance dualism and its application to the particular issue in hand (barring the modification concerning the simplicity of souls).

A Sheddian-traducian who is also a modified Cartesian substance dualist might accede to the following argument: souls are fissile; souls are (normally speaking) human persons; so human persons are fissile. But I presume that one of the main attractions of a Cartesian view of the mind-body problem is that it offers a way of making sense of diachronic personal identity. It is, on the Cartesian way of thinking, the soul that perdures through bodily changes. Cartesian dualists deny that personal identity across time can be made out on the basis of any merely material constitution of the body e.g. a hemisphere of the brain, the whole brain, the central nervous system, or whatever.[45] Cartesians

---

[42] I say 'normally speaking' (here and below) because I think that the Incarnation is an exception to this rule. At the Incarnation, a body-soul composite is assumed by the Second Person of the Trinity. But, according to catholic Christology this soul-body composite cannot be a person distinct from the Word of God - that is the heresy of Nestorianism, the notion that Christ is two persons, one divine and one human.

[43] Compare Chisholm: 'According to the principle of mereological essentialism, if a thing P is a part of a whole W, then W is necessarily such that P is a part of W. From this principle it follows that, if W is possibly such that it has no parts, then W has no parts and it, therefore, simple.' From 'On the Simplicity of the Soul, p. 177.

[44] This is exactly what Swinburne does claim in 'Personal Identity: The Dualist Theory', p. 439.

[45] One reason that is given for this is the *ens successiva* argument favoured by Roderick Chisholm, amongst others. If material objects are constantly gaining and losing matter, then they are, in Dean Zimmerman's memorable phrase, 'ontologically incontinent'. But if a material object gains and loses 'bits' of matter all the time, how can we be sure that

also deny that memory is a sufficient condition for persistence through time of a human person.[46] However, once one concedes to the Sheddian-traducian that souls (i.e. human persons, normally speaking) are fissile, one has a very good reason for thinking that the soul *cannot* provide the necessary persistence conditions for the identity across time of human persons. An entity liable, under certain conditions, to split into two further entities one of which may, or may not, be identical to the entity that existed prior to the split, presents a host of very difficult problems for the persistence-through-time of that entity that can hardly be a welcome prospect for the traducian who is a (modified) Cartesian dualist.

We can spell this problem out in the following way. First a premise, which if not unassailable, is at least widely accepted: personal identity is a transitive relation. If P at time t1 is personally identical with Q at t2, and Q is personally identical with R at t3, then P is identical with R. But what if at t2 Q is divided into two parts, so that at t3 we have, not merely R, but R1 and R2 respectively? Which (if either) of R1 or R2 are identical to P? If the Sheddian replies, 'the one that remains (somehow) related to the body of the parent is identical with P and the one that is 'split-off' from the parent and forms a new human being (i.e. a child) is the soul of the offspring' it should not be surprising if the creationist finds this inadequate. The fact that one product of an instance of soul-fission, say, R1, remains related (in some attenuated, non-physical sense) to the body of the parent, whilst the other, R2, is somehow transmitted – presumably with its counterpart from the second parent - to form a the new soul of the offspring, does not explain why we should think the soul-stuff that remains 'with' the first parent is identical to P. Such a Sheddian response (although, of course, Shedd himself does not make it) is rather like the Magician who, upon sawing his assistant in two, explains 'I know the piece of Debbie from the hips down that remains in this half of the box is identical with Debbie prior to my cutting of her, because it is the piece of her that I find most attractive.' I suspect his audience would find such a pronouncement fatuous. And with good reason - the fact that the Magician stipulates that Debbie-from-the-waist-down in the first half-box is identical with the whole Debbie that existed prior to sawing the poor woman in two offers no explanation as to why anyone else should think of the

---

the object at one moment is the same as (what appears to be) the same object at a later time? For discussion of this, see Zimmerman, 'Material People' in *The Oxford Handbook of Metaphysics,* (eds.) Michael J. Loux and Dean Zimmerman (Oxford: Oxford University Press, 2003).

[46] The *locus classicus* of this view is John Locke's *Essay Concerning Human Understanding*, Bk. II, ch. 27. The problems with memory as a criterion of identity across time are well known and I need not rehearse them here in detail. The basic problem is that memory is too unreliable to provide the persistence condition for personal identity. I frequently forget things that have happened to me – does this mean that those events in the past happened to someone other than me? Swinburne does a good job of recapitulating these criticisms in 'Personal Identity: The Dualist Theory'.

one half of Debbie as identical with the whole Debbie rather than the other half (or neither halves).

But the Sheddian could respond to this by claiming that souls are not fissile, but rather, parturient. Perhaps souls can extrude themselves in the generation of new souls, although they cannot divide into two. Then, the traducian could argue that souls are capable of generating new souls, not by soul-fission, but by soul-parturition. This would involve some story about the way in which souls are 'carriers' of soul-stuff that they are able to pass on, rather like physical organisms such as human bodies, are 'carriers' of DNA which is passed on via parents to children through human seed. Aspects of what Shedd does say seems to comport with this, or something like it. But it does require that souls are compound rather than simple substances. It also requires some explanation of how such a view avoids accusations of what we might call 'incorporeal incontinence'. If souls gain and lose parts (or are capable of gaining and losing parts), then what are the persistence conditions of souls? How can such souls avoid something like Chisholm's *ens successiva* argument, according to which an entity that has a part at one time, which it loses at another, is not the same entity, but a successor to the previous one?

Well, perhaps the Sheddian-traducian who takes this sort of view can come up with counterarguments to these objections, as materialists have done when analogous criticisms have been raised with their arguments in favour of human persons being corporeal beings. These things are hard to judge – and I do not pretend to have offered anything like a watertight argument against Shedd's traducianism.

Of course, traducians need not be modified Cartesian substance dualists – perhaps Sheddians need not either. One obvious alternative is a version of hylomorphism, where the human person (normally) consists of body-soul composite. On this view, or family of views, the soul alone is not a person, strictly speaking. So the same problems concerning soul-fission that face the Cartesian-traducian would not necessarily apply to the hylomorphist-traducian. But, if anything, this presents even more difficulties for the Sheddian to overcome. For the same sort of argument that was given against the Cartesian-traducian can be run against the hylomorphist-traducian, minor changes having been made. Does the soul, as the form of the body, constitute that which guarantees identity-across-time of a particular human person? If it does, then the same problems with soul-fission apply as apply with the Cartesian-traducian. If not, and personal identity across time is constituted by, say, the soul-body composite (rather than the soul alone), then further questions arise concerning whether an object that is partially composed of matter can be said to perdure, when this object is constantly gaining and losing matter. I do not propose to argue this in detail here.[47] I merely point out that if the

---

[47] I direct readers once more to Dean Zimmerman's discussion of this in 'Material People', in *The Oxford Handbook of Metaphysics*.

hylomorphist-traducian goes down the road of locating persistence conditions in the body-soul composite that is human nature (according to Shedd), then this raises a number of the problems for material persistence that are raised for materialist accounts of identity-through-time. It does not seem to me to be a preferable state of affairs for the traducian to have to provide some reason for thinking that the material part of a human person is one part of what it is that perdures, the other part being the soul, or form, of the body. This seems to have all the drawbacks of both materialist and (modified) Cartesian accounts of identity-through-time without any of the advantages of coming down on one side or the other on this matter.

Creationism and Imputed Sin

We come, more briefly, to the third issue raised by Shedd's discussion of traducianism (the first that we dealt with in the previous section of the paper). This was Shedd's claim that creationism cannot offer a just argument for the imputation of Adam's sin. Shedd argues that if God creates souls out of nothing for each new human person, then, according to a traditional account of original sin, you and I are punishable for a sin we are not guilty of. And this seems unjust.

This is an important problem in the doctrine of sin. But I think Shedd is mistaken in thinking that his criticism applies to *all* versions of creationism. Shedd's comments are, for the most part, directed towards those in the Reformed tradition who are creationists and think that the imputation of Adam's sin to his progeny is a matter of divine convention. God treats Adam's offspring, you and me included, as if we were guilty of Adam's sin and imputes original sin to us accordingly.[48] But a creationist need not also be a representationalist in his or her understanding of the means by which original sin is imputed to Adam's progeny. It is perfectly consistent for a creationist to be an Augustinian realist. Naturally, such a creationist-realist would have to give some satisfactory explanation about how it is just for God to create new souls *ex nihilo* for new human persons, as required, that have a sinful condition justly conferred upon them. But such an explanation can be given. There is not space to develop it in detail here, but an outline may suffice:

The first moment a given human person begins to exist is the moment God creates his soul *ex nihilo*. Now, assume that God constitutes things so that he may treat certain sorts of things that may be spatially and/or temporally scattered as one object. Alternatively, God ordains things such that spatio-temporally scattered things may constitute one object – since this is merely a sketch of an alternative to Shedd's account, I will not take sides on whether or not God constitutes things this way, or merely treats things as if this were the case. If this were a detailed examination of this way of thinking about the imputation of sin we would have to spend some time teasing these distinctions

---

[48] A matter to which we shall return in the next chapter.

out.[49] (Is this unjust? Well that depends, amongst other things, on whether you think a metaphysical version of voluntarism is true or not - the doctrine that certain things depend upon the divine will for their existence. This is a controversial notion, but I think it is at least plausible to assume that there are certain things, perhaps even what it is that constitutes certain sorts of metaphysical entity, that are contingent upon the divine will. For the sake of argument let us grant that this is so, and that it applies to the constitution of souls.[50]) To return to the main point, God ordains that each soul as it is created is part of a larger metaphysical whole, or is treated as such. This whole comprises some number of human beings – not the whole number, because some humans, such as Adam and Eve before the Fall, Christ, perhaps his mother, and certainly those in the eschaton, are without original sin. So, God constitutes some number of human beings less than the total number of human beings that forms the relevant metaphysical whole. This metaphysical whole includes Adam from the moment of his fall and all other fallen humans, despite the fact that they are temporally and spatially scattered.[51]

Is this story realist? I think it is. Augustinian realism only requires that somehow God constitutes Adam and his progeny one metaphysical entity for the purposes of imputing, or transmitting, original sin. There is nothing about Augustinian realism that stipulates the *mode* of this transmission, or the precise *nature* of the metaphysical arrangement concerned (although this is a point

---

[49] One problem here is that it is one thing to say God *constitutes* or *ordains* that such and such is the case, and another to say God acts *as if* such and such were the case. The former carries an ontological payload: these things are so. The latter does not – it is a kind of divinely ordained fiction.

[50] Objection: if voluntarism is granted here, surely the creationist can appeal to it and claim that her view is just that God wills that it is just that I am punished for Adam's sin. Reply: it might be that there is a divine conventionalism that applies to objects (God gerrymanders certain hunks of matter into objects, say), but that such conventionalism cannot apply to the imputation of sin without violating a deep-seated moral intuition: that such an action is unjust because undeserved.

[51] Earlier I remarked that I found Shedd's use of the notion of a species-nature unhelpful. Is this story not smuggling in just such a notion in order to make sense of the divine gerrymandering of souls into some metaphysical entity (or fictional entity)? Well, yes. This story implies something like a doctrine of temporal parts, where temporal worms are concrete particulars. This is the notion that objects that persist through time are composed of aggregates of temporal, as well as physical parts, that form a four-dimensional whole (or 'temporal worm') when taken together. But there is an important difference with Shedd's view. On the story I am laying out it is not the case that the whole of humanity comprises the temporal worm all of whose parts have the property of original sin. Only some of humanity make this worm up, because not all humans have original sin (e.g. Adam prior to the Fall, the glorified in the eschaton ,etc.). Shedd's view is that *qua* species, there is a shared nature that is a concrete particular. My story requires only that those parts of humanity that have the property of original sin form a temporal worm that is divinely constituted.

often overlooked by friends and foes of the doctrine).

Shedd's argument against creationism relies on each newly created soul having no metaphysical connection with other souls going back to Adam. And this is one of the main reasons why he opts for the combination of traducianism + Augustinian realism. But the story I have just sketched out is consistent with a version of Augustinian realism, and creationism. And this, I think, offers one promising alternative to Shedd's account that is a sort of metaphysical hybrid, which is Augustinian realist and creationist. In fact, it may be more promising than Shedd's account, since Shedd does not address the problem of the identity of Adam and his progeny.[52] On his version of realism Adam and his progeny share a common nature, but they are not numerically identical. Yet much of the force of his criticisms of creationism appear to rely on the fact that creationism denies the numerical identity of Adam and his progeny, yet still applies punishment for Adam's sin in the absence of culpability. If Shedd's view is not clearly an instance of numerical identity between Adam and his progeny, then the same argument applies, the relevant changes having been made, to Shedd himself. However, it need not apply to the revised creationist-Augustinian realist hybrid I have sketched out, because on this view numerical identity is not required for the imputation of sin. Identity, on this view, is a matter of a perduring space-time worm that has different temporal parts that are numerically distinct 'temporal counterparts' that, taken together, 'form', or are 'fused into' one particular entity.[53]

Conclusions

Arguments against traducianism that are worthy of serious consideration are not easy to come by. An assessment of Shedd's version of traducianism only underlines this fact. But perhaps this should not be terribly surprising. The question of the origin of the soul has taxed some of the greatest minds in Christendom. In this chapter, I have argued that, although there are objections to Shedd's account that are insufficient or question begging, there are also difficulties for Shedd's traducianism that are not easily answered and are on target. This is especially true of the problems that the simplicity of the soul poses for Shedd's view. I have also argued that Shedd's objection to

---

[52] It might be objected that the story just told is just as 'baroque' as the ontology Shedd presupposes. Well, perhaps. But it seems to me that this story has certain advantages over Shedd's view that makes this bullet worth biting.

[53] The literature in this area is recent and growing. Representative examples amongst those taking a doctrine of temporal parts include Katherine Hawley, *How Things Persist* (Oxford: Oxford University Press, 2001), Mark Heller, *The Ontology of Physical Objects* (Cambridge: Cambridge University Press, 1990) and Theodore Sider, *Four Dimensionalism* (Oxford: Oxford University Press, 2001).

creationism based on the question of the imputation of sin does not apply to all forms of creationism, as he seems to think, and that the problem of identity-across-time that motivates his argument against creationism can be applied to his own version of Augustinian realism. Although Shedd's arguments may not be convincing, they are important and interesting. At the very least, Shedd's discussion of these matters shows that there are still intriguing problems to be explored concerning traducianism, Augustinian realism, and the nature of sin. We turn to the consideration of one such problem in the next chapter, which considers the relation between Shedd's Augustinian realism and the imputation of sin.

CHAPTER 2

Augustinian Realism and the Imputation of Sin

The doctrine of original sin has a perennial theological fascination. In the second half of the nineteenth century several Calvinistic divines sought to answer the problem that the question of the transmission of original sin poses, to wit, How is it just that God imputes Adam's sin to his posterity? They sought to answer this problem by recourse to versions of Augustinian realism, the doctrine that Adam's posterity is somehow metaphysically one entity with Adam such that Adam's sin just is the sin of the whole of humanity. In this chapter, I want to examine the arguments of two of these divines. One of them is, of course, William Shedd. The other is Shedd's near contemporary, the Baptist theologian Augustus Strong. We will consider their arguments as they bear upon the question of the imputation of Adam's sin. As a foil to their views, I shall also examine what the Princetonian theologian Charles Hodge had to say on the matter. (His views on this issue are within the federalist tradition of Reformed theology.) We shall see that there was a lively and theologically interesting debate about the nature and transmission of sin in this period, which has important implications for contemporary discussion of this same topic.

The argument proceeds in four stages. To begin with, we shall set out some terms of reference for what follows. We shall then be in a position to consider the views of these three theologians. This analysis will be split into two sections. In the first of these, we shall consider two claims made in the dogmatic theologies of Shedd and Strong and show that these need not entail an obviously false version of realism. Although one of these claims presents problems, the other can be used as the basis for a theologically interesting realist doctrine. The second section deals with Hodge's somewhat idiosyncratic defence of representationalism with respect to the doctrine of sin.[1] Having examined and assessed the relative strengths and weaknesses of each of these nineteenth century approaches to imputed sin, I shall close with some comments on the extent to which this discussion may be helpful for ongoing theological reflection in this area.

---

[1] Representationalism is the view favoured by those Reformed theologians who are also federal theologians. It states that Adam is the federal head of humanity and the representative of the race. He acts on behalf of humanity, and in the place of humanity.

Some Terms of Reference

All three of these nineteenth century divines assumed a traditional, full-orbed doctrine of original sin, inherited from their theological forebears in Reformed dogmatics. It is therefore important to clarify what the constituents of this traditional view are in order to make sense of the views expressed by Shedd, Strong and Hodge. We shall consider the doctrine of original sin that arose out of Reformed Orthodox theology,[2] the tradition that in varying degrees influenced the work of theologians like Shedd, Strong and Hodge.[3] The full-orbed doctrine of original sin comprises two aspects.[4] These are original corruption and original guilt. Original corruption has two parts: the lack or privation of original righteousness enjoyed by Adam and Eve before the Fall, and the vitiated moral nature that all human beings post-Fall are cursed with. For our purposes, original righteousness is that deposit of divine grace given to the morally upright Adam and Eve at their creation, which enabled them not to sin. It did not preclude the possibility of sinning. That is, it did not confer *impeccability* upon the recipient of this grace. Adam and Eve could (and did) sin. The point is that the state of original righteousness was one where Adam

---

[2] In what follows I shall distinguish between Reformed Orthodoxy, the dogmatic tradition of the post-Reformation theological tradition allied to Calvinism, and Scholasticism, the theological method deployed by these theologians, who took their cue from the Medieval schoolmen in this regard. Where I refer to classical theology, this means theologians in the broadly Augustinian tradition, including the Medievals. I am taking my cue here from recent work in post-Reformation theology that has distinguished the terms 'Reformed Orthodox' and 'Reformed Scholasticism'. See, for example, Richard Muller *After Calvin* (Oxford: Oxford University Press, 2003), ch. 2.

[3] Of course, there is not a single, unified doctrine of original sin in the Christian tradition. Nor is there a single doctrine of original sin in Post-Reformation scholastic theology. There are a number of versions of the doctrine of original sin in the tradition, and important variations on a central core of agreement amongst the Reformed Orthodox. It is the agreed broad structures of the doctrine in Reformed theology that I am concerned with here. I shall not deal with other versions of the full-orbed doctrine that are found before Post-Reformation scholastic theology. For a good recent discussion of the development of the doctrine of original sin, see Tatha Wiley, *Original Sin, Origins, Developments, Contemporary Meanings* (New York: Paulist Press, 2002).

[4] These two aspects are clearly delineated in Reformed confessional standards. For instance, the *Westminster Shorter Catechism.* Q. 18 states: 'wherein consists the sinfulness of that estate whereinto man fell?' To which the following response is made: 'The sinfulness of that estate whereinto man fell, consists in the guilt of Adam's first sin [first aspect], the want of original righteousness, and the corruption of his whole nature, which is commonly called Original Sin [second aspect]; together with all actual transgressions which proceed from it.' It seems to me that actual sin, that is sin proceeding from a vitiated moral nature, is not an aspect of original sin *per se*, but a consequence of original sin.

and Eve were *sinless* and *able not to sin*.⁵ As the Reformed Orthodox put it, Adam was created with a *natura integra* (morally upright nature) such that it was true that he was *posse non peccare et posse peccare* (able not to sin and able to sin).⁶ But in addition to the loss of this grace at the moment of the Fall, Adam and Eve gained a morally depraved nature or *macula*. Spiritual pollution could be considered an effect of a privation, like an infection is the result of ill health. This would mean that the individual sinner loses original righteousness and the resulting privation of this state gives rise to the *macula* (blemished nature). The Reformed Orthodox thought of the morally depraved nature Adam and his posterity are left with after the Fall as a deformed nature (*deformitas naturae*) that is spiritually polluted (*pollutio spiritualis*). This could be taken to mean a deformed and spiritually polluted human nature is the direct result of the privation of the integrity and moral uprightness enjoyed by Adam pre-Fall. But it may not be taken this way. One could see this change of moral state as merely the exchange of one property, or quality – moral uprightness – for another, moral deformation and spiritual pollution. Either way, the effects of the Fall upon human nature means that all humanity (bar Christ) are deprived of original righteousness and instead have a polluted and deformed moral nature. (Although the way in which this is brought about is different, depending on whether one opts for the privative view of these things, or not.)

Original guilt is the other component of a doctrine of original sin. As we shall see, this particular aspect of a full-orbed doctrine of original sin brings into focus a number of the problems that there are with the doctrine of original sin espoused by Shedd and Strong – both Augustinian realists. There have been several ways in which the notion of original guilt has been understood in the tradition. For the purposes of this essay, I shall assume that original guilt comprises a *reatus*, or liability. Classical theologians have disputed quite what the sinner is liable for, and here is not the place to enter into that discussion in

---

⁵ There is not the space to go into the question, why Adam and Eve sinned in the first place if they were created morally upright with original righteousness. For an interesting account of the way in which one great theologian struggled with this problem, see John Kearney, 'Jonathan Edwards' Account of Adam's First Sin' in *Scottish Bulletin of Evangelical Theology* 15 (1997): 135-136. A brief exposition of the Reformed confessions on this matter can be found in Jan Rohls, *Reformed Confessions, Theology from Zurich to Barmen* (trans.) John Hoffmeyer (Louisville, KT: Westminster John Knox Press, 1998), pp. 68 ff.

⁶ Some of the Reformed , following the Scotists, claimed that Adam pre-Fall was in a purely natural moral condition, dependent on his abilities, rather than upon some deposit of divine grace. This is known as the *status purorum naturalium* (purely natural moral condition). However, most of the Reformed maintained that prior to the Fall Adam was given *iustitia originalis* (original righteousness), which he needed in order to perform any action that was meritorious. See Heinrich Heppe, *Reformed Dogmatics* (trans.) G. T. Thompson (Grand Rapids, MI: Baker, 1950), ch. XV.

detail.⁷ Suffice it to say that some theologians refer to a two-fold *reatus*, of guilt (*reatus culpae*) and of punishment (*reatus poenae*). Others, in the Reformed Orthodox tradition, speak of a potential and actual guilt. Still others, perplexed by these fine distinctions, have opted for a concept of guilt *simpliciter*, which arises from the fact of sin.⁸ (There are also those who, like the contemporary philosophical theologian Richard Swinburne, have rejected original guilt altogether because it seems so problematic.⁹) The chief problem with original guilt is that it is very difficult to see how one person could be liable for the guilt of another. This theological problem goes to the heart of the versions of Augustinian realism defended by Shedd and Strong.

Typically, theologians in the Reformed tradition have claimed that Adam's sin and the guilt for that sin were immediately imputed from Adam to his posterity. (Some Reformed divines have claimed that this imputation is mediate,¹⁰ others that it only involves liability to punishment, but these are minority reports in the tradition.¹¹) What is important to note for our purposes, is that the traditional Reformed doctrine of the imputation of Adam's sin, based on the view that Adam is a federal head of humanity involves a kind of legal fiction. The nineteenth century Scottish theologian, William Cunningham explains:

> In virtue of the federal headship or representative identity, established by God between Adam and all descending from him by ordinary generation, his first sin is

---

⁷ I have spelt this out in 'Scholastic Theology, Augustinian Realism and Original Guilt' in the *European Journal of Theology* 13 (2004): 17-28. The discussion of these issues here depends upon the argument of this previous essay.

⁸ For a brief discussion of these different views with respect to original guilt in the tradition, see Louis Berkhof, *Systematic Theology* (Edinburgh: Banner of Truth, 1939), p. 245 ff.

⁹ Richard Swinburne, *Responsibility and Atonement* (Oxford: Oxford University Press, 1989), pp. 144-145.

¹⁰ The immediate imputation of sin is, roughly, the notion that God imputes sin directly to each individual sinner on the basis of Adam's sin. Mediate imputation is the notion that God 'imputes' sin via natural generation. That is, original sin is passed down the generations 'mediately'. This was the view of the French Saumur School of theology, following Joshua Placaeus. For more on this distinction, see Oliver D. Crisp, 'On the theological pedigree of Jonathan Edwards' doctrine of imputation' in *Scottish Journal of Theology* 56 (2003): 308-327.

¹¹ This, as we shall see presently, is the view of Charles Hodge. He says, '[t]o impute sin, in Scriptural and theological language, is to impute the guilt of sin. And by guilt is meant not criminality or moral ill-desert, or demerit, much less moral pollution, but the judicial obligation to satisfy justice. Hence the evil consequent on the imputation is not an arbitrary infliction; not merely a misfortune or calamity; not a chastisement in the proper sense of that word, but a punishment, i.e., an evil inflicted in execution of the penalty of law and for the satisfaction of divine justice.' *Systematic Theology*, Vol. II, Pt. II, ch. VIII § 9 (Grand Rapids, MI: Eerdmans, 1968 [reprint]), p. 194.

imputed to them, or put down to their account; and they are regarded and treated by God as if they had all committed it in their own person, to the effect of their being subjected to its legal and penal consequences – so that, in this sense, they may be truly said to have sinned in him and fallen with him in his first transgression.[12]

The imputation of Adam's sin to his posterity, according to these Reformed theologians, involves no real transference of properties from Adam to his posterity. Adam's posterity does not gain the property of Adam's sin and guilt as the deposit of original sin. Rather, God arranges things such that Adam's progeny are treated *as if* they had sinned with Adam and *as if* they had Adam's guilt. This is the basis of the representational or federalist view of the imputation of Adam's sin. In particular, the federal view means that God makes Adam's posterity morally responsible for a sin that they did not commit. Worse still, God constitutes things such that, by way of the legal fiction of representationalism in federal theology, all of Adam's posterity must suffer as if they had committed his sin, solely because he has been appointed by God as their federal head.[13] We shall see that both Shedd and Strong pose arguments that may be used to show how Adam's guilt could also be my guilt without incurring the problem that the representationalist view involves a legal fiction.

A complete doctrine of original sin has to deal with the problems associated with the origin and nature of sin as well as its transmission. However, we shall restrict ourselves to the problems associated with the question of transmission just mentioned, touching upon the other aspects of the doctrine only tangentially. The problem of the transmission of sin has to do with two related issues, which we shall call *the question of injustice* and *the question of plausibility* respectively. First, on the question of injustice, it seems monumentally unjust that God should condemn me for the sin of another, particularly for the sin of a long dead ancestor. Why, we might ask, should I be

---

[12] William Cunningham, *The Reformers and The Theology of The Reformation* (Edinburgh: Banner of Truth, 1967 [1862]), p. 374. This is a standard Reformed position. Compare John Murray, who says that Adam's posterity 'came to have property in Adam's disobedience with the result that their judicial status is that belonging to the disobedience in which they have property. The disobedience of Adam is brought to bear upon posterity in such a way that the judgment registered upon them is the judgment which the disobedience of Adam elicits and demands.' *The Imputation of Adam's Sin* (Grand Rapids, MI: Eerdmans, 1959), pp. 87-88.

[13] I am not arguing that there is no theological basis for some form of representationalism, nor that federal theology is false. My point is that, in the matter of the imputation of Adam's sin, all traditional federal theologians have to base their arguments on, is the claim that Adam is the federal head and chosen representative of humanity. This alone simply cannot bear the theological weight of imputed sin. Something more is needed to explain how sin may be imputed from Adam to me in a way that is *just*.

punished for the sin of Adam? The other issue, the question of plausibility, has to do with whether any solution to the problem of injustice can be found which offers a plausible way in which Adam's sin could justly and fairly be said to be mine. A viable solution to this problem will have to overcome both the injustice and plausibility problems that the imputation of sin involves. This is no small task, as we shall see.

Augustinian Realism in Shedd and Strong

The major theological alternative to the federalist theory of imputed sin is realism. The term itself has come to be associated with Augustine as its chief proponent, and it has to do with the way in which Adam's progeny were somehow *really* present with Adam at the point of his first sin. Hence Augustinian *realism*.[14] As we have just noted, one of the criticisms often raised against a full-orbed doctrine of original sin is that it is unjust that the sin of Adam is imputed or imparted to me. How can I be held responsible for the sin of some distant ancestor of mine whom I never knew? Augustinian realism responds to this charge of injustice by claiming that all human beings were somehow metaphysically present with Adam at the moment of Adam's sin. Because all humanity is somehow present with Adam at the moment of his first sin, the original sin of Adam is properly the sin of all his posterity too. Thus, a central insight into the doctrine of original sin provided by Augustinian realism is that Adam's sin is not mine because it is imputed to me; it is imputed to me because it is mine. In fact, as we shall see, even this is not strictly speaking correct, since on at least one version of realism nothing is imputed at all if all humanity is joined with Adam in his first sin. Augustine puts it like this:

> In fact, because of the magnitude of that offence, the condemnation changed human nature for the worse; so that what first happened as a matter of punishment in the case of the first human beings, continued in their posterity as something natural and congenital.... Therefore the whole human race was in the first man, and it was to pass from him through the woman into his progeny, when the married pair had received the divine sentence of condemnation. And it was not man as first made, but what man became after his sin and punishment, that was thus begotten, as far as concerns the origin of sin and death.[15]

---

[14] There are a variety of ways in which the word 'realism' has been used in philosophy and theology. In what follows, when the term 'realism' is used, it should be taken to mean Augustinian realism.

[15] Augustine, *City of God* Bk. XIII: III, trans. Henry Bettenson (Harmondsworth: Penguin, 1984), p. 512. Augustine's doctrine is not always easy to discern, and it is not always clear that he advocates an unambiguous version of realism as John Murray points out, in his volume on *The Imputation of Adam's Sin*, p. 31. For our purposes, it is

If, as at least one traditional understanding of this doctrine has maintained, this means that Adam's posterity was somehow seminally present in his loins at the moment of primal sin, this is plainly false.[16] However, this is not the only way to construe Augustine's words here.[17] It could be, for instance, that for the purposes of imputation human nature is (or perhaps, is treated as) one metaphysical entity, that is as Adam-plus-progeny. This could be understood in several ways. One way that some Augustinian realists have understood the union of Adam and his progeny maintains that Adam and his posterity are separate individuals that share a common fallen human nature. If this human nature is corrupted by Adam's first sin, then it is corrupted in the subsequent individualization of that nature in an infralapsarian state. Consequently, all humanity actually or really sinned 'in' Adam, since all humanity actually or really share in this one substance of human nature.[18] Let us call this the *common human nature version* of Augustinian realism, or 'common nature version' for short. This account of imputation may, as we shall see, point in the direction of a solution to the injustice problem, but it does not, as it stands, provide a satisfactory account of how it is that God may justly impute the sin of Adam to his posterity. For it is not clear thus far, on this view, how it is that God is able to treat Adam and his posterity, as generically and numerically one metaphysical unit for the purposes of the imputation of sin.

So, let us flesh out how this common nature view might go. First, all of humanity was somehow 'with' or 'in' Adam when he committed his primal sin. This is often taken to mean that somehow all of humanity post-Adam was

---

sufficient that Augustine has traditionally been regarded as an exemplar of realism, though perhaps this is not as clear cut as is sometimes thought.

[16] There does seem, *prima facie*, to be some support for the seminal version of Augustinian realism in Scripture. For instance, Hebrews 7: 9-10 says 'One might even say that Levi, who collects the tenth [tithe], paid the tenth through Abraham [to Melchizedek], because when Melchizedek met Abraham, Levi was still in the body of his ancestor.' But even if this is presumed to lend support to the seminal version of realism, the passage cannot be taken seriously as a statement of some biological or metaphysical fact. It is consistent with some poetic or metaphorical understanding of 'being seminally present with x'. I assume no responsible contemporary theologian would take this passage literally. This leaves open the metaphorical interpretation, or some other non-seminal version of realism.

[17] This, despite the fact that a number of important theologians have claimed that the seminal view, or something very like it, just is the realist view. See, for instance, Charles Hodge who comments, 'Others again adopt the realistic theory, and teach that as generic humanity existed whole and entire in the persons of Adam and Eve, their sin was the sin of the entire race.... We literally sinned in Adam, and consequently the guilt of that sin is our personal guilt and the consequent corruption of nature is the effect of our own voluntary act.' *Systematic Theology, Vol. II,* Part II, ch. VIII, § 9, p. 193. As we shall see, Hodge is mistaken in this claim.

[18] For a standard theological recapitulation of this point, see Louis Berkhof, *Systematic Theology*, p. 241.

present with Adam at the time of his primal sin. However, this is not the only way in which we could understand this phrase. It could be taken to mean something more like all post-Adamic humanity was constituted one metaphysical entity 'with' (or, less helpfully, perhaps, 'in') Adam by God. Then Adam and his posterity are one metaphysical entity, or God treats Adam and his progeny as one metaphysical entity for the purposes of original sin, rather like the temporal parts version of realism and creationism suggested in chapter one. It is important to see that this common nature version of Augustinian realism need not entail that post-Adam humanity is somehow physically or spiritually present with Adam at the time of his sin. All that is required on this view is that we share the same nature with Adam so that when Adam sins, his sin affects human nature, and all subsequent instances of that nature in his posterity. In this particular way we are 'parts of' Adam. Second, this construal of the common nature version of Augustinian realism does not entail that all humanity is somehow 'seminally' present in or with Adam. It only requires that there is some strong metaphysical union between Adam and his progeny in the human nature that they share.

But what sort of metaphysical union is envisaged here? Perhaps something like the following story. Industrial spies gain access to the prototype for a new generation of automobile and tamper with it, rendering one or more of its specifications dangerous. These damaged specifications are entered into the blueprints for the new vehicle. The upshot of this is that all the production-line models of that automobile made according to the blueprints of the damaged prototype will have the same design problems as the damaged prototype. In a similar way, if Adam's sin affects human nature for the worse, then all subsequent instances of the same human nature will be adversely affected, as the production-line models based on the prototype, Adam. But what does this mean for the imputation of sin? It is not exactly that the very nature Adam has is the nature I am in union with if I am to be a member of the human race of which Adam is the head. It is rather that Adam's sin affects the sort of human nature all humanity post-Adam has because he is the head of the race. In this way, all human beings after Adam share in the same kind of nature as Adam does. And if they have the same sort of nature, then they share in the same sin and its consequences. For, consider the automobile example once more. The production models share the same design-specifications as the marred prototype. This means that all of the production models have the same dangerous design faults as the prototype, in fact, exactly the same design faults, although they are different instances of the same sort of car. In the same way Adam's progeny all share the same human nature – that is, they share the same kind-essence. But they are different instances of the kind, humanity.[19] Thus

---

[19] Recall from the previous chapter that a kind essence is the set of properties a thing has to have in order to be an instance of a particular kind of thing, such as a horse, a man, or a Martian.

they can share the same property of original sin as Adam in virtue of sharing the same kind-nature as Adam. But they have different individual natures that distinguish one person from another (I am not you, although both you and I are human beings and both you and I are fallen human beings, because of Adam's sin.) So this is a moderate version of Augustinian realism.

Certain things Shedd says concerning the transmission of original sin sound like the common nature version of Augustinian realism, although, in fact, from what we have already seen of Shedd's view in the previous chapter it should be clear that Shedd's position is considerably stronger than the common nature doctrine. But, to give an example of the sort of passage where Shedd could be taken to be a defender of the common nature view, consider the following lines that come at the end of his discussion of original sin:

> Scripture is clear that the sin of Adam is the sin of us all, not only by propagation and communication (whereby not his singular [individual] fault, but something of the same nature [with it] is derived unto us), but also by an imputation of his actual transgression unto us all, his singular [individual] transgression being by this means made ours.

He goes on to clarify this position:

> The grounds of imputation are: 1. That we were then in him and parts of him. 2. That he sustained the place of our whole nature in the covenant God made with him. When divines affirm that by Adam's sin we are guilty of damnation, they do not mean that any are damned for his particular act, but that by his sin and our sinning in him, by God's most just ordination we have contracted that exceeding pravity and sinfulness of nature which deserveth the curse of God and eternal damnation.[20]

There are stronger versions of Augustinian realism than that offered by the common nature view. One such is given in the work of the Baptist theologian Augustus Strong at the beginning of the twentieth century. He says,

> God imputes the sin of Adam immediately to all his posterity, in virtue of that organic unity of mankind by which the whole race at the time of Adam's transgression existed, not individually, but seminally, in him as its head. The total life of humanity was then in Adam; the race as yet had its being only in him. Its essence was not yet individualized.... In Adam's free act, the will of the race revolted from God and the nature of the race corrupted itself.

Moreover,

---

[20] DT: 602, n. 4. 5. 1.

Adam's sin is imputed to us immediately, therefore, not as something foreign to us, but because it is ours – we and all other men having existed as one moral person or one moral whole, in him, and, as the result of that transgression, possessing a nature destitute of love to God and prone to evil.

He makes clear what his realism entails in the following:

> Our realism then only asserts the real historical connection of each member of the race with its first father and head, and such a derivation of each from him as makes us partakers of the character which he formed. Adam was once the race; and when he fell, the race fell.[21]

In this passage Strong seems to be closer to the seminal view often attributed to Augustine. We could say, with Strong, that there was a sense in which Adam *was* the human race, because he was the first human being, and what he did as the first human being was something that affected the whole of the race stemming from him. Just as we might say, in a rather poetic way, that the whole life of a person is 'contained' in the foetus that develops in the womb, so Adam 'contained' the whole life of the human race. But Strong is saying something more than this. He speaks of members of the whole human race being somehow *present* in Adam, but without being *individualized*. And here Strong's commitment to traducianism is apparent.[22] Augustine seems to teach something similar:

> Made an exile from thence after his sin, he [Adam] bound also his offspring, whom by sinning he had marred in himself as root in the penalty and death of damnation: with the result that all the children born of him ... were infected with original sin.[23]

How are we to understand this? Strong (and, perhaps, Augustine), are claiming that the way to understand the notion, expressed in Romans 5: 12, that 'just as sin entered the world through one man, and death through sin, and in this way death came to all men because all sinned', is to say that somehow all humanity were present at the moment of sin in Adam (via traducianism). All humanity was somehow present in Adam as a whole entity, rather than as individual human beings – which echoes Shedd's account of traducianism. There is, in this respect, an 'organic unity' between Adam as the head of the race, and all those human beings who come after him. In a similar fashion, we might say, the beauty of the fully developed daffodil is 'present' in the bulb that

---

[21] Augustus Strong, *Systematic Theology, Vol. II* (Philadelphia, PA: The Griffith and Rowland Press, 1907), pp. 619, 620 and 621 respectively.

[22] Compare Strong, *Systematic Theology, Vol. II*, pp. 493-497.

[23] Augustine, *Enchiridion* (trans) Ernest Evans (London: SPCK, 1953), ch. 26, p. 24.

is planted in the earth months beforehand. The whole entity of the fully formed daffodil is present in the bulb from which it sprouts. Likewise, the fall of Adam is transmitted to the whole of the race that is present in him as an unindividualized whole at the moment of his sin, resulting in the original sin present in each human individual thereafter.

So, on this argument for realism, traducianism is implied. But the idea that all humanity are somehow 'seminally' present 'in' Adam – a notion Shedd appeals to and Strong appears to endorse – need not mean anything more than that human nature, taken as an unindividualized mass, was present in Adam. In which case, there is some sense in which both the physical and 'psychical' or immaterial parts of my human nature were present 'in' Adam when he sinned, and only individualized at some later date, through natural generation. On this construal of Augustinian realism there are two ways of referring to the human race, either as the whole race that is present and unindividualized in Adam, or to the set of individual human beings consisting of Adam and Eve and all who in fact proceed from them. The two ways of referring to humanity in this argument may have different senses (of the whole unindividualized whole, or of all the individuals proceeding from Adam and Eve), but the same reference: the human race. Let us call this the *unindividualized whole of humanity version of Augustinian realism*, or 'unindividualized version' for short.

That Shedd held to this doctrine can be demonstrated easily enough:

> The very important discussion of St. Paul in Rom. 5: 12-19 teaches (1) that the death which came upon all men as a punishment came because of one sin and only one and (2) that this sin was the one committed by Adam and his posterity as a unity. (DT: 558)

And,

> The total guilt of the first sin, thus committed by the entire race in Adam, is imputed to each individual of the race because of the indivisibility of guilt.... The first sin of Adam, being a common, not an individual sin, is deservedly and justly imputed to the posterity of Adam upon the same principle upon which all sin is deservedly and justly imputed, namely, that it was committed by those to whom it is imputed.... It is just to impute the first sin of Adam to his posterity, while it would be unjust to impute it to the fallen angels because Adam and his posterity were a unity when the first sin was committed, but Adam and the fallen angels were not. (DT: 560-561)

The clincher comes in Shedd's discussion of creation, where he says this:

> The posterity [of Adam] were not vicariously represented in the first sin, but they

sinned the very first sin being seminally existent and present; and this first sin is deservedly imputed to them, because in this generic manner it was committed by them. (DT: 435)

This version of realism, shared by Shedd and Strong, is distinct from the common nature version (although, I suppose, one could hold both together, and it seems at times that Shedd did, indeed, hold something like a combination of both views).[24] The common nature version of Augustinian realism preserves the central idea that the whole race is in some strong sense metaphysically united with Adam in virtue of sharing the same kind essence as Adam. But it does not do so via the notion that the race is present with Adam as some undifferentiated whole, rather than as a group of individual human beings. Instead, the common nature view seems to be that Adam's sin affects human nature, and that this vitiated human nature is what is transferred to each individual human being thereafter. Once this generic human nature is corrupted in Adam, every other individualization of that nature in each subsequent individual member of the human race will carry the same imprint of corruption. Put another way, on the common nature version of realism sin is transmitted via a generic human nature shared with Adam. In this way, one could hold to a common nature version of realism without commitment to traducianism, or, at least, without commitment to the sort of traducian doctrine Strong, Shedd (and perhaps Augustine) envisaged, which may seem problematic to modern ears. In the second version, the unindividualized version, there is no transmission of sin involved because original sin affects all of humanity before it is differentiated into different individuals. And this requires some form of traducianism.[25]

But how is the common nature version of realism just? It still looks as if God has unjustly imputed the sin of Adam to me via the fact that I belong to the same natural kind as Adam, namely, humanity. But this is just because Adam is the first human being and therefore his action has important implications for the whole race in a way that my own actions cannot. (For instance, my sin today cannot affect all those human beings who are dead and buried. Adam's sin affects all human beings because all the rest of humanity post-date him.) The common nature version of realism shows that the implication of Adam's first sin is that something really changes with respect to human nature. In this sense, this argument for realism is stronger, and perhaps more plausible, than traditional federalist arguments for imputed sin. Such federalist arguments rely on the same sort of intuition about the justness of the arrangement between

---

[24] This is not an obvious point. Some theologians seem to think that there is one generic version of realism. See, for example, Anthony Hoekema, *In God's Image* (Grand Rapids: Eerdmans, 1986), p.158. In fact, realism could be parsed more finely than we have done here. But these distinctions will serve the present purpose.

[25] The ideas Shedd and Strong share in common on this matter is perhaps an interesting instance of the way in which certain concepts seem fashionable at particular times in the history of the church.

Adam and his posterity, but cash this intuition out in an argument that depends in crucial respects, on a fiction. (I mean, the fiction of God treating humanity as if they were guilty of Adam's sin.)

By contrast, the unindividualized version of realism involves the peculiar idea that human beings are corrupted 'in' Adam, as an undifferentiated whole, present in Adam. This latter, traducian claim is obscure, and has led a number of theologians, including some contemporary theologians, to reject this theory of original sin as hopelessly unclear and counterintuitive, and, in the seminal version, downright false. Thus, for example, Henri Blocher in one recent account of original sin says, 'the realist explanation is fraught with a number of difficulties. "Realizing" the idea of nature so strongly that it becomes numerically one, as a substance, with a history of its own, demands a rather extreme form of Platonism [.]' [26]

It is important to see that Augustinian realism need not be taken in this way, although Shedd and Strong do. One could maintain the common nature claim about realism without the unindividualized version that poses problems for the realist. The important insight that Shedd and Strong bring to the discussion is that if Adam's sin is my sin, we must be somehow really united together. A doctrine that amounts to a mere legal fiction on this question of imputed sin, such as is presented by traditional federal theologians simply cannot make this claim. Some theologians will no doubt concede this point quite happily, including, one presumes, the federalists. But then they must give an account of imputed sin that is able to show how it is that God is just in imputing the sin of Adam to me, in a way that is plausible and consistent with their federalism.

Charles Hodge's Idiosyncratic Federalism

Hodge thought he had provided such an argument. His position, whilst not a response to those of Shedd and Strong (their systematic theologies post-dated his own), takes seriously the problems often expressed by realists. In particular, he is keenly aware of the injustice problem and the plausibility problem and seeks to address them in his own federalist account of sin. However, in so doing, he develops a version of federalism that is not entirely in accord with the Reformed Orthodox consensus on this subject. It is therefore worth considering his views as a foil to the realist arguments of Shedd and Strong, even though they were not intended to rebut exactly the arguments Shedd and Strong developed.

I begin this section by setting Hodge's views in some historical context. It is often thought that Calvin is a proponent of federalism in some embryonic form. For this reason federalism is often referred to as 'Calvinistic federalism'. This is a half-truth that is misleading. It is half-true because in the post-Reformation

---

[26] Henri Blocher, *Original Sin, Illuminating the Riddle* (Leicester: IVP, 1997), p. 115.

period, Reformed Orthodox dogmaticians did take this view. So it is properly 'Calvin*istic*'. But it is misleading because Calvin is not unambiguously a proponent of this view. In the course of his discussion of original sin in his *Institutes*, Calvin says,

> For, since it is said that we became subject to God's judgment through Adam's sin, we are to understand it not as if we guiltless and undeserving, bore the guilt of his offence but in the sense that, since we through his transgression have become entangled in the curse, he is said to have made us guilty.[27]

This excerpt shows that Calvin's view, unlike later Calvinists, is not forthrightly federalist. From passages such as this, it is clear that Calvin's debt to Augustine extends to his theory of the spread of sin, although the extent of this debt is difficult to discern.[28] However, amongst the post-Reformation Reformed Orthodox theologians things are more clearly defined. Take, for instance, Francis Turretin's articulation of federalist doctrine:

> For the bond between Adam and his posterity is twofold: (1) natural, as he is the father, and we are his children; (2) political and forensic, as he was the prince and representative head of the whole human race. Therefore the foundation of imputation is not only the natural connection which exists between us and Adam (since, in that case, all his sins might be imputed to us), but mainly the moral and federal (in virtue of which God entered into covenant with him as our head.) Hence Adam stood in that sin not as a private person, but as a public and representative person - representing all his posterity in that action and whose demerit equally pertains to all.[29]

Here the injustice problem is dealt with by claiming that Adam acts on behalf of the rest of humanity when he acts sinfully in the Garden of Eden. He is the representative of humanity in this respect. Analogues to this notion of representation are not hard to find. Jones may appoint Smith as his representative with the power to act on his own behalf in the acquisition of

---

[27] Calvin, *Institutes* II: I: 8, (ed.) John T. McNeill, (trans.) Ford Lewis Battles (Philadelphia, PA: Westminster Press, 1960), p. 251.

[28] Calvin's commentary on Romans 5: 12 and 19 does not offer any greater clarity on this matter, as far as I can make out. See *Calvin's Commentaries, Vol. XIX, Commentary on The Epistle to The Romans* (trans.) John Owen [Calvin Translation Society Edition] (Grand Rapids, MI: Baker, 1979 [reprint]), p. 200: 'For as Adam at his creation had received for us as well as for himself the gifts of God's favour, so by falling from the Lord, he in himself corrupted, vitiated, depraved, and ruined our nature; for having been divested of God's likeness, he could not have generated seed but what was like himself. Hence we have all sinned; for we are all imbued with natural corruption, and so are become sinful and wicked.'

[29] Turretin, *Institutes of Elenctic Theology, Vol. I,* trans. George Musgrove Giger, ed. James T. Dennison, Jnr. (Philipsburg, NJ: Presbyterian and Reformed, 1992), p. 616.

Botticelli's 'the Birth of Venus' at Christies. In such circumstances, where Smith bids a particular sum for Botticelli's painting, he is representing his employer in this regard, whose money he is bidding with.

However, the problem with this sort of scenario applied to the case of Adam, is clear: unlike the Smith and Jones situation, I have not authorized Adam to act on my behalf. Perhaps God has ordained matters in such a way that Adam acts on my behalf, and this seems the most fitting way in which God can actualize the federalist scenario. But this appears arbitrary, to say the least. On the question of plausibility, the federalist position does seem, at face value, to be more plausible than Augustinian realism. But it still appears to be a rather peculiar state of affairs wherein God ordains that one person represents everybody else, and commits a sin that everybody else has to suffer for.

Defenders of federalism usually respond to this sort of criticism by way of the twofold distinction in Adam's position, outlined by Turretin. This involves claiming that what is important in this representational view is not that it was the particular individual, Adam, who was the representative, but that Adam was the first human being. Someone else could have been created as the first human being, perhaps you or me.[30] But the net result would have been the same because whoever was the first human being, and therefore the natural head of the human race, would also have represented the rest of the race before God, and eventually sinned as Adam did. Such sin would, like Adam's sin, have had serious consequences for the rest of humanity. Thus, the argument goes, whoever occupied the position of the first human being would have sinned like Adam.

This seems right. In fact, this seems to be one of the key insights of the representational aspect of the federal view. It is Adam's place as the first human being that makes him the representative of the whole race, not the fact that it happened to be this human being who is called Adam who was given this place. Or, perhaps better, not just because of this – I presume God has a reason for making this person the first person. However, this does nothing to alleviate the embarrassment caused by the problem of injustice that the federal view seems to entail. Nor does it provide a conclusive argument in favour of the plausibility of the federal theory.[31]

This brings us to Hodge. He seems to have felt something of this problem with federalism, and structured his argument on imputed sin accordingly. In

---

[30] If this is so, then perhaps an entirely different human race would have resulted, that is, a race descended from whoever God had made the first human being, rather than Adam. This is related to the issue of the necessity of origin, discussed by Saul Kripke in *Naming and Necessity* (Oxford: Blackwell, 1980).

[31] From the foregoing it should be clear that 'Reformed' and 'federalist' are not synonyms. There are theologians in the Reformed tradition who do not take a federalist view of imputed sin, including those Calvinistic theologians like Shedd, who defend a version of realism.

particular, Hodge's defence of the immediate imputation of Adam's sin to his posterity led him to revise the concept of original guilt used by federal theologians.

Let us examine his argument. First, Hodge claims that imputation is to reckon or lay something to someone else's account. Imputing sin entails imputing guilt for that sin:

> And by guilt is meant not criminality or moral ill-desert, or demerit, much less moral pollution, but the judicial obligation to satisfy justice. Hence the evil consequent on the imputation is not an arbitrary infliction; not merely a misfortune or calamity; not a chastisement in the proper sense of that word, but a punishment, i.e., an evil inflicted in execution of the penalty of law and for the satisfaction of divine justice.[32]

This is a significant admission. Hodge is affirming that there is a strong connection between original sin and original guilt on the one hand, whilst rejecting the claim that the *reatus*, or liability involved in original guilt, is grounded in the *culpa* or guilt of Adam, on the other. To put it another way, the traditional Reformed doctrine states that all Adam's posterity have original sin and original guilt imputed directly and immediately to them by God. The guilt that original sin involves is Adam's own guilt, the *culpa*, for which there is a corresponding punishment based on the liability for punishment this involves (*reatus poenae*). Hodge denies that the guilt involved in original sin is grounded in Adam's guilt. He maintains it is merely the liability for punishment on the basis of original sin. Each member of Adam's progeny has Adam's original sin imputed immediately to them, and each individual sinner is thereby liable for punishment according to divine justice. But - and this is crucial - *not* on account of the fact that each individual sinner is guilty of Adam's guilt, but merely on the basis of the fact that each of Adam's posterity have original sin.

John Murray claims that Hodge makes this theological move for two reasons.[33] First, he was responding to the claim that immediate imputation had two consequences that were damaging to the legal fiction involved in the federalist case for imputed sin. These consequences are that (a) somehow it means Adam's posterity are personally and voluntarily involved in Adam's sin,

---

[32] *Systematic Theology Vol. II*, p. 194. Murray points out that this is a claim Hodge made elsewhere. For instance, ' "And if there is anything in which Calvinists are agreed, it is in saying that when they affirm 'that the guilt of Adam's sin has come upon us,' they mean, exposure to punishment on account of that sin"', from *Theological Essays: Reprinted from The Princeton Review* (New York, 1846), p. 140, cited in *The Imputation of Adam's Sin*, p. 74, n. 119.

[33] See *The Imputation of Adam's Sin*, p. 77. Murray thinks that Hodge was mistaken in making this move, and should have retained a traditional, federal doctrine of original guilt.

and (b) immediate imputation seems to imply the transference of moral properties from Adam to his posterity. The second reason for making this move was the implications it had for the imputation of Christ's righteousness. Like the imputation of sin, this too is a species of legal fiction according to the federalist account. Christ does not literally take on the sins of all Adam's posterity. He is their substitute, but this does not entail taking on their sin and guilt. In order to counteract both these perceived problems with the doctrine of immediate imputation as it stood, Hodge dropped the *culpa* aspect of original guilt, retaining only the *reatus*, derived solely from possession of original sin itself.

Let us assume that Murray is right about this. If this is right, then Hodge, like the realists, seems to be acknowledging that his federalism has a problem with injustice. As we have already noted, Augustinian realists like Shedd and Strong say it makes no sense to suffer for someone else's sin. So God imputes Adam's sin to me immediately, such that Adam's sin is my sin on account of the metaphysics involved. And just as Adam's sin is my sin, so also, according to this argument, Adam's guilt is my guilt. Hodge is saying that there is a problem here with immediate imputation because it seems to mean Adam's sin is my sin via his guilt being my guilt. How can this be resolved without embracing realism? By denying that Adam's posterity are punishable on account of having Adam's actual guilt imputed to them (or his sin, for that matter). Rather, Adam's posterity is punishable merely on account of, as Hodge says, 'an evil inflicted in execution of the penalty of law and for the satisfaction of divine justice'. But this does not seem to lead to a more robust version of federalism.

Consider the following federalist reasoning, consistent with Hodge's claim about imputed sin and guilt. Original sin is imputed from Adam to his posterity, such that God treats Adam's posterity 'as if' they were sinners because Adam is their representative. Why is guilt imputed, then? Adam's descendants are not themselves guilty of Adam's sin, just as they are not themselves the one's who committed the original sin. Yet God treats them 'as if' they were both the one sinning and thereby the one guilty for that sin. Hodge sees that if he concedes that God imputes guilt immediately, then it might appear that I am somehow guilty of Adam's sin. He averts this outcome by denying that immediate imputation has this consequence. All that guilt involves in this case, he claims, is liability to punishment, not, in addition, liability to guilt (because the guilt of the first sin was Adam's guilt, not mine). But this is just to say God imputes someone else's sin to me and treats me as the sinner, punishing me for it. The problem with this should be obvious: treating one person as if they have committed another person's crime, and then acting upon that assumption, punishing them as if they were the guilty party, is simply monumentally unjust. Far from solving the problem of immediate imputation and the injustice problem by adjusting the federalist argument to make it consistent with the 'as if' clause of legal fiction, Hodge undercuts his own federalism. What he ends up with is a legal fiction that comprises both imputed sin and imputed guilt, and that is morally indefensible.

In order to avoid falling into the arms of the realists, Hodge claims that the legal fiction of imputation extends to sin and only that aspect of guilt that is compatible with imputation being a legal fiction. (The assumption being that the *reatus* applies only to the punishable aspect of guilt, not to some liability for guilt itself, as per medieval discussion of the subject.) This seems rather a high price to pay to retain federalism. Hodge denies the obvious consequence of a full-blooded doctrine of original sin with respect to original guilt. This is that if one is truly guilty of Adam's sin one must participate in that sin. Far better, it seems to me, to simply concede the injustice question and embrace the fact that Adam's sin and guilt are (somehow) my sin and guilt for which I am culpable, as per realism.

Conclusions

What can we say about these three views of the imputation of Adam's sin? First, it is important to note the considerable conceptual overlap between the realist and federalist solutions to the problem we have examined. Shedd, Strong, and Hodge all shared a debt to a common theological heritage and seem to have been happy to remain within the boundaries of the full-orbed doctrine of original sin bequeathed to them by Reformed Orthodoxy (even if they repudiated something of the method of scholasticism).[34]

Second, there is a desire to take seriously the problem of imputed sin. Shedd and Strong sought to *defuse* this problem by explaining how Adam's sin just is the sin of his posterity via arguments for realism. Hodge sought to *deflect* the problem by explaining how it could be that federalism is consistent with divine justice in this area. But in order to do so, he took a view of original guilt that was not typical of other Reformed theologians and entails a truncated, if not downright peculiar doctrine of original guilt that pertains to punishment only, not, in addition to this, to the crime committed.

It seems to me that Hodge was unsuccessful in his attempt to rehabilitate a purely federalist understanding of the imputation problem. But the unindividualized version of realism offered by Shedd and Strong also presents conceptual difficulties that appear insuperable, to do with the way in which they construe all humanity being 'seminally' present in Adam as some

---

[34] In this respect, these three theologians are quite unlike their contemporary counterparts. Even theologians like Piet Schoonenberg amongst the Roman Catholics, and Reinhold Niebuhr amongst Protestants, who have attempted to come to terms with a doctrine of original sin in the parlance of contemporary theology, have felt the need to distance themselves from some of the defining structures of the previous discussion. See Tatha Wiley, *Original Sin*, ch. 6.

unindividualized mass. However, a chastened version of realism that uses the common nature argument of Shedd without the unindividualized argument as well, might provide a way forward in this discussion that circumvents the obviously unpalatable aspects of the strong version of realism, and is able to offer a solution where federalism cannot. Such a solution to the problem of imputation would also have the advantage (if it is an advantage) of remaining within the boundaries of the traditional doctrine of original sin, without necessarily committing oneself to a view of sin that is theologically otiose.[35] I hope this is possible, and have tried to indicate elsewhere how this might be done.[36] If this is possible, then it would represent a real contribution to our understanding of theological anthropology and may open up new ways of thinking about the imputation of Christ's righteousness too.[37] Thus, a realist solution to imputed sin offers the prospect of a realist solution to not just one, but potentially two central issues in dogmatic theology, a matter to which we shall return in chapter five. But before this we will need to consider Shedd's understanding of the person of Christ and how Christ is without sin, the subjects of the next two chapters. Just as Shedd's commitment to traducianism has implications for his doctrine of the transmission of sin, so it also affects what he says about the theanthropic constitution of Christ's person. It is this matter to which we turn next.

---

[35] That is, one could endorse a version of realism along the lines suggested here, which does not entail anything that is obviously false in the way that the seminal version of realism does.

[36] See 'Scholastic Theology, Augustinian Realism and Original Guilt', which offers a sketch of how this might go. This article utilizes contemporary essentialist metaphysics to plug the conceptual gap in Shedd's argument. I hope to offer a more complete account of the doctrine of original sin and this problem in particular, in a monograph on this subject entitled, *An Essay on Original Sin*.

[37] However, as I pointed out in 'Scholastic Theology, Augustinian Realism and Original Guilt', there is still a serious problem for Christology with respect to original guilt. I hope to overcome this problem in *An Essay on Original Sin*.

CHAPTER 3

The Theanthropic Person of Christ

In this chapter, we shall consider some central issues in Shedd's understanding of the theanthropic person of Christ. Shedd's contribution in this area of Christology is worthy of consideration for a number of reasons. First, although he took a classical view of the person of Christ, there are a number of ways in which his view is untraditional, or, perhaps better, relies upon minority reports in the tradition at crucial points in the development of his account.[1] In this respect his systematic theology is distinct from that of his Presbyterian contemporary Charles Hodge, and more like that of the Baptist theologian, Augustus Strong, as we have already had cause to note. Second, Shedd's Christology has a theologically interesting application of two trademark doctrines that Shedd espoused, and that we have already considered, namely, Augustinian realism and traducianism. Thus, his understanding of the person of Christ reflects two important overarching themes in his dogmatics.

This chapter proceeds in several stages that reflect these hallmarks of Shedd's account of the person of Christ. To begin with, we shall sketch out the ways in which Shedd allies himself with classical theology in his exposition of the doctrine of the theanthropic person of Christ. We shall see that, although the language Shedd uses to explain the two-natures doctrine of the hypostatic union is rather misleading, it can be expressed in a way that is compatible with one traditional account of the human nature of Christ. Then, secondly, we shall examine several key issues in Shedd's Christology that comprise his particular contribution to the doctrine. In the course of this discussion, we shall see that his defence of Augustinian realism and traducianism play an important role in the metaphysics of the Incarnation as he understands it.

There is much more to Shedd's account of the theanthropic person of Christ than we can take account of here. For instance, Shedd has interesting things to say about the hypostatic union, and in particular, the way in which Christ's two

---

[1] In his introduction to DT, Shedd remarks that 'the general type of doctrine is Augustino-Calvinistic. Upon a few points, the elder Calvinism [i.e. Augustinianism] has been followed in preference to the later. This, probably, is the principal difference between this treatise and contemporary ones of the Calvinistic class.' DT: 37. The 'few points' to which he refers, are, as he goes on to explain, his traducianism and Augustinian realism – central and defining doctrines in his theological anthropology and Christology, as we shall see.

wills and two centres of action (as defined by the sixth ecumenical council at Constantinople in AD 681) correspond to two ranges of consciousness in one single consciousness of the Word. But we cannot enter into these matters here. We will be sufficiently occupied in trying to make sense of the material in hand as it is.[2]

Shedd*ing* the Classical Doctrine of the Person of Christ

In his editorial introduction to his recent edition of Shedd's *Dogmatic Theology*, Alan Gomes says Shedd did not hold that 'the two natures of Christ combine to form a person.' Rather, 'Shedd believed that the second person of the Trinity assumed a human nature, not that two unpersonalized natures formed a theanthropic person.'[3] This is certainly true if one is speaking of the Chalcedonian two-natures doctrine of the person of Christ, as found in Shedd's Christology. Shedd does not claim that Christ is composed of two unpersonalized natures comprising the divine nature of the Word and the human nature of Christ that, when joined in hypostatic union together form a theanthropic person since one of those natures, the divine nature of the Word, is not assumed at the Incarnation and is not unpersonalized prior to the Incarnation – it is, after all, the nature of the divine person of the Word. What Shedd says is that the Word in becoming Incarnate assumes a body-soul composite that is the human nature of Christ. However, this body-soul composite consists of two 'natures', namely, the human body and the human soul of Christ. These two 'natures' *are* unpersonalized until assumed by the Word in the Incarnation. So, although Gomes is right if one is talking about the two natures doctrine of Chalcedonian Christology as found in Shedd's thought, there is a sense in which Shedd affirms that the Word assumes two unpersonalized 'natures' in the Incarnation, where this means the two parts of human nature consisting of a human body and human soul. (In what follows, I shall distinguish Shedd's idiosyncratic use of the term nature from the traditional way the term is deployed in the two-natures doctrine of Chalcedonian Christology, by placing Shedd's term in speech marks, thus: 'nature'.) In this first section, we shall give a critical account of the two natures doctrine that Shedd adopts. Although the language he uses is idiosyncratic, it expresses one traditional version of the nature of the two natures doctrine of Chalcedonian Christology.

It is certainly the case that Shedd, in common with classical theologians generally, affirms the *anhypostasia-enhypostasia* distinction with respect to the human nature of Christ. (But he does so without using the theologoumenon

---

[2] What he has to say about the sinlessness of Christ and the temptations of God Incarnate are the subject of the next chapter. Such matters have an important bearing upon our two themes of sin and salvation.
[3] Alan Gomes, *Editor's Introduction* to DT.

'*anhypostasia-enhypostasia*' common in contemporary discussions of this distinction.) Very roughly, this distinction states that the human nature of Christ does not constitute a human person on its own. It does not exist independently of the person of Christ, but is 'personalized', so to speak, as a 'part' of the person of Christ which is brought about by the assumption by the Word of human nature in the Incarnation.[4] Shedd says:

> He [the Word] did not acquire personality by union with a human nature. The incarnation was not necessary in order that the trinitarian Son of God might be self-conscious. On the contrary, the human nature which he assumed to himself acquired personality by its union with him.[5]

Shedd's use of 'nature' to denote the human body and soul of Christ is compatible with the *anhypostasia-enhypostasia* distinction, although it does mean that Christ assumes a particular human nature (i.e. concrete particular consisting of a body and soul distinct from the Word), rather than merely assuming the property of being human that is common to all human beings. (Although, as we shall see, Shedd's traducianism means that the human nature of Christ does exist prior to his Incarnation.)[6] In order to make these issues clear, we will need to explain where Shedd's view fits amongst the classical theological positions on the human nature of Christ.

There are, broadly speaking, two ways in which the human nature of Christ has traditionally been understood. (I do not say these are the *only* two ways to think of the human nature of Christ. But these are two traditional positions that are compatible with Chalcedonian Christology, the theological benchmark for classical theologians in matters Christological. We shall not consider traditional ways in which unorthodox views of the Incarnation have been expressed.) The first of these views claims that Christ is composed of two 'parts', the Word and the human body he assumes in the Incarnation.[7] Sometimes this is spoken of in

---

[4] I am not suggesting that the human nature of Christ is literally a 'part' of Christ; just that, in some way analogous to a whole object that has parts, the Word, in assuming human nature at the Incarnation, 'expands' himself, as it were, to include the 'parts' of human nature. 'Parts' Christologies have been discussed in detail by Richard Cross in *The Metaphysics of the Incarnation* (Oxford: Oxford University Press, 2002). By 'parts' Christologies, Cross means those Christologies which use an analogy with the relation between a normal human body and soul to understand the 'parts' of God Incarnate: the Word, his human body and his distinct human soul. This is similar to what I am getting at here.

[5] DT: 617.

[6] See DT: 489-490; 626-627; 630-631; 637-640.

[7] Here and in what follows, I shall assume the traditional Christian view, that human beings are normally composed of two substances, a human body and a soul. I shall not discuss the recent Christian forms of materialism, where human beings are taken to be material beings with no immaterial soul, (e.g. Peter van Inwagen's, *Material Beings* [Ithaca, NY: Cornell University Press, 1990], or *In Search of The Soul, Four Views of*

terms of the Word assuming the property of human nature. Where this is the case, the Word takes on that property that is necessary and sufficient for being human, including a human body, making up a two-parts Christology of Word + human body. But it is the Word who occupies the place of a human soul. This view – let us call it, for the sake of the argument, the two-part view[8] - is often thought to be Apollinarian because it affirms a two-part Christology, where human nature is just a property, including the property, 'having a human body', but without a human soul that is distinct from, and in addition to, the divine nature of the Word. However, this need not be Apollinarian, if, rather than taking the place of a human soul, the Word becomes a human soul in addition to being the divine Word.[9]

This is rather like saying Mary takes on the property of motherhood when she becomes a mother. She does not cease to be the person she was because of this event. What happens is that she begins to have a property that she did not have previously. In a similar way, on this view, the Word assumes the property of being human in addition to having the essential property of being divine. He does not give up his divinity in order to become human.[10] If this is the case, then, in assuming the property or properties of human nature the Word takes on the property (or property conjunct) of 'being a human soul'. This view may still be problematic. For instance, it is often thought that a two-part view of Christ's human nature entails monothelitism, the notion that Christ had only one will and one centre of action (as canonized by the sixth ecumenical council of Constantinople in AD 681) – a matter that I have attended to elsewhere.[11] Whether or not this is the case, the two-part approach to Christology is at least

---

The Mind-Body Problem, eds. Joel B. Green and Stuart L. Palmer [Downers Grove, IL: IVP, 2005]). Shedd also assumes a version of substance dualism (that human beings are normally composed of a body and soul.) Of course, this does not mean human beings cannot be disembodied. Only that normally speaking, human beings are embodied.

[8] Sometimes the two-part view is identified with Alexandrian Christology of the pre-Chalcedonian period. However, it seems to me that (a) the Alexandrian Christology is a very rough and ready collection of differing views, not one monolithic entity as is sometimes claimed and (b) an Alexandrian Christologist need not be committed to a two-part Christology. So, I have resisted the urge to call the two-part view, the Alexandrian view. For a standard presentation of the early pre-Chalcedonian Christological controversy in these terms, see Daniel Migliore's introduction to systematic theology, *Faith Seeking Understanding, Second Edition* (Grand Rapids, MI: Eerdmans, 2004 [1991]), pp. 169-173 and Otto Weber, *Foundations of Dogmatics Vol. 2*, (trans.) Darrell L. Guder (Grand Rapids, MI: Eerdmans, 1983), pp. 111-114.

[9] This has been defended in the recent literature by Alvin Plantinga in 'On Heresy, Mind, and Truth' *Faith and Philosophy* 16 (1999): 182-193.

[10] It is precisely at this point that kenotic Christologists take their leave of Chalcedonian Christology.

[11] See *Divinity and Humanity: The Incarnation Reconsidered* (Cambridge: Cambridge University Press, 2007), ch. 2.

prima facie compatible with the Chalcedonian definition of Christology. That is sufficient for present purposes.

The alternative to this two-part Christology is that often associated with what, for the sake of the argument, we shall dub three-part Christology.[12] On this view, Christ comprises three 'parts': the Word, the human body of Christ and the human soul of Christ, which is distinct from the divine nature of the Word. The Word assumes not just a property at the Incarnation, but also a body + soul composite, or concrete particular. This body + soul composite is not a distinct human person because, so this story goes, the Word assumes this human nature before it becomes a distinct human person. Instead, with Brian Leftow,[13] we could call the human nature assumed by the Word on this view, the *natural endowment* of a human person. That is, it has all the components of a complete human person, but in the case of the Incarnation, does not become a human person until it is assumed by the Word (assuming for the present that, without an Incarnation, the body + soul of the human that becomes Christ in the Incarnation, could have become some human being other than Christ, if it had become a human being at all – although we will have cause to question this assumption in the next chapter).[14] This view is often thought to imply Nestorianism, the heresy which states Christ is composed of two distinct persons, one divine and the other human. But this need not be the case if the three-part Christologist is able to show that the Word assumes the human nature of Christ before it becomes a human person.[15] This view also seems, *prima facie*, compatible with Chalcedonian Christology, expressed in the so-called Chalcedonian definition of AD 451. It may be that the three-part view is easier to reconcile with dyothelitism than (some versions of) the two-part view. Dyothelitism is the idea that Christ has two wills and two centres of action,

---

[12] This three-part view of Christology is often conflated with Antiochene Christology in the literature. But this characterization suffers from the same problems as conflating the two-part view with Alexandrian Christology, namely, that the Antiochene view is not a clearly defined group of theological ideas, and that it is not clear an Antiochene Christologist is committed to a three-part view of the theanthropic person of Christ. Therefore, I have resisted the temptation to speak of three-part Christology as Antiochene Christology.

[13] Brian Leftow, 'A Timeless God Incarnate', in Stephen T. Davis, Daniel Kendall and Gerald O'Collins (eds.) *The Incarnation* (Oxford: Oxford University Press, 2002).

[14] Thus the Word assumes a complete human nature, but not a complete human person, thereby avoiding Nestorianism, and retaining the notion, essential to orthodox Christology, that the Word assumes a complete human nature at the Incarnation. I should also add that, on the version of the Antiochene view I am expounding, there is no temporal lag between the creation of the human nature of Christ and its assumption by the Word. These events are simultaneous.

[15] For a recent attempt to do this, see Leftow, 'A Timeless God Incarnate' I have also dealt with this in *Divinity and Humanity*, ch. 2.

affirmed by the sixth ecumenical council at Constantinople in AD 681 as an extrapolation of the basic Chalcedonian position.

Having given a thumbnail sketch of these two traditional alternatives on the human nature of Christ, we are now in a position to ascertain which of these two views (if either) Shedd opts for. Let us see what Shedd says for himself:

> The distinctive characteristic of the incarnation is the union of two diverse natures, a divine and a human, so as to constitute one single person. A single person may consist of one nature or of two natures or of three. A Trinitarian person has only one nature, namely, the divine essence. A human person has two natures, namely, a material body and an immaterial soul. A theanthropic person has three natures, namely, the divine essence, a human soul, and a human body. By the incarnation, not a God, not a man, but a God-man is constituted. A theanthropic person is a Trinitarian person modified by union with a human nature. (DT: 617)

Similarly,

> A theanthropic person, again, is yet more complex than a human person. He has three divers natures, each yielding their diverse experiences or modes of consciousness, and yet only a single self-consciousness. The Lord Jesus Christ is constituted of three substances, distinct and different in kind from each other. He is constituted of one infinite spirit, one finite spirit, and one finite body. (DT: 644, n. 5. 1. 8)

He also speaks of the 'unification ... of three factors – the Logos, the human soul, and the human body – which was effected in the miraculous conception and which continued through the whole earthly life of our Lord'.[16] And again,

> The union of two natures in Christ's person is denominated hypostatic, that is, personal. The two natures or substances (*ousiai*) constitute one personal substistence (*hypostasis*). (DT: 656)

From these citations the following tenets of Shedd's position are clear. First, Shedd stands squarely within what we have called the three-part tradition of Christology. He affirms, with the three-parters, that Christ's theanthropic person (that is, his fully divine and fully human person) is composed of three 'parts': the Word, a human body and a human soul (distinct from the Word).

Second, the theanthropic person of Christ is fundamentally a divine person 'modified' by a human nature.[17] That is, it is the divine nature of the Word that

---

[16] DT: 619.

is the 'root' of the person of Christ (something which Gomes is at pains to point out in his introduction to Shedd's *Dogmatic Theology*). It is not the case, on Shedd's view, that Christ is a just human person who has been divinized in some way, or a human person who has a divine aspect or part (where part is understood in the conventional sense, as some fraction of a whole object). It is rather, that Christ is a divine person, the Word, who has become human by taking on the components of human nature. It is in virtue of this union that Christ can be said to have all the predicates requisite to humanity and divinity.

Third, although Shedd speaks at times of two natures and at other times of three natures, it seems from what he says that the three natures are three elements of the person of Christ that are distinct substances: a human body, a human soul and the Word (the human body and soul comprising the concrete particular of Christ's human nature). What he means by this twofold use of the term 'nature' here, is that there are two natures involved in the hypostatic union, but three 'natures' if we are counting the two parts of Christ's human nature as substances in their own right. It may help to re-cast Shedd's concepts in slightly different language to avoid potential misunderstanding. Let us say that the Incarnation involves the Word, and the human nature he assumes. (These two are what is usually denominated the two natures of Christ in Christologies that take their point of departure from Chalcedon.) The divine nature of the Word has no proper parts. But the human nature of Christ is a concrete particular that has 'parts' in our extended sense of parts: the human body and human soul of Christ. Together these two 'parts' form the human nature of Christ that is assumed by the Word. It is clear from what he says that Shedd holds to a version of substance dualism, the notion that a human being is composed of two substances, a body and soul. Since Christ is fully human, his human nature is a body + soul composite. It is also clear that Shedd takes this to mean that Christ has a human soul distinct from the Word.[18] But this seems to have certain undesirable consequences for this theanthropic view of the person of Christ.

Here is one such potentially undesirable consequence (if it is a consequence of Shedd's views). What Shedd says seems to imply that the Word and the Christ are distinct entities. If Shedd is saying that there are three substances involved in the Incarnation, the Word, the human body of Christ and the distinct human soul of Christ, it looks like Christ has properties the Word does not have. Christ has a distinct human soul and a human body; the Word (apparently) does not. So Christ has the properties, 'having a human body' and

---

[17] 'It is the divine nature and not the human which is the base of Christ's person.' DT, 617. Compare Shedd, *HCD2:* 406.

[18] Alternatively, we could construe Shedd as saying there is the Word (first substance) and the human nature of Christ, which is a compound substance composed of two distinct substances, the human soul and human body of Christ. This sounds like what he says in the first citation given earlier.

'having a distinct human soul', which the Word does not have. But then, in what sense is the Word the same as the Christ? Or, consider another, related problem. It seems that, according to Shedd's view Christ has proper parts, whereas the Word does not. Christ has the proper parts, the Word, the human body and the human soul. But the Word has no parts whatsoever (or at least, on one traditional view of the Word, he has no proper parts). But then, Christ has this property that the Word does not: 'having proper parts'.

To my knowledge Shedd does not directly address this problem in his Christology. But one could develop a response that is compatible with Shedd's stated views on the matter. For instance, one could claim that in some way one can retain both divine simplicity (which Shedd defends) and the Incarnation, such that the 'parts' assumed by the Word at the Incarnation do not involve any essential change to the nature of the Word (again, something Shedd endorses), where the Word is timelessly God Incarnate. Then, Christ is born in 4 BC, but this does not mean that the Word begins to have human nature at that moment, because if he is timeless, there is no 'before-' for the Word. What we can say is that before the human body and soul of Christ began to exist, it was timelessly the case that God the Son was human, as well as divine. So, on the timeless view, there is a timeline of history in which Jesus of Nazareth can be placed – he has a birth, life and death in temporal succession. But there is no corresponding timeline for the Word. The relation he has to the human Jesus is an atemporal one. The upshot of this is that if one takes the timelessness view of the Incarnation, then the Word is timelessly God Incarnate, but at some time Christ begins to exist.[19] But this does nothing to solve the whole-parts problem of the Incarnation. It just shows that it can be re-cast in terms of divine timelessness. It is still the case on a timeless view of the Incarnation that the act of becoming incarnate, even if it is a timeless act, means that the Word has human parts. And this was our initial concern. How can we say both that the Word is simple in the strong sense of metaphysically simple associated with traditional accounts of divine simplicity, and that the Word takes on human parts in the Incarnation?[20] Perhaps we can say the Word has no essential parts but that in the Incarnation he assumes accidental parts. Then we have no essential change in the person of the Word and no parts to the Word that are essential parts. Still, this seems incompatible with divine simplicity, if it means that the Word Incarnate has parts that the Word *simpliciter* does not. Nevertheless, perhaps this argument (or one like it) could be defended in order

---

[19] This is not Nestorian because the Word assumes the natural endowment of a human being, not a human being *per se*. This is the case on the atemporal view as well as the temporal one, although the relations involved in the assumption of this human nature are different.

[20] The relevant aspect of the traditional account of divine simplicity is the notion that God has no parts, not even any distinct properties.

to safeguard some strong account of divine simplicity – it is just that Shedd does not offer such an argument in his *Dogmatic Theology*.

Or, one could simply concede the simplicity claim (something which Shedd would not agree to[21]). It is not obviously incoherent to suppose that the Word enlarges himself to include human nature that has proper parts at this first moment of Incarnation. We could argue as follows: My tie is tartan. It has parts, some of which are not tartan, for instance, the cobalt strands in the tie that make up one of the colours of the plaid. So the tartan tie has parts that are not tartan. But the whole tie is tartan plaid, and only the whole is tartan. Perhaps we can say something similar about the Incarnation. Christ (the whole 'person of Christ') is the Word Incarnate. Parts of Christ, specifically, the human body and soul of Christ, are parts of the Word Incarnate, specifically, the human parts of the Word. But only when taken together with the Word is the resulting whole the Word Incarnate.[22]

This is commensurate with the claim that at the Incarnation the Word enlarges himself to include human nature. And it is commensurate with the claim that the parts of the human nature of Christ are parts of the Word. In which case the Word, from the moment of Incarnation onwards, has proper parts. This may seem undesirable to some, Shedd included. It may seem peculiar to others. But it is not obviously incoherent. Nor, it seems to me, is it unorthodox, although it would mean someone who defends this view would have to give up (at least some versions of) divine simplicity, a notion that is deeply embedded in the tradition, and which Shedd upholds.

The fourth aspect of Shedd's Christology follows on from this. The composite substance of the human body and soul of Christ comprises the human nature of Christ, which is not a human person until it is united with the Word. At the first moment of Incarnation and thereafter, we may speak of the human person of Christ, meaning the divine person of the Word united to the human nature of Christ to form one theanthropic person. Shedd affirms this in *A History of Christian Doctrine*, where he cites Richard Hooker as follows:

> The Son of God did not assume a man's *person* into his own [person], but a man's *nature* to his own person.... The flesh and the conjunction of the flesh with God, began both at one instant; his making and taking to himself our flesh was but one act, so that in Christ there is no personal subsistence but one, and that from everlasting.[23]

So, it seems Shedd affirms that the Word assumes a human nature, that is, a concrete particular, not just the property of human nature, although clearly he does affirm this too. The point is that, if the Word assumes human nature he assumes a concrete particular not just the property of human nature. Moreover,

---

[21] DT: 276.

[22] Leftow is good on this point. See 'A Timeless God Incarnate'.

[23] Shedd, *HCD1:* 407, citing Hooker, *Ecclesiastical Polity* (1597), Bk. V, ch. liii.

the human nature assumed by the Word is unpersonalized as per the *anhypostasia-enhypostasia* distinction. But the divine nature of Christ was always personal because his divine nature is just the nature of the Word, who is one of the divine persons of the Trinity. Thus, Gomes is right that Shedd does not teach that the Word assumes two unpersonalized natures in the Incarnation, if he is referring to Shedd's defence of the traditional Chalcedonian two-natures doctrine.[24] But it is also the case that, on Shedd's view, the Incarnation involves the assumption of two unpersonalized natures, if one is thinking in terms of the elements of the human body-soul composite the Word assumes in taking on human nature. Then, somehow, the human body and soul of Christ is not made a human person until assumed by the Word at the moment they are generated, in the Incarnation. (This does not imply that there is a time at which the human nature of Christ exists, but has not yet been assumed by the Word – which is Nestorian and Adoptionist,[25] and which we have just seen Shedd denies. Rather, this means that the Word assumes this human nature at the moment of Incarnation, and that this human nature has no existence prior to, or independent of the Word. Then there is no time at which the human nature – that is, the human body and soul - of Christ existed, without the Word.)

Once this is clarified, it is apparent that what we might call the hard core of Shedd's doctrine of the theanthropic person of Christ is straightforwardly three-partist. It is also clearly not Nestorian. The Word assumes a concrete particular at the Incarnation that is the human nature of Christ, composed of a human body and a human soul. But nothing Shedd says commits him to the notion that the Word assumes an already existing person at the Incarnation. Nor does it require that the hypostatic union is a union of two distinct persons. He explicitly states that, 'at the instant when it [the human nature of Christ] was assumed, it was human nature unindividualized, not a distinct individual person.' (DT: 626-627)

Shedd also affirms other key aspects to classical Christology. For instance, he affirms the traditional doctrine of the Virgin Birth and that the Incarnation does not affect any change in the divine essence of the Trinity. He is committed to the claim that the Incarnation does not involve the assumption of a human nature into the divine essence, but only the assumption of a human nature by one of the persons of the divine Trinity. It is not the case that, because the Word becomes Incarnate, the divine essence becomes Incarnate. Rather, the person of the Word assumes human nature in the Incarnation. This scholastic distinction is a staple of Protestant Orthodoxy, and Shedd simply reiterates it in

---

[24] Viz. the citation from Gomes's editor's introduction to DT, cited a the beginning of this chapter.

[25] Adoptionism is the view that, at some moment later than the first moment of his existence, the human person Jesus of Nazareth is possessed by the second person of the Trinity. This means that there are moments at which Jesus exists, but without being the Word Incarnate.

his own discussion. He also advocates a doctrine of the communication of attributes (*communicatio idiomatum*), where, in keeping with the Reformed tradition and contrary to the Lutheran Orthodox, he maintains that the properties belonging to one or other of the two natures may be predicated of the person of Christ. This, of course, is a constituent of his position on the hypostatic union (*unio personalis*). These additional claims are important, and not uncontroversial. But I do not propose to enter into discussion of Shedd's justification of them here. I mention them in order to show that Shedd's understanding of the theanthropic person of Christ is staunchly classical and clearly Chalcedonian.

Traducianism, Realism and Christ's Human Nature

We come now to consider the particular aspects of Shedd's understanding of the person of Christ that constitute his own particular contribution to the doctrine. As was mentioned earlier, it is not that Shedd's own contribution is novel or innovative in the sense that he develops an entirely new way of understanding a particular aspect of the person of Christ. Rather, what is particular to Shedd is the way in which he takes elements in the tradition, sometimes elements that have not been popular within his own Reformed tradition, and forges them together into his own understanding of the person of Christ.

There are two theses intertwined in the theological superstructure of Shedd's thought, forming two of the main pillars in his dogmatics, which have a particular application in his understanding of the person of Christ. I am referring to his defence of traducianism and Augustinian realism. Shedd's traducian-realist argument has an application to his understanding of the theanthropic person of Christ in the following way. Christ's human nature is generated from the Virgin Mary through the agency of the Holy Spirit:

> Jesus was really and truly the Son of Mary. He was bone of her bone and flesh of her flesh. He was of her substance and of her blood. He was consubstantial with her, in as full as sense as an ordinary child is consubstantial with an ordinary mother. And she was the mother of his human soul, as well as of his human body. (DT: 639)

He is quite clear that this means 'the body and soul of Christ were formed simultaneously and by one act of the Holy Spirit out of the psychico-physical substance of the mother.' (DT: 638, n. 72) According to this traducian strand of Shedd's theology all human natures partake of original sin via the generation of the soul of one human from its parents. This is also true of the body + soul composite assumed by the Word in the Incarnation. However, what prevents Christ from having a sinful human nature is the miraculous sanctifying work of the Holy Spirit accompanying his conception. This means that Christ's human body and soul are only sinless because, in generating Christ's human nature from that of the Virgin Mary, The Holy Spirit somehow removes or cleanses it of sin. As Shedd puts it, without the agency of the Holy Spirit, what was formed from the 'substance' of Mary would have been corrupt. (DT: 637)

Shedd approaches his Christological discussion of realism by attempting to make clear what he thinks the distinction between 'nature' and 'person' is in the Incarnation. We have already seen that his broadly Antiochene Christology means human nature is not just a property, but a concrete particular consisting of a human body and soul distinct from and in addition to, the Word. Now, in explaining what a nature is, Shedd says,

> When we speak of a human nature, a real substance having physical, rational, moral, and spiritual properties is meant. This human nature or substance is capable of becoming a human person, but yet is not one. It requires to be personalized in order to be a self-conscious individual man. A human person is a fractional part of a specific human nature or substance, which has been separated from the common mass and formed into a distinct and separate individual by the process of generation. Prior to this separation and formation, this fractional portion of the common human nature has all the qualities of the common mass of which it is a part, but is not yet individualized. It is potentially, not actually personal. (DT: 630)

Shedd also says that, 'a nature cannot be distinguished from another nature, but a person can be from another person'. (DT: 632) Taken together with his commitment to traducianism, it is clear that Shedd applies his realism unflinchingly to the human nature of Christ as a part or 'fraction' as he says, of the whole mass of human nature that exists in some unindividualized mass that is gradually individualized by successive division over time through generation (e.g. DT: 631).

We can express the Christological application of his traducianism and realism in the following propositions about the person of Christ:

1. One human nature is not distinguishable from another in the same way that one person is distinguishable from another.

Why not? Because (as we have already seen in the first two chapters) for Shedd human nature exists as an unindividualized mass, prior to the generation of each new human individual. This means:

2. The human nature of Christ is derived from the mass of human nature that is tainted with sin because of the fall of Adam and that is individualized in concrete particulars by natural generation.
3. The human nature of Christ is a fraction of this human nature, which is personalized by being united with the Word.

4. The Holy Spirit generated the human nature of Christ (comprising his human body and human soul) from the Virgin Mary's human nature.
5. The human nature thus generated is prevented from being tainted with original sin by the special work of the Holy Spirit in generation.

There are several problems with Shedd's use of realism and traducianism. The first of these has to do with the fact that, on Shedd's account, the human nature of Christ pre-exists his Incarnation as part of the mass of unindividualized human nature that exists in the person of the Virgin Mary and is therefore has the property of original sin. Christ's human nature, as part of this mass of human nature possessed by Adam and Eve, is subject to the Curse, and has the property of being fallen. But, if one affirms with Protestant Orthodoxy that being fallen is itself a sin, then the human nature of Christ in this attenuated, pre-existent state, is not only fallen but sinful, just as the whole mass of human nature, which is subject to the Curse, is both fallen and sinful. Shedd sees this implication of his view, and embraces it:

> So far, then, as the guilt of Adam's sin rested upon that unindividualized portion of the common fallen nature of Adam assumed by the Logos, it was expiated by the one sacrifice on Calvary. The human nature of Christ was prepared for the personal union with the Logos by being justified as well as sanctified.... The justification in this instance, like that of the Old Testament believers, was proleptic, in view of the future atoning death of Christ. (DT: 476)

His reasoning is this. If Christ's human nature needs to be sanctified by the work of the Holy Spirit before the Incarnation can take place, then his human nature must also need to be justified by Christ's finished work on the cross. The fact that Christ's human nature needed to be sanctified by the Holy Spirit prior to Incarnation implies that it required sanctification before the Incarnation could take place. This must be because, without such sanctification, Christ's human nature would have been sinful (bearing, through generation – although generation of a miraculous kind – the marks of original sin). Why is this? For the simple reason that prior to Christ's human conception, his human nature existed as an unindividualized part of the common human nature, which has the property of original sin. So, Christ's human nature pre-exists the Incarnation, needs to be sanctified in order for the Incarnation to take place, and requires justification just as all other human natures require justification. This seems to be internally consistent with what he says in defence of traducianism and realism. But it does require the application of sanctification and justification to the human nature of Christ.[26]

---

[26] Prof. Michael Rea has pointed out to me that Shedd's view of the sanctification of Christ's human nature seems to be independent of the work of Christ, which raises the question, If the Holy Spirit can sanctify Christ's human nature without the need for the

Secondly, the traducian-realism Shedd adopts means he can tell a consistent story about the transmission of sin to all humanity, Christ's pre-existent human nature included. Transmitted sin is not a legal fiction imputed to Adam's progeny, whereby God treats Adam's progeny (Christ included) *as if* they were culpable for Adam's sin. This is the federalist view of imputation found in high Calvinism. Instead, Adam's progeny (Christ included) really were present in Adam in the unindividualized mass of human nature possessed by Adam and Eve. On this basis, Shedd can argue that the human nature of Christ was really and truly fallen and sinful prior to the Incarnation because it shares in the guilt of the unindividualized mass of human nature. So what the Word assumes in becoming Incarnate is a human nature like that of any other human being, apart from the fact that it has been miraculously sanctified by the Holy Spirit and (proleptically) justified by Christ's own work on the cross. It is a holy human nature fit for the Word, although it has been made holy by the special work of the Holy Spirit and the Word. But this is not to say that the Word assumes a fallen or sinful human nature, in the way affirmed by Barth or Edward Irving.[27] The human nature of Christ is sinless at the moment of Incarnation and at all subsequent moments, although it was not sinless prior to the moment of Incarnation, when it was just part of the mass of sinful, unindividualized human nature as possessed by the Virgin Mary. However, there is a crucial issue that remains unresolved in Shedd's account: how can being part of an unindividualized mass of human nature prior to individualization be sufficient for possession of the guilt of Adam's sin? To this question Shedd provides no adequate response.

A third problem with Shedd's argument has to do with Christ's human nature being one of the means and object of salvation. This *seems* circular. How can sanctification and justification be applied to the human nature of Christ if sanctification and justification are the fruits of the work of Christ for which Christ's being both fully human and fully divine are necessary conditions? Shedd appears to think that he can get around this problem with respect to the justification of Christ's human nature by saying that Christ's human nature is justified proleptically, as the Old Testament saints were.[28] It might be objected that the difference between Christ and the Old Testament saints makes this untenable. The reason usually given for thinking that the Old Testament saints

---

work of Christ, why not yours and mine too? At the very least, this makes the pervasiveness of sin rather mysterious.

[27] See Karl Barth, *Church Dogmatics* I/2 eds. G. W. Bromiley and T. F. Torrance (Edinburgh: T&T Clark, 1957-1969), pp. 147-159 and Edward Irving, *The Orthodox and Catholic Doctrine of Our Lord's Human Nature* (London: Baldwin and Cradock, 1830).

[28] 'The justification [of Christ's human nature] in this instance, like that of the Old Testament believers, was proleptic, in view of the future atoning death of Christ.' DT, 476.

were justified proleptically is that they hoped for the salvation that was to come for their sins. But Christ is the means of that salvation! If Christ comes to redeem human beings, but his own human nature requires redemption, in what sense can he offer himself up as a redeeming sacrifice for sin (to borrow certain Reformation-inspired language that Shedd was familiar with), if his own human nature requires justification too? The human nature of Christ cannot be both one of the objects of Christ's saving work and the means by which that saving work is brought about.

However, a defender of Shedd could respond in the following way. The suffering and death of a sinless God-Man suffices for the salvation of all human creatures, including the retroactive justification of his own human nature. This may sound odd, but it is not incoherent. This is rather like my applying for a job that requires accreditation with some professional body. I do not have the accreditation, but am able to assure my prospective employer that I will be able to secure the accreditation in due course. I am employed, and, sure enough, obtain the accreditation shortly thereafter. But, even if this example does go some way to explaining Shedd's position, it still seems odd to say that Christ's work justifies his human nature. If his human nature is sinless by the power of the Holy Spirit, why does it need to be justified at all?

Fourthly, Shedd's claim that human natures are not distinguishable one from another seems to conflict with what he says about the human nature of Christ consisting of a human body and human soul. Surely one body + soul is different from another in more than merely trivial ways. Each body + soul composite has properties that are shared in common with other human beings, like 'being human'. But there are a myriad of properties that different concrete particulars do not share. This body + soul composite has the property 'being the product of the union of parents x and y' which only its siblings can have. And it has many other properties which no other individual can have, such as 'being the human nature generated by these two parents, x and y at time t_n', where t_n is some particular time. Shedd himself admits, 'the proper statement is that the Logos united himself with a human nature, not with the human nature.' (DT: 633) It is a particular human nature with which the Word is united in the Incarnation. But this particular human nature must be distinguished from some property of human nature (as per the Alexandrian Christology) that is just a property or set of properties that is shared with all other human beings. We might say that one way of thinking about two-part Christology is to picture Christ's human nature in terms of a set of universals that comprise human nature. (Universals are properties, that is, abstract objects like 'redness' that are exemplified by all objects which have this property.) Such a nature is a 'kind essence', or generic nature,[29] that is, a set of properties that all members of a particular natural kind, such as the kind 'human' or the kind 'horse' possess. But three-part

---

[29] Thomas V. Morris, *The Logic of God Incarnate* (Ithaca, NY: Cornell University Press, 1986), p. 66 ff.

Christologists affirm that Christ's human nature is a concrete particular; a human body and soul. It is not just a kind essence. That is, it is not just a set of properties that all members of the kind 'human' possess. It is a particular body and soul; the body and soul of Christ. The problem this poses for Shedd is that he cannot consistently affirm both the Antiochene tripartite view of the Incarnation (Word + human body + human soul) and say that the human nature of Christ is indistinguishable from other human natures. For one thing, this sounds like a lapse into the language of two-part Christologists, where, (if the two-partist espouses the view that properties are universals), the human nature of Christ is just a kind essence, or universal shared by all human beings.[30] For another, if it is not such a lapse, it is not clear what Shedd can mean, since a given human body + soul composite is distinguishable from another body + soul composite that is human. It is not possible to have distinct body + soul composite human natures that are not distinguishable precisely because they are distinct concrete particulars, not a set of abstract objects, like properties. It seems to me that Shedd is just confused in this matter.

Fifthly, and finally, it could be objected: If Adam has a human nature that is created *ex nihilo* by God, why cannot Christ also have a human nature created *ex nihilo* by God? Why apply traducianism to Christ? I suppose Shedd's response would be that if Christ's human nature is created out of nothing by God, then it is not 'born of a virgin' as the creeds say. It is generated out of nothing in the womb of a virgin, which is not the same thing at all. What Shedd's argument tries to do is preserve the link between the human nature of Christ and the rest of humanity by underlining the need for a virgin birth where the virgin supplies not just the matter from which Christ's body is formed, but the substance from which his human soul is fashioned too. And this, for Shedd, means that Christ must have a human nature that is composed of the same stuff as the human natures generated from the primeval unindividualized mass possessed by Adam and Eve.

But, we might ask, why must Christ have the same human nature as Adam in order to redeem Adam's fallen progeny? If one thinks that Christ has to have a human nature in order to save human beings (along the lines of an Anselmian *Cur Deus Homo*-type argument, perhaps), why should this mean Christ has to

---

[30] This view that properties are universals is often called 'realism'. The word realism has a number of applications in theology and philosophy, including the Augustinian realism Shedd defends. In order not to confuse the reader by using realism in two quite different senses in the space of a few pages, I have refrained from referring to the view that properties are universals as 'realism'. An Alexandrian Christologist need not be a realist with respect to properties. Such a Christologist could opt for nominalism, the view that properties are predicates we apply to one object alone because there are no universals. On this view, when we say 'this hat is red' we mean something like, 'this particular hat is red' not 'this hat exemplified the universal of redness'. There are various theories of universals and particulars, but we need not enter into this discussion here. See, E. J. Lowe, *A Survey of Metaphysics* (Oxford: Oxford University Press, 2002), chs. 19-20.

have the *same* human nature as Adam? Why not simply a human nature *simpliciter*, that is, a human nature created by God out of nothing? What more is gained by stipulating that Christ's human nature has to be the same human nature as Adam? Perhaps Shedd thought that retaining some strong notion of the solidarity of Christ with humanity, understood in terms of having the same human nature as the rest of fallen humanity, is important in an adequate account of the Incarnation. But this could be understood in several ways. I suppose that for Shedd the idea is that only if Christ has the same human nature as Adam can Christ's human nature be said to be sinful and in need of redemption, just as the rest of human nature in the rest of humanity is. So original sin picks out the theologically relevant difference between Adamic human nature (the unindividualized human nature) and some human nature God creates in the act of parthenogenesis in the Virgin's womb, which involves the creation of a new soul for this body *ex nihilo*.

But the property of original sin is not a property God Incarnate shares with the rest of humanity, on Shedd's account, even though it is a property that the pre-existing, unindividualized human nature of Christ shares with the rest of fallen humanity. Yet surely it would have been simpler had God created Christ's human soul out of nothing in the act of virginal conception, and used Mary's physical substance to supply the raw materials for Christ's human body. If he had done so, Christ's human nature could have been sinless – his body subject to corruption, but his human soul created out of nothing and sinless - the result Shedd needs to remain orthodox, but without the need for this particular Christological application of traducianism. All that is lost without the traducian element that is *theologically* relevant is, it seems, this complicated argument for the human nature of Christ pre-existing the Incarnation in some unindividualized state, sharing original sin with the rest of this common human nature, and then having this original sin removed by the sanctifying work of the Holy Spirit in order for the Word to become Incarnate in a human nature he has to then redeem by his own work at Calvary. But then, the net result of Shedd's view is the same as the case of the human nature of Christ that has a physical part created from the physical substance of Mary, and an immaterial soul created *ex nihilo* and sinless by the Holy Spirit.

It might be thought that there is still an important difference between Christs's human nature and the human nature of Adamic humanity if we opt for the creation-out-of-nothing view of Christ's human nature over Shedd's explanation. The different is that, on this creation-out-of-nothing view, Christ's human nature is not the same human nature as that shared with Adam and his progeny. This is true. But then, once a human nature is individualized on Shedd's account, it is no longer part of the common unindividualized whole that is diffused down through the ages from Adam to his descendents. It may, on Shedd's view, be more than just an individual human nature (for it carries within it the 'seed' of many more such individuals that are diffused from this individual human nature). But the point is that each new human being has a human nature that is an individual human nature once they have been formed as an individual human being. They are no longer linked to the common human nature of which they were once parts. So, once he is Incarnate, the human nature of the Word is no longer part of the common human nature of Adam's progeny either, even if one takes Shedd's account of the matter. And the human nature of Christ does not diffuse itself further by procreation (even if this is possible, on Shedd's view). So, whether Christ's human nature is generated *in toto* from the Virgin Mary by the Holy Spirit according to Shedd's Christological application of traducianism, or created partially from Mary's substance (physical body) and partially *ex nihilo* by God (immaterial soul), the result is the same: a sinless human nature, which is distinct, and that is personalized by the Word. In both cases, it seems to me, we have an important sense in which Christ's human nature is shared in common with the rest of humanity. For Shedd, this is because of his traducianism. For the creation-out-of-nothing view, this is because the human body of Christ is generated from the physical substance of Mary. But the advantage of the creation-out-of-nothing account is that it removes the need for Christ's human soul to be sanctified by the Holy Spirit. Yet it leaves room for the idea that Christ's human body suffers from the effects of the Fall because it is generated from the physical substance of Mary. It also offers a simpler account of the way in which God brings this about, without the need for the traducian theory about the propagation of human nature.

Conclusions

I have tried to show that Shedd's doctrine of the theanthropic person of Christ is theologically interesting in a number of key areas, whilst remaining orthodox. This is no mean achievement. Shedd thought creatively through the doctrine of the person of Christ and sought to apply to it two central tenets of his theological architechtonic, namely his realism and traducianism. It is a testimony to his consistency that he did not baulk at the prospect of doing so, even though it drove him to take rather strange views about the pre-existence of Christ's human nature, and its sinfulness prior to the Incarnation. I have taken issue with this Christological application of traducianism in particular, because it seems to me that Shedd's traducianism has several theological implications that are peculiar, not least that it means Christ's human nature pre-exists the Incarnation as a part of some unindividualized mass. I have also been critical of his unindividualized version of Augustinian realism that is the corollary of his traducian position. However, this should not be taken to mean that I think there is no useful theological application of realism, including an application to Christology – there are, after all, versions of realism other than the unindividualized version Shedd defends in his Christology and theological anthropology.[31] What Shedd achieves is an account of the person of Christ that is largely, although, not entirely, consistent with his stated theological principles (his traducian and realist views). But it will only be a convincing account for those willing to follow him down the path his metaphysical commitments take him. I for one cannot do so.

---

[31] As was pointed out in ch. 2. One such version is offered by Jonathan Edwards in *Original Sin, The Works of Jonathan Edwards, Volume 3*, (ed.) Clyde A. Holbrook (New Haven, CN: Yale University Press, 1970), IV. III.

CHAPTER 4

The Impeccability of Christ

This chapter explores a Sheddian account of Christ's impeccability. I say the argument offered here is Shedd*ian* because there are aspects of Shedd's case in his *Dogmatic Theology* that are incomplete, which we will need to supply in order to overcome certain problems with a Shedd-like view that have been raised in the recent literature. We shall proceed in several stages. In the initial stage, Shedd's argument for the claim that Christ is impeccable *qua* divine but peccable *qua* human is set forth. There are several components of this argument, and we will have to consider each in turn. Then, in the second stage, we shall consider three problems this argument faces. (I do not say these are the only problems one could raise; but they are three that are obvious, and that present a serious challenge to this view.) The first of these has to do with what it means to say the human *nature* of Christ is peccable. The second has to do with what it means to say the human nature of Christ is *peccable*. In the recent literature Thomas Morris has argued that an impeccable person cannot have a peccable human nature. However, with Shedd, I shall suggest that Christ could have a peccable human nature and an impeccable divine nature. This is not so much a departure from, as an amendment to, Morris's way of thinking. But a third problem has to do with what it means to say Christ's temptations are morally innocent, a difficulty common to all orthodox explanations of Christ's sinlessness. Shedd is right to state that Christ's temptations must be morally innocent, but does not satisfactorily explain how a temptation could be morally innocent.

The Argument from Scripture and the Person of Christ

The epistle to the Hebrews tells us, 'we do not have a High Priest who cannot sympathize with our weaknesses, but was in all points tempted as we are, yet without sin' (Heb. 4: 15). This verse clearly teaches that Christ was without sin. But does this mean that Christ was sinless, or impeccable? That is, was it the case that Christ could have succumbed to temptation, but did not? Or is it that he was *incapable of succumbing to temptation*? If the latter of these two views is right, Christ was impeccable rather than just sinless. One traditional objection to the notion that Christ was impeccable is that impeccability is incompatible with being able to be tempted to sin. If someone is impeccable, so this objection goes, then that person cannot be tempted to sin; they are incapable of being tempted to sin by anything. (The idea here is that for something to be a temptation it must be possible – usually understood, I think, to mean, metaphysically possible – for the person tempted to succumb to that temptation on at least some occasions. But, so those who present this objection maintain, someone who is impeccable is incapable of yielding to temptation.)

According to Shedd's way of thinking, this is to misunderstand the application of impeccability to Christ.[1] Christ can be tempted to do certain sorts of things (but not all sorts of things; some temptations require the person tempted to be in a prior state of sin). Nevertheless, he is not able to succumb to the temptations proffered to him. How can this be? The reason has to do with Christ being impeccable *qua* divine and peccable *qua* human. This notion needs some unpacking (or perhaps, this notion needs some Shedd*ing*). We begin with some explanation of sinlessness and impeccability.

Sinlessness is a moral state in which a person is able not to sin and able to sin (*posse peccare et posse non peccare*). Adam was in this moral state before the Fall. However, those in this moral state are not incapable of sinning, as the story of the Fall shows in Genesis 1-3. It is just that persons in this state can refrain from sinning and are not sinful provided they continue to refrain from sinning. Adam and Eve are examples of two sinless persons who did yield to temptation, and sinned. So someone who is sinless is also peccable. Impeccability is a stronger moral state than sinlessness. Someone who is impeccable is sinless; but someone who is sinless is not (necessarily) impeccable. This is the case where an impeccable person (in the technical sense of the term we are using here) is someone who is incapable of succumbing to temptation and sinning. It is not possible for such a person to sin because he or she is not able to sin (*non posse peccare*). So impeccability, like sinlessness, is a modal notion.

Shedd thinks that Christ is like Adam in that he is sinless, and cites Hebrews 4: 15 to show that this is the biblical view of Christ's moral nature. However, unlike Adam, there is, according to Shedd, no possibility of Christ sinning:

> That he [Christ] was sinless is generally acknowledged. But the holiness of the God-man is more than sinlessness. The last Adam differs from the first Adam by reason of his impeccability.[2]

This, according to Shedd, is the biblical view too. (He makes the strong claim that impeccability can be *proved* from Scripture.) So, for instance, Hebrews 13: 8 says that Christ is the same yesterday, today and forever. This, according to Shedd, applies to the whole character of Christ. All his attributes are immutable: 'the immutability of Christ taught in Heb. 13: 8 pertains to all the

---

[1] See DT, part 5, chapter 5.
[2] DT: 659.

characteristics of his person.'[3] (It is clear from what Shedd says about divine immutability elsewhere, that this should be taken to mean God essentially changes if one of his essential properties changes.[4]) What is more, Christ is holy. But if his holiness is like that of Adam, only a contingent holiness, then Christ could lose his state of holiness just as Adam lost his in sinning. Then, were he to sin, Christ would not be the same yesterday, today and forever; he would change from being sinless to being a sinner, at the moment of his first sin. But this cannot be the case, so Christ's sinless state must be a constituent of his immutability, which means he must be essentially holy. God cannot cease to be holy, nor can Christ, as the God-man, cease to be holy. So Christ cannot sin.[5]

Shedd offers two other reasons for thinking Christ is impeccable. First, Christ is omnipotent. But an omnipotent being cannot be overcome by temptation (i.e. deprived of impeccability). Second, Christ is omniscient and therefore incapable of being deceived. 'The omniscience which characterizes the God-man made his apostasy from good impossible.'[6] But, says Shedd, the success of a temptation depends, in part, upon the deception of the person tempted.[7] Now, an omniscient being is incapable of being deceived. The God-Man is divine. He is also omniscient (in his divine nature). So he cannot be deceived either. Thus Shedd: 'A finite intelligence may be deceived, but an infinite intelligence cannot be. Therefore, the omniscience which characterizes the God-man made this apostasy from good impossible.'[8]

One way of making sense of this (not supplied by Shedd, but consistent with what he does say) would be the following: if I am tempted to sin this is due, at least in part, to the fact that I am deceived into thinking – or I deceive myself into thinking - the sinful act that is presented to me is a good thing to do. But, even if it is a good thing in itself, it is not a good thing all things considered, because it is a sin. So I must in some sense be deceived (or self-deceived) into

---

[3] DT: 659.

[4] Compare DT: 284: 'the immutability of God is the unchangeableness of his essence, attributes, purposes, and consciousness. Immutability results from eternity as omnipresence does from immensity. That which has no evolution and no succession is *the same yesterday, today, and forever.*' (Emphasis added.) This, coupled with Shedd's endorsement of a traditional doctrine of divine simplicity means God is immutable in a strong sense.

[5] An example to make this point: I am essentially human. So I have the property 'being human' essentially. It is not possible that I exist without being human. I could not be a cat, say, or an iguana. But then 'being human' is an essential property that I possess.

[6] DT: 660.

[7] DT: 660.

[8] DT: 660. Shedd also cites Jonathan Edwards's argument that the biblical promises of a messiah who would save his people are only true if the messiah really will save his people. If it were possible that the messiah would fail in his mission, God would be a liar. So it is impossible that the messiah fail in his mission by, say, sinning. See DT: 670.

thinking that the sin in question is a good thing, even though it is not a good thing, either on its own (given a deontological view of sin), or all things considered. The paradigmatic biblical example of this is Eve in 1 Timothy 2: 14, (cited by Shedd) 'Adam was not deceived, but the woman being deceived fell into transgression.' In this case, Eve was tempted to take the fruit of the tree of the knowledge of good and evil because it was purportedly able to make one wise. It is a good thing to be wise. So, one would think, it is a good thing to eat the fruit of a tree that makes one wise. However, the sinuous words of the serpent in the Garden of Eden were deceptive - even if the fruit of this particular tree were able to make one wise if eaten, God had specifically commanded Adam and Eve not to eat of it. So it was a bad idea to eat the fruit, all things considered.

In addition to reasons for Christ's impeccability drawn from Scripture, Shedd also deals with considerations from the constitution of Christ's person. The first of these has to do with the hypostatic union of the two natures of Christ. Shedd says

> his [Christ's] strength to prevent a lapse from holiness is to be estimated by his divinity, not by his humanity, because the former and not the latter is the base of his personality and dominates the whole complex person. Consequently, what might be done by the human nature if alone and by itself cannot be done by it in this union with omnipotent holiness. (DT: 660)

The idea here is that the human nature of Christ cannot sin because it is in hypostatic union with the divine nature of Christ. The divine nature of the second person of the Trinity is incapable of sinning. It is impeccable. But the Incarnation is just the assumption of human nature by the second person of the Trinity. The Incarnation does not mean that the Word of God suddenly becomes susceptible to sin in a way that he was not before the Incarnation. If he was susceptible to sin, then possibly he could sin. But this is metaphysically impossible because God is impeccable. However, according to Shedd, this does not mean that the human nature the Word assumes at the Incarnation has to be impeccable too. Thus Shedd:

> The omnipotence of the Logos preserves the finite human nature from falling, however great may be the stress of temptation to which this finite nature is exposed. Consequently, Christ while having a peccable human nature in his constitution was an impeccable person. Impeccability characterizes the God-man as a totality, while peccability is a property of his humanity. (DT: 661)

So it seems Shedd believes the human nature of Christ could sin without the interposition of the divine nature of Christ to prevent this outcome.[9]

---

[9] For an interesting contrast to this view, see Alan Spence on John Owen's Christology, 'Christ's Humanity and Ours: John Owen' in Christoph Schwöbel and Colin Gunton

Nevertheless, because the divine nature is somehow more fundamental than the human nature in the hypostatic union, or perhaps, dominates the human nature in some way, the human nature of Christ is incapable of sinning.[10] The Word is, on Shedd's view, responsible for the human nature of Christ from the first moment of hypostatic union onwards:

> When the Logos goes into union with the human nature, so as to constitute a single person with it, he becomes responsible for all that this person does through the instrumentality of his nature.... If, therefore, the Logos should make no resistance to the temptation with which Satan assailed the human nature in the wilderness and should permit the humanity to yield to it and commit sin, he would be implicated in the apostasy and sin. The guilt would not be confined to the human nature. It would attach to the whole theanthropic person. And since the Logos is the root and base of the person, it would attach to him in an eminent manner. (DT: 661)

Shedd speaks of the human nature of Christ as he does here because he believes it is a body-soul composite, as we note in the previous chapter.[11] In fact, he believes that the whole human nature of Christ (body and soul) is generated by the Holy Spirit from the substance of the Virgin Mary. It is not just a property that the Word assumes at the Incarnation. The human nature of Christ is a concrete particular, personalized or hypostatized by the Word in the Incarnation.[12]

Shedd resists any attempt to conflate this understanding of the peccable human nature of Christ being preserved sinless by the impeccable Word with a doctrine of the communication of attributes (*communicatio idiomatum*). This latter doctrine comes in several varieties. The Reformed doctrine of the communication of attributes, with which Shedd aligned himself, states that we can predicate apparently contradictory attributes to the person of Christ on the

---

(eds.) *Persons, Divine and Human: King's College Essays in Theological Anthropology* (Edinburgh: T&T Clark, 1991). Owen maintained that it was the Holy Spirit that prevented Christ from sinning.

[10] But, it might be asked, How does the divine nature of Christ act in such a way that it prevents the human nature from sinning? This is mysterious, and Shedd does not attempt to explain it. One possible answer has to do with the perichoresis or coinherence involved in the hypostatic union. It might be that the perichoretic relation the Word has to his human nature is such that it prevents the human nature from sinning.

[11] See DT, part 5, chapters 1-4.

[12] But how can it be that the Word personalizes the human nature he assumes at the Incarnation, if it is created *in toto* by the work of the Holy Spirit in Mary's womb? Perhaps if one holds to a doctrine of *enhypostasia*, according to which the Word takes a human nature into his person, thereby 'personalizing' it, sense can be made of this. It is no part of Shedd's doctrine (or any orthodox doctrine of the Incarnation) that the human nature the Holy Spirit creates is a *person* prior to its assumption by the Word. That would be Nestorianism.

basis of a two-natures doctrine of the Incarnation. So, we can say both that Christ is finite and Christ is infinite because we mean to predicate of the person of Christ attributes that belong to one or other of the natures of Christ. He is finite in his human nature and infinite in his divine nature. It is not clear to me why Shedd resists the application of this doctrine to the impeccability of Christ. There appears to be no reason why the logic of the Reformed doctrine of the communication of attributes could not be applied to the person of Christ to explain the impeccable divine nature and peccable human nature posited by Shedd.[13]

This understanding of what we might call, somewhat paradoxically, a humanly-peccable-but-divinely-impeccable hypostatic union does not mean that Christ does not suffer or feel the effects of the Fall. Shedd reaffirms the traditional Augustinian view that Christ *qua* human weeps, suffers and knows the privations that have been brought about by the Fall. But he does not know the sinful condition that usually accompanies these privations. He maintains that, 'all the innocent defects and limitations of the finite may be attributed to Jesus Christ, but not its culpable defects and limitations. The God-man may be weak or sorrowful or hungry or weary; he may be crucified, dead, and buried; but he may not be sinful and guilty.'[14]

How an Impeccable Christ can be Tempted

With this sketch of the biblical and theological reasons why Shedd holds to

---

[13] Shedd says he resists this application of the communication of attributes because the divine nature cannot leave the human nature to its own finiteness without support as it can in other instances (DT: 661). But I am at a loss to know what this means. Alan Gomes has suggested to me in private correspondence that Shedd may have thought there is a difference between Christ in the state of humiliation having attributed to his person the properties of a human as well as a divine nature, and Christ having attributed to his person the peccability of his human nature. But I do not see why attributing peccability to the person of Christ in the communication of attributes is any more serious than attributing limited power or knowledge.

[14] DT: 661-662. Shedd also claims that his understanding of Christ's impeccability is compatible with the doctrine that Christ has two wills (dyothelitism), provided it means the human will submits to, and obeys, the divine will of Christ. I do not intend to enter into discussion of dyothelitism here. Nevertheless, it is important to see that Shedd believes commitment to dyothelitism does not mean the peccable human nature of Christ conflicts with his divine will, it 'obeys it invariably and perfectly' DT: 662. For discussion of the historical context of dyothelitism, see for example Wolfhart Pannenberg, *Jesus – God and Man, Second Edition,* trans. Lewis L. Wilkins and Duane A. Priebe (Philadelphia, PA.: Westminster Press, 1968), pp. 293-295 and Robert W. Jenson, *Systematic Theology Volume 1, The Triune God* (New York: Oxford University Press, 1997), pp. 134 ff.

Christ's impeccability, we can turn to the question of whether such an impeccable Christ can be tempted. Shedd's immediate answer is in the affirmative. The temptation of the impeccable person of Christ is no more problematic than the notion of attacking an unconquerable army. Or, to add an illustration of my own, it is like Joe Average stepping into the ring with an invincible pugilist. There may be a struggle, but the outcome is a foregone conclusion – the boxer will be victorious.

But this needs to be fleshed out. An illustration does not an argument make. Shedd supplies two interrelated points to support this claim. The first develops what he says about the constitution of the theanthropic person of Christ. The second involves what he calls 'innocent' and 'sinful', temptations.

On the question of the constitution of Christ's person, Shedd says there is a distinction between having a constitutional susceptibility to temptation and being impeccable because one successfully wills to remain sinless. Christ 'was open to all forms of human temptation excepting those that spring out of lust or corruption of nature'.[15] This seems to be a consequence of the fact that his human nature is peccable (considered in abstraction from its union in his person). But even here there are areas of sin that Christ's human nature could not be tempted to yield to, because they require a prior corruption of character, such as lust. So, according to this way of thinking, Christ could not be tempted to fornication because this would require him to have a corrupt, lustful moral nature. Without a corrupt moral nature, he would have no inclination to commit such an action. Shedd says,

> his peccability, or the possibility of being overcome by these temptations, would depend upon the amount of voluntary resistance which he was able to bring to bear against them. Those temptations were very strong, but if the self-determination of his holy will was stronger than they, then they could not induce him to sin, and he would be impeccable. And yet plainly he would be temptable. (DT: 662-663)

It is the holy will of the impeccable divine nature of Christ that prevents his peccable human nature from succumbing to temptations that are offered to him, and which his human nature is susceptible to, but do not require a prior corrupt moral nature. And because the Word is an omnipotent being, he is incapable of being overcome by temptation. Shedd is clear that the only reason the human nature of Christ does not succumb to temptation as all other human beings would without the interposition of divine grace, is because of Christ's divine nature: 'there may be the very greatest degree of temptation where there is no possibility at all of its succeeding; there may be the highest temptability and absolute impeccability. Such we suppose to have been the case in the God-man.'[16] So temptation admits of degrees and a perfectly virtuous (and in this

---

[15] DT: 662.
[16] DT: 664.

case, omnipotent) person may be so constituted that they are impervious to even the strongest temptations.[17]

However, this should not be taken to mean that Christ's temptations were therefore less severe than the temptations suffered by other, fallen human beings - quite the opposite. 'An innocent temptation may be greater in its force than a sinful one', says Shedd. 'Christ was solicited by sinless temptation more strongly than any man ever was by sinful temptation. No drunkard or sensualist was ever allured by vicious appetite so fiercely as Christ was by innocent appetite, when after forty days "he was hungered".'[18] By this he means that because Christ was humanly sinless and divinely impeccable, the trials he underwent had to be more severe than those undergone by merely human beings, in order for them to be able to present a real temptation to him. A drunk needs little temptation to take up the bottle because he is already disposed to yield to the temptation presented to him; he is physically and psychologically addicted to alcohol. But someone who is without sin will need to be presented with a formidable temptation to even feel the 'pull', so to speak, of what the temptation offers.[19]

But what does it mean to speak of the 'pull' of temptation in the case of a sinless person? Clearly, the 'pull' of temptation does not include acting upon temptation. It means being inclined to do what is tempted. If I am tempted to go and watch a film rather than doing some work, I am inclined to go to the film. I am attracted by the allure of what this prospect offers: relaxation rather than labour, enjoyment rather than work, and so on. But this is not the same as actually yielding to the temptation and going to see the film.[20] (This seems to be in line with what Shedd says about the 'innocent' nature of Christ's temptations, about which, more presently.) In the case of Christ, on Shedd's account, the 'pull' of the temptations he endures will only apply to his human nature. It is his divine nature that prevents the human nature from succumbing to those temptations that are offered. Or, possibly, his human nature resists the temptation successfully without the interposition of his divine nature, although if his human nature were to be about to succumb to temptation, his divine nature would prevent that outcome.

---

[17] I say persons, not human persons here, because Shedd believes that the angels were tempted by sin and some fell. Indeed, according to Shedd there are two inlets of temptation: the body and the soul. So some immaterial persons are not necessarily immune from temptation. See DT: 663-664.

[18] DT: 665.

[19] I suppose one could argue, although Shedd does not do so here, that 'an innocent temptation may be greater in its force than a sinful one' means something like this: the temptations of Christ were more deeply offensive to Christ than they would have been to you or me because he is sinless and free from self-deception.

[20] This is, of course, nothing like a complete explanation of the difference between feeling the 'pull' of temptation and yielding to it. But it is sufficient for the purpose of showing that the 'pull' of temptation is not the same as yielding to temptation.

Moreover, Shedd thinks that the fact Christ consistently resisted all the temptations offered to him means that the trials he endured as a result of being tempted were that much more severe than they are in the case of human beings who are sinful:

> Temptations that are accompanied with struggle and opposition against them are fiercer than those that are not so accompanied. The good man, in this way, often feels the distress of temptation far more than the bad man. The latter yields supinely and making no opposition does not experience the anguish of a struggle. The former is greatly wearied and strained by his temptation, though he is not conquered by it. Christ "resisted unto blood, striving against sin, and offered up prayers and supplications with strong crying and tears unto him that was able to save him from death." But his people "have not so resisted" (Heb. 12: 4; 5: 7). (DT: 665)

It seems plausible to suppose that a person who is sinless will have to be presented with a formidable temptation in order to feel its 'pull'. Would a sinless person immediately feel the 'pull' of the least temptation because he sees its nature and tendency? I think not. It may be that a sinless person would see the nature and tendency of some lesser temptation that is presented to him. But this need not mean that he feels the 'pull' of such a lesser temptation.

It also makes sense to suggest that someone who is already a sinner has a predisposition to sin, and is therefore more likely to yield to a lesser temptation than that offered to a sinless person. But does anything morally relevant follow from the *degree* of temptation for the case of an impeccable person? It might be thought that nothing morally relevant follows for an impeccable person not least because such a person is, as Shedd points out, *constitutionally incapable* of yielding to temptation. However strong the temptation offered to such a person, he or she will never succumb to it.

One might think that Shedd's reasoning here is only morally relevant to someone who is in a qualitatively similar moral state to Adam, that is, a state where it is possible for such a person to sin (a sinless state). But Shedd has already denied that Christ is in such a state, even though he is willing to concede that his human nature is in such a state. This is rather like protecting a fragile crystal wine glass in polystyrene, which effectively prevents it from being broken. Christ's human nature may be hamartiologically fragile (as it were), like the glass. But it is protected from being damaged by the surrounding divine nature of the Word.[21] If Christ is constitutionally incapable of sinning,

---

[21] A similar analogy is offered by Richard Sturch. Imagine a cricket pitch with a boundary-wall, part of which is made of glass. Even if no cricket ball ever actually came into contact with the glass portion of the wall, it would be foolish to make this part of the wall glass, hoping that no ball would hit it. But if this portion of the wall is protected somehow, so that is cannot be hit by a cricket ball in any circumstances, then the situation is rather different. In a similar way, Christ's human nature, if peccable, could

then it is hard to see how any amount of temptation would ever make a subjective impression upon him – he would never feel the 'pull' of such temptations. His relation to temptation would be similar to Superman's invulnerability to bullets: the temptation 'bounces' off him, just as the bullets ricochet off the Kryptonian hide of the Man of Steel. And this reasoning would apply, irrespective of whether or not one temptation was offered to Christ, or a barrage of temptations over the period of his earthly ministry. As Superman's body is supposed to be able to withstand any number of bullets being fired at it because it is invulnerable, so Christ's impeccability would keep him from ever feeling the 'pull' of temptation, however many times he was assailed.

But this is to misunderstand the novel way in which Shedd conceives of the theanthropic person of Christ. What Shedd wants to affirm is that the peccability of Christ's human nature means Christ can be tempted, provided the temptation in view does not require original sin. It is precisely because Christ's human nature is in the same moral state as Adam prior to the Fall that he is able to feel the 'pull' of temptation as Adam did. But unlike Adam, Christ's divine nature prevents the fall of his human nature from occurring. So, there is, according to Shedd, a morally relevant sense in which Christ is so constituted that he does feel the 'pull' of temptation, although he is incapable of succumbing to temptation.

Let us turn to the second aspect of Shedd's account of tempting an impeccable person. He maintains that there is an important distinction to be made between innocent and sinful, or culpable, temptations. 'Christ's temptations', he says, 'were all ... sinless, but very many of the temptations of fallen man are sinful: that is, they are the hankering and solicitation of forbidden and wicked desire.'[22] Shedd thinks that Hebrews 4: 15, 'we have a high priest who was in all points tempted as we are, yet without sin', means, amongst other things, that Christ cannot have sinful temptations.

Sinful temptations, it seems, apply only when the person concerned is already a sinner, whose sinful condition means certain sorts of things will be temptations to them that would simply not be temptations for someone who was without sin. There seem to be two conditions involved in Shedd's account that make a temptation sinful. These are, (a) certain things are only temptations because the person tempted by them is already in a sinful condition, and (b) being tempted by such things, even if one does not act upon the temptation proffered, is itself sinful. This is analogous to the claim, made in classical theology, that being in a sinful moral condition is itself heinous in the sight of God, irrespective of whether or not a sinful person commits actual sin. In this case, Shedd is claiming that there is a certain class of temptations that are

---

be like the glass portion of the wall: it is protected by the presence of the Word, so that it is never damaged. See Richard Sturch, *The Word and The Christ, An Essay in Analytic Christology* (Oxford: Oxford University Press, 1991), Excursus IV.

[22] DT: 665.

themselves sinful irrespective of whether or not the person tempted yields to them and actually sins. This broad brush distinction between sinful and innocent temptations needs some filling out, but seems *prima facie*, to have some plausibility.

To see this, let us apply a Sheddian account to a paradigm case of sinful temptation. Being tempted to abuse a child looks like one such case. Irrespective of whether or not a person who is tempted by this act carries out this act, they have committed a sin. The idea here is that being tempted to do such a thing implies the presence of certain conditions (not all of which are spelt out by Shedd) in order for the temptation to be one for which the person concerned is morally culpable. First, there must exist a situation that, objectively speaking, presents a temptation to the person concerned (even if the object of temptation does not intend to offer a temptation to the subject of the temptation, as I suppose a child does not intend to tempt another to abuse him or her). Second, the person concerned – the temptee, so to speak – needs to be in a morally vitiated state in order to find such an act appealing or alluring (as Shedd makes clear). A third condition is that the temptee is, subjectively speaking, in a position to recognize that he is being tempted. And fourth, the temptee needs to be culpable for finding such an act enticing, independently of whether or not he or she acts upon this temptation. (Indeed, one could argue that acting upon such a temptation would constitute grounds for guilt in addition to the guilt of being tempted by such an act.)

In commenting on Hebrews 4: 15, Shedd speaks of a difference in *moral quality* between sinful and innocent temptations and the fact that Christ's temptations were different in their *source* and *nature*, not just in the resulting action:

> This text teaches that the temptations of Christ were "without sin" in their source and nature and not merely, as the passage is sometimes explained, that they were "without sin" in their result. The meaning is not that our Lord was tempted in every respect exactly as fallen man is – by inward lust as well as by other temptations – only he did not outwardly yield to any temptation; but that he was tempted in every way that man is, excepting by that class of temptations that are sinful because originating in evil and forbidden desire.... Temptations from evil desire have a different moral quality from those presented through innocent desire. (DT: 666-667)

I am suggesting, in Sheddian fashion, that the moral quality that differentiates a sinful from an innocent temptation has to do with the fact that a sinful temptation is itself morally culpable, irrespective of whether or not a person yields to it and actually sins. The source and nature, not just the result, of a particular temptation, are important in distinguishing the different moral qualities of temptations. (The 'source' being a sinful or sinless moral nature and the 'nature' of the temptation being whether the temptation is itself morally culpable or morally innocent, independent of any action taken as a result of being tempted.)

What, then, constitutes an innocent temptation? According to Shedd, that class of temptations that does not require the person being tempted to possess a sinful moral nature in order to feel the 'pull' of temptation. There might be several sorts of innocent temptations. One sort would involve being tempted to do something that does not require a prior sinful disposition, where the temptation itself is not a sin, but committing the action would be. For instance, the temptation to turn stones into bread that Christ suffers in the wilderness. Another sort would involve being tempted to choose between two options that are both good things, where one of those things is better, all things considered. As Richard Swinburne observes, 'God the Son could subject himself to temptation, but only to do a lesser good, not to do wrong.'[23] The temptation to do an action falling within the bounds of these two sorts of temptation would not require the person concerned to have a prior sinful moral nature. Nor, following Shedd's suggestion, would it mean that the person concerned sins just by being tempted by the particular thing in question.

But it might be objected, if Christ is incapable of being tempted with sinful temptations, he is not tempted in *every* way as we are, sin excepted. In response to this criticism, Shedd observes that Christ is the ideal, unfallen, sinless man, and not some fallen, sinful, wicked man. 'He must be truly human in order to be assailable by temptation and thereby able to sympathize with every tempted man.' But, 'in order to sympathize with a person, it is not necessary to have had exactly the same affliction the he has. It is only necessary to have been afflicted. A different kind of affliction may make a man all the more sympathetic.'[24] In this regard, Shedd explains that Christ's sympathy for sinful human beings is disinterested. That is, it does not require the sympathizer to have undergone the same experience as the sinner. In fact, as Shedd points out, Christ would not be better off for having had sinful experiences. One drunk may sympathize with another. But neither offers the other the prospect of salvation because both are in the same sinful moral condition.

What, then, are the reasons for Christ's temptations? Shedd suggests two considerations. First, being tempted was part of Christ's work of humiliation, meaning, that part of his work which required him to humble himself in becoming 'like us in every way, sin excepted'. Second, in submitting to temptation, Christ sets an example to his disciples in a life of unbroken holiness (compare Hebrews 12: 2-3).

---

[23] Richard Swinburne, *The Christian God* (Oxford: Oxford University Press, 1994), p. 207. See also the previous discussion from p. 204.
[24] DT: 669.

Three Problems for Shedd's Account

Can Christ's Human Nature be Peccable?
Shedd's account of Christ's impeccability is attractive. But it is not without problems. Let us consider three of the most important. First, Shedd's argument depends upon the human nature of Christ being peccable. But, it might be asked, what does it mean to suggest that a *nature*, rather than a *person*, is peccable or impeccable? As we have seen, Shedd says that Christ's human nature is a concrete particular, composed of a body and soul distinct from the Word.[25] But, although a body and soul composite is normally sufficient for human personhood, in the case of Christ it is not. Only when conjoined with the Word in Incarnation, is the human nature personalized.[26] To import the language of medieval theology, a human nature is usually a *suppositum*, that is, a fundamental substance that is the subject of predication. But, as Thomas Flint points out, this, uniquely, is not the case in the Incarnation:

> Rather, in this unique case [viz. the case of the Incarnation], what we must say is that this individual human nature, this particular body-soul composite (or whatever), is *not* a suppositum; the ultimate subject of any of its properties is not it, but rather the Son, the person who is united to and sustains in being this individual human nature.[27]

Although Shedd does not use the language of medieval theology (he does not speak of 'supposits' for instance), his discussion of these matters does share with the medievals the idea that Christ's human nature is a concrete particular composed of a body and distinct human soul. Let us assume, for the sake of the argument and in concert with Shedd and the Medievals, that the human nature of Christ is a concrete particular, but only a person because of the hypostatic union with the Word. What would it mean to say that Christ's human *nature* is peccable on such an understanding of Christ's humanity? Perhaps Shedd means something like this (and here, I am attempting merely to make sense of Shedd's views – we are, we might say, 'trying to get inside the Shedd'). Christ is so constituted that he may be tempted by the class of innocent temptations that the Word alone could not be tempted by. Earlier in his discussion of the theanthropic person of Christ, Shedd says that there is a twofold consciousness in God Incarnate, corresponding to his two wills, although this twofold

---

[25] See DT, 613 ff.

[26] For a recent robust defence of this sort of view, see Brian Leftow, 'A Timeless God Incarnate', in *The Incarnation*, (eds.) Stephen T. Davis, Daniel Kendall and Gerald O'Collins (Oxford: Oxford University Press, 2002). For historical discussion of the same sort of view in the medieval period, see Richard Cross, *The Metaphysics of the Incarnation* (Oxford: Oxford University Press, 2002).

[27] Thomas P. Flint, ' "A Death He Freely Accepted": Molinist Reflections on The Incarnation' in *Faith and Philosophy* 18 (2001): 5.

consciousness is somehow 'contained' in the one consciousness of the Son of God:

> The God-man is both unlimited and limited, illocal and local. He has consequently a twofold consciousness: infinite and finite. He thinks like God; and he thinks like man. He has the eternal, all-comprehending and successionless consciousness of God; and he has the imperfect, gradual, and sequacious consciousness of man.

Moreover,

> The two different modes or forms of consciousness – the divine and the human – in the God-man do not constitute two self-consciousnesses or two persons, any more than two or more different forms of consciousness in a man constitute two or more self-consciousnesses or persons. A man at one moment has a sensuous form of consciousness and at another moment a spiritual form; but he is one and the same person in both instances and has but a single self-consciousness. (DT: 625-626) [28]

Shedd thinks that it is according to this human consciousness that Christ can be said to be peccable, whilst remaining impeccable in the divine consciousness. So it seems to me that it is in the context of this discussion of two ranges of consciousness corresponding to the two nature of Christ, that we should situate what Shedd says about the human nature of Christ being peccable. It sounds strange to say that a nature is peccable, rather than a person. But if, as Shedd and the medievals claim, the human nature of Christ is a concrete particular that can be said to have a range of consciousness, will certain things, and so forth, it does not seem any more strange to suggest that this nature is peccable too.

Can Christ's Human Nature be Peccable?

But there is a second potential problem with Shedd's view. This has to do with what it means to say that Christ's human nature is *peccable*. In his work on two-minds Christology, Thomas Morris argues that to say Christ was tempted by sin is to say Christ believed himself capable of sin. It is the merely epistemic possibility of sinning that is in view here. There was no metaphysical possibility of Christ sinning. Thus Morris:

> Some Christian theists are tempted to try to solve this problem merely by adverting to the two-natures model and the reduplicative form of proposition. They attempt to specify *qua* God, or with respect to his divine nature, he was not able to sin, whereas *qua* man, or with respect to his divine nature, he was able to sin, and thus able to be tempted. But could it have been that God the Son was

---

[28] I do not think the illustration from 'sensuous' and 'spiritual' consciousness works. But, this does not matter. What we are interested in here is the distinction Shedd makes between the two ranges of consciousness in the person of Christ.

necessarily good *qua* God whilst only contingently good *qua* man? [29]

And, of course, the answer given is negative: it is metaphysically *impossible* that the human nature of Christ be only contingently good.[30]

The argument here seems to be this: If Christ was only contingently good *qua* human being then it is metaphysically possible for Christ to sin. But it is not metaphysically possible for Christ to sin because his divine nature is impeccable. So, it cannot be the case that Christ's human nature was only contingently good. But what Shedd's account shows is that it is possible for Christ's human nature to be constitutionally capable of sin in abstraction, as it were, from the hypostatic union, and yet be rendered incapable of sinning in virtue of that union with the divine nature of the Word of God. So the fact that Christ's human nature is only contingently good does not necessarily mean that the whole theanthropic person of Christ is capable of sinning. Nor does this mean Christ is incapable of being tempted. For, as we have seen, there is a distinction to be made between being tempted and succumbing to temptation. One can be truly tempted and not succumb, otherwise, what would it mean to say 'x was tempted and resisted that temptation'? To put it another way, there is nothing about the notion of temptation that requires that the person who is being tempted succumbs to that temptation. So, on the Sheddian way of thinking, all the following statements are true:

1. Christ's human nature was constitutionally sinless but not impeccable (in abstraction from the hypostatic union).
2. Christ's human nature was rendered impeccable through the hypostatic union with the Word of God (who is constitutionally incapable of sinning).
3. Christ was capable of being tempted (by a certain class of temptations, namely, innocent temptations).
4. Christ was incapable of succumbing to temptation.

But, interestingly, Shedd's account may actually provide a broadly Morrisian sort of argument for the merely epistemic possibility of Christ's temptation that is not committed to Morris' view that if Christ has a peccable human nature then it is metaphysically possible for him to sin.

To see this, let us adapt Morris's reasoning so that it corresponds to Shedd's

---

[29] Thomas V. Morris, *The Logic of God Incarnate* (Ithaca, NY.: Cornell University Press, 1986), p. 146.

[30] Shedd affirms that the human nature of Christ was ignorant of many things that were withheld from the human nature by the divine nature (DT, 620). In this respect, Shedd's notion of two ranges of consciousness in Christ sounds rather like Morris's claim that the human mind of Christ is 'contained' in the divine mind, between which there exists an asymmetrical accessing relation.

account. Morris uses an example of Jesus being tempted to commit adultery in order to show that it is metaphysically impossible that his human nature is peccable. But we have already seen that this sort of example is ruled out by Shedd's account: it would constitute a sinful temptation, requiring a prior morally corrupt nature. Let us grant this to Shedd. Nevertheless, there are other putative temptations that could apply to Christ. One such, adverted to earlier, is disobeying a divine command, where the person tempted does not have a prior morally corrupt moral nature. Suppose Christ, according to his human nature, could have been tempted to disobey a divine command without that temptation being morally culpable in and of itself (independently of whether it is acted upon). Being tempted to succumb to the temptation concerned (that is, feeling the 'pull' of the temptation) is itself non-culpable, although it is presented to Christ as an action he could perform, and which, if he did perform, would be culpable. In other words, suppose Christ is, in Shedd's terminology, 'innocently' tempted. It is not difficult to see that the logic of Shedd's position is that Christ may be subject to such 'innocent' temptations and yet not sin. Adam may have been in a parallel situation prior to his primal sin. Perhaps his primal sin was not the first instance of temptation that had beset him, but was merely the first temptation he succumbed to. Previous to his primal sin, Adam had successfully resisted the temptations put to him (presuming there were prior temptations). If Christ has a human nature that is constitutionally sinless, then presumably, like Adam, the human nature of Christ may repulse innocent temptations. Now, were it possible to decouple Christ's human nature from the hypostatic union (a controversial idea, to be sure) then possibly, the human nature that had been the human nature of the Word of God would form a supposit – a human person – and may then sin. But this does not mean that the theanthropic person of Christ may sin. For, as we have already seen, Shedd maintains that, though constitutionally capable of sinning absent union with the Word of God (and having formed a supposit independently of the Word of God), there is no possibility of Christ's human nature sinning when in union with the Word of God. The Word of God renders his human nature impeccable through his assumption of that human nature. Or, perhaps, his divine nature would prevent his human nature from sinning, were it ever the case that his human nature was about to succumb to some innocent temptation. For, as Morris also points out, there is nothing incoherent in supposing that the human nature of Christ, though tempted by sin, never actually succumbs to temptation. It might be that his human nature, unlike Adams', resisted all temptations that Christ was presented with.

It is at this point that Shedd's argument may be used to amend, or extend, a broadly Morrisian-style account of Christ's impeccability. Shedd's claim that Christ is rendered impeccable though his human nature is constitutionally peccable (absent the hypostatic union) does not necessarily mean it was metaphysically possible for Christ to sin. Shedd's position is compatible with Morris's claim that there was only ever an epistemic possibility of Christ sinning. When presented with innocent temptations, Christ's human nature may have believed it possible to sin. But, in fact, he was incapable of sinning. For either his divine nature would have prevented this outcome, or he would have successfully resisted this temptation, *qua* human, without the interposition of his divine nature to ensure this. Either way, Christ is metaphysically incapable of sinning, though he is epistemically capable of being tempted.

This raises three further issues: in what way is Shedd's account preferable to Morris's account; does this mean Christ held false beliefs about being able to succumb to temptation; and in what way can Christ be said to be truly tempted as per Hebrews 4: 15, if there is no metaphysical possibility of him ever sinning on Shedd's view?

As to the first question, Shedd's account is preferable to Morris's because he is able to make sense of the intuition, shared by a number of classical divines but denied by Morris, that Christ must be capable of sinning *qua* human. Admittedly, at first glance Shedd's reasoning seems somewhat beside the point: Christ is incapable of sin, but, in abstraction from the hypostatic union, Christ's human nature is like any other human nature absent original sin. His human nature is sinless, but capable of sinning – as Adam's human nature was prior to the Fall. This might be thought beside the point because it denies that Christ is able to sin, whilst affirming that his human nature *would be able to sin if it were not the human nature of Christ*. For, if it were possible for Christ's human nature to be decoupled from the hypostatic union, then the human nature concerned would no longer be the human nature of the Word of God. It would be the human nature of some human person that would be formed the moment this decoupling took place (according to the medieval account of the human person of Christ which we have brought to bear upon the metaphysics of the Incarnation Shedd sets forth). And, if there are possible worlds at which there exists a human nature that would have been the human nature of Christ had the Second Person of the Trinity assumed that human nature – but did not - then in those worlds the same reasoning would apply: the human nature that is unassumed by the Word of God (but is assumed by him in all those worlds at which he does become incarnate[31]) forms a human person, and, in at least some of this galaxy of worlds, sins.[32] But this has no bearing upon the incarnation

---

[31] Assuming that the Second Person of the Trinity assumes the same human nature in all those possible worlds at which he assumes human nature at all.

[32] A galaxy of possible worlds is just a group of possible worlds determined by a certain creaturely world type. A creaturely world-type is a complete set of creaturely counterfactuals of freedom that God knows to be true. The galaxy of possible worlds that are relevant in this case comprise all those worlds at which the human nature of Christ exists, which contain the relevant counterfactuals of freedom that God knows to be true. I am assuming, that God *makes truth* in these matters; it is not the case that certain worlds are infeasible for God because they are possible but not actualisable. All possible worlds seem actualisable given theological compatibilism. And Shedd was a theological compatibilist. So there are no infeasible worlds on this view. See Flint,

precisely because, even if this sort of scenario is possible, it does not obtain in the case of the Incarnation. Christ is impeccable because his peccable human nature is rendered impeccable by union with the Word of God. Hence, if this sort of reasoning stands behind Shedd's way of conceiving of the peccability of Christ's human nature, then it misses its mark.

But, there is no reason to think Shedd is committed to this way of thinking. And even if he were, the logic of the position he espouses does not necessarily lead in this direction. For the sort of modal story just told depends upon a highly contentious thesis, that the human nature of Christ is only contingently related to his divine nature. The medieval theologians William Occam and John Duns Scotus defended this view.[33] But Shedd need not. He, like Thomas Aquinas, might opt instead for the idea that the human nature of Christ is necessarily such that it is sustained by a divine person.[34] In which case, talk of possible worlds at which Christ's human nature is decoupled from his divine nature for some period, or is unassumed by the Second Person of the Trinity and forms a person distinct from the Word of God, is idle. There can be no such possible worlds because in every world at which the human nature of Christ exists, it is united to the Second Person of the Trinity.

If this Thomist way of conceiving the relation between the human nature of Christ and the Second Person of the Trinity is right, then what Shedd's view amounts to is the claim that, like the human natures of Adam and Eve prior to their primal sin, Christ's human nature is constitutionally capable of sinning, although this capacity or disposition, is overridden or rendered inoperative by union with the Word of God. Recall the example, used earlier, of the glass encased in polystyrene. We might say that the glass is constitutionally fragile, or that it has the dispositional property 'being breakable'. It shares this property with every other glass object that exists because this is a property that is essential to 'glassness'. But suppose that there are no possible worlds at which this particular glass is without its polystyrene casing, and suppose that this casing renders the glass incapable of being broken. Then, there are no worlds at which this particular glass can 'realize' its dispositional property, and be broken.

This, I suggest, is something like the story motivating Shedd's account of

---

Divine Providence, The Molinist Account (Ithaca, NY.: Cornell University Press, 1992), ch. 2, where these terms are laid out.

[33] Alfred Freddoso has discussed this point in detail in 'Human Nature, Potency and The Incarnation', *Faith and Philosophy* 3 (1986): 27-53.

[34] At least, this is the view Freddoso attributes to Thomas, with some pretty convincing exegesis in the appendix to his paper, 'Human Nature, Potency and The Incarnation'. Even if this is not Thomas' view, it is certainly one that Shedd could adopt. The idea that the human nature of Christ is necessarily such that it is sustained by a divine person should be distinguished from the notion that the divine nature of the Second Person of the Trinity freely became incarnate. This means the relation between the Word of God and his human nature is a contingent one.

Christ's impeccability. Or, at least, it is a story consistent with what Shedd does say, that does not fall foul of the objection that Shedd's position is merely sophistical. But how is this preferable to Morris's analysis of impeccability? It is preferable because it retains a place for the classical notion that Christ was peccable *qua* human, whilst impeccable *qua* divine. And it does this without sacrificing Morris's notion that Christ can only ever have believed himself capable of sin as a human. There was never any metaphysical possibility of Christ actually succumbing to temptation and sinning.

But, secondly, does Shedd's account mean Christ held false beliefs? On Morris' view, it looks like he does. Christ's human range of consciousness does not include an awareness of being impeccable (at least, not at those moments at which he is tempted to sin). But, presumably, this means that any belief of the form 'I may succumb to temptation x' that he may have held *qua* human was, strictly speaking, a false belief. However, it might be thought that Shedd's view is not subject to the same objection because it allows that Christ's human nature was constitutionally capable of sin, though it was rendered impeccable by the hypostatic union. Beliefs of the form 'I may succumb to temptation x' that Christ may have held at those moments when he was tempted were false with reference to the hypostatic union, but were not false with reference to the way in which the human nature of Christ was constituted. It is true on Shedd's view that the human nature Christ has would be capable of sin without union with the Word of God, even if it were a necessary truth that at any world in which this human nature exists it is united to the Word of God.[35]

But there is a problem with Shedd's view at this juncture parallel to the sophistry objection just considered. This is that his reasoning appears to rely on a metaphysical sleight of hand. The metaphysically relevant context here is the Incarnation. The notion that the human nature of Christ would sin were it not assumed by the Second Person of the Trinity is not modally relevant because (a) this state of affairs is metaphysically impossible if the human nature of Christ is necessarily such that it is united to the Second Person of the Trinity in all those possible worlds at which it exists, and (b) even if this state of affairs were metaphysically possible, the human nature concerned would not be the human nature of Christ, but a human person distinct from the Word of God (assuming the medieval picture of the metaphysics of the Incarnation, outlined earlier). So it would seem that Shedd's solution to the problem with Morris's argument for the impeccability of Christ suffers from difficulties at least as

---

[35] Shedd's argument also provides a solution to an objection raised by David Werther. He argues that if Jesus is essentially good and only his divine nature prevents him from succumbing to temptation, then he is not necessarily good (i.e., he is not impeccable). But we have seen that, given Shedd's account, Christ can be both necessarily good and yet constitutionally peccable according to his human nature (considered in abstraction from the Incarnation). See Werther, 'The Temptation of God Incarnate' in *Religious Studies* 29 (1993): 47-50.

problematic as those attending Morris's reasoning.

However, I do not think this is quite right. It is true that the Incarnation is the modally relevant context for the discussion, not some putative human nature that forms a supposit and exists as a human person distinct from the Word of God, in a possible world where the Incarnation does not take place. But return to the example of the glass in polystyrene: It would surely be true to say of the glass that it has the dispositional property of being breakable even if there are no circumstances in which this particular glass exists without its polystyrene packing, in order for it to be broken. (Where the individual glass is necessarily such that it is encased in this polystyrene packing at all worlds at which it exists.)

Perhaps Shedd, or a Sheddian, might reason in a parallel way concerning the Incarnation. There are no possible worlds at which the human nature of Christ exists without being united to the Word of God. So there are no possible worlds at which the human nature of Christ may sin. But this does not mean that the human nature of Christ ceases to have the dispositional property 'being capable of sin absent the hypostatic union'. And perhaps this is all that is needed for the Sheddian to be able to circumvent this difficulty: Christ in his human range of consciousness (a phrase Shedd shares in common with Morris) conceives that he may succumb to innocent temptation x. He believes this because he knows himself to be a human being who, *qua* human, is constitutionally sinless. What his human consciousness may not be aware of (at least, during moments of temptation) is that he is actually rendered impeccable because of the hypostatic union with the Word of God. And this does not necessarily commit the Sheddian to the idea that Christ had false beliefs about his capacity to sin.

This brings us to the question of how Christ can be said to be truly tempted as per Hebrews 4: 15, if there is no metaphysical possibility of him ever sinning on Shedd's view. In this respect, Shedd and Morris share a common problem, and one that has been mooted in the current literature.[36] Earlier, in setting out Shedd's position, we noted that he claims Christ can only be tempted by innocent temptations that do not require Christ to be in a prior state of sin to feel the 'pull' of the temptation concerned, and where the very act of being tempted is not itself a sinful act. Let us grant this to Shedd. We now see that his position means Christ cannot sin under any circumstances. Nevertheless, this is consistent with being truly tempted. What needs to be kept in mind is that being tempted and succumbing to temptation are two different acts, and that succumbing is not entailed by the notion of temptation. Otherwise, in every instance of temptation, the person being tempted would inevitably succumb. But this is obviously false. For then sentences of the form 'x resisted the temptation' would be meaningless. Once this is granted, the real import of Hebrews 4: 15 becomes clear: Christ was capable of being truly tempted but

---

[36] Richard Swinburne raises a similar point in criticism of Morris's two-minds Christology. See *The Christian God,* p. 205, n. 14.

not of succumbing to temptation, rather like the invincible pugilist may be truly tested in the ring by an opponent, and have to defend himself against attack, although there is no possibility of him ever being overcome or defeated.

The Paradox of Innocent Temptation

There is one final problem with Shedd's view. This is an issue that Shedd does not entirely resolve. However, it is a problem he shares with all orthodox accounts of Christ's moral nature. The problem has to do with how any temptation can be innocent. We are faced with two, apparently contradictory, sets of biblical data. On the one hand, there are those passages that state quite clearly that Christ is without sin. We have already mentioned Hebrews 4: 15, but there are other places where this seems to be implied, e.g. Hebrews 7: 26, 9: 14; 2 Corinthians 5: 21; 1 Peter 2: 22, 3: 18; and 1 John 3: 5. Then there are those places where Christ is said to have been tempted. Apart from Hebrews 4: 15, these include the synoptic accounts of Christ's temptations, the Gospel accounts of the temptation by Peter in, e.g. Matthew 16, and the anguish in the Garden of Gethsemane. But how can Christ be both tempted *and* sinless? Shedd's response, as we have seen, is to make a distinction between innocent and sinful temptations. And surely the theological motivation behind this manoeuvre is correct. If Christ is both sinless and tempted, his temptations cannot themselves constitute a sin independently of his acting upon those temptations, otherwise Christ sins in being tempted, even if he does not act upon the temptation proffered.

But it might be thought that the notion of temptation includes some idea of doing wrong. On one understanding of temptation, once a person is tempted he or she is already committed to thinking of the object of temptation as the subject of a possible action that it is within his or her power to perform.[37] But then it seems that it is too late to speak of 'innocent' temptations; the person concerned is responsible for considering the object of temptation as the subject of a possible action. It has been claimed that there are temptations that involve wrongs that are not moral wrongs, strictly speaking, for instance, wrongs that are merely prudential or legal but not moral.[38] But I do not think that Shedd thought like this, nor do I think it plausible to say one can be truly *tempted* to do something that is not morally, but only legally, or aesthetically, wrong.

---

[37] Assuming that it is within the power of this person to perform the action in question.

[38] So, J. P. Day says, 'one must distinguish yielding to temptation, which is always morally wrong, from the wrongness of that which TE [that is, the temptee] is tempted to do, which must be wrong in *some* way (e.g. prudentially, legally, or aesthetically), but need not be wrong morally.' From 'Temptation' in *American Philosophical Quarterly* 30 (1993): 177. His example involves someone being tempted to break the speed limit for ten pounds. Succumbing to the temptation is morally wrong, but driving at one mile-per-hour over the speed limit is not – it is only legally wrong. But it seems to me that for the Christian, this is also morally wrong (Romans 13: 1).

Temptation is an irreducibly moral notion – at least, this is how it has been traditionally understood in Christian theology.

Is someone culpable for merely considering a particular course of action that is a temptation, even if he or she does not act upon this deliberation and yield to temptation? Perhaps. Consideration and deliberation are mental actions. It seems plausible to claim that I am morally responsible for my own actions, including mental actions (other things being equal). In which case, I am morally responsible for considering or deliberating about, a given temptation. If a temptation is the enticement to do something that is morally wrong, then considering whether to yield to the enticement to do something wrong might itself be wrong.[39]

This seems to raise a problem for a Sheddian account of 'innocent' temptations. Even if Christ was only faced with a temptation to do some supererogatory action less than a better supererogatory action, the very fact that he is tempted to do such a thing looks like a moral failing, on this way of thinking about temptation. Shedd says, 'the temptations of Christ were "without sin" *in their source and nature* and not merely as the passage is sometime explained, that they were "without sin" *in their result.*'[40] This seems right given the biblical data. But it does not constitute an *explanation* of what it means to say there is a class of temptations that are innocent.[41]

Conclusions

Shedd's treatment of the impeccability of Christ turns out to be one version of a traditional argument in favour of Christ's impeccability that explains the temptability of Christ in terms of the peccability of his sinless human nature. We have dealt with three problems for this view. The first has to do with the human nature of Christ being peccable. However, if one is willing to accept that Christ's human nature is a concrete particular, there does not seem to be anything particularly strange about saying that this nature might be peccable

---

[39] Of course some people do say things like 'I was tempted to go to Church today', but usually the context of such an utterance makes it clear that the person saying it does not literally mean the hearer to think that going to church is a temptation, or, as J. P. Day puts it, such an example 'is not a serious use of "tempt"', 'Temptation', p. 177.

[40] DT: 666, emphasis added.

[41] Shedd's position is complicated by what he has to say about the temptation of Adam: 'Such being the facts in the case, it is evident that inward lust or sinful desire did not contribute to the force of temptation in the instance of unfallen Adam as it does in that of his fallen posterity, nor can it be postulated as helping to explain his fall. Sinful desire was begun by an act of pure self-determination and therefore could not have been the cause of this act. Unfallen Adam was not "drawn away of his own lust and enticed," as his fallen posterity now are. He willfully and wantonly yielded to an external suggestion of Satan which had by no means the violent strength of an internal desire.' DT: 539. I am grateful to Alan Gomes for drawing my attention to this passage.

any more than when we say it was the blackness of the ink that was indelible. Second, we have seen that a Sheddian argument may augment, or correct a view broadly in keeping with several central tenets of the views expressed by Thomas Morris on the peccability of Christ's human nature. Though there may be residual problems with this way of construing a broadly Morrisian position on the impeccability of Christ, Shedd's account points out some important issues pertaining to the consistency of claiming Christ was both impeccable and tempted, that, like Morris, devolves upon that temptation being a merely epistemic, rather than metaphysical possibility. However like other, similar orthodox arguments for Christ's impeccability, Shedd's view offers no satisfactory explanation of how Christ can be innocently tempted, an important constituent of his proposed solution to this theological problem. For this reason, his account is only partially successful.

CHAPTER 5

Sin, Atonement and Representationalism

Dogmatic Preamble

There are many doctrines of the atonement in the history of Christian thought. One of the most important and enduring of these is the theory that Christ's atoning work is a penal substitution. Put briefly (and somewhat roughly), this is the idea that Christ stands in the place of the sinner, the penal consequences of whose sin he takes upon himself at the cross, being punished in place of the sinner. Crucially, for the logic of this view of the atonement, although Christ is not the one guilty of sinning, God treats him as if he is the guilty party, punishing him in place of the guilty parties, namely sinful human beings (or some number of sinful human beings less than the total number of humanity). This is the central notion behind the theory of penal substitution, and it depends on what we might call a *forensic fiction*. (It is forensic because the theory concerned is penal, or judicial; it is a fiction because Christ is not literally guilty of sin, but is treated as if he were, for the sake of atonement.) Different advocates of penal substitution construe this in different ways, with different emphases, but they all share this common core understanding of the nature of the atonement.

One of the key differences between different defenders of this theory of the atonement involves a distinction between the imputations of human sin from Adam to his progeny on the one hand, and from the sinner to Christ on the other. (There is also a further matter, related to these two, which has to do with the way in which Christ's righteousness is imputed to the sinner.) There are those defenders of penal substitution who think that Adam's sin is imputed to his progeny because Adam acts as the representative of the human race such that when Adam sins, his sin may be justly imputed to those whom he represents. This representational view is sometimes called 'federalism', on account of the fact that it means Adam is the federal head, or representative of the human race. But there are other defenders of penal substitution who are Augustinian realists, like Shedd. For such theologians, the imputation of Adam's sin is not merely a matter of representation. Rather, Adam and humanity are somehow one metaphysical entity. Adam's sin, on this second view really is my sin, because Adam and I are somehow two parts of one metaphysical whole – issues we have already attended to in this study.

These are not the only views on the matter of the imputation of Adam's sin in the Christian tradition, but they are the two views relevant for our purposes. Those who are representationalists about the imputation of Adam's sin are usually also representationalists about the matter of the atonement. (This is an historical fact, not a point of logic – representationalism in hamartiology does not entail representationalism in soteriology.) Theologians who take this sort of view think that as Adam acts as the representative of the human race, such that when Adam sins, the rest of humanity are punished for that sin by having original sin imputed to them, just so, in the case of the atonement, Christ acts as my representative, standing in my place to take the punishment for sin due to me. Thus, God the Father punishes Christ in my place, treating him as if it were me he was punishing.

There is, therefore, a certain symmetry between the two representatives of the human race on this sort of view, which ties in with a particular way of understanding biblical texts such as Romans 5: 12-19. In that passage, Paul lays out his comparison between the 'two Adams', that is, Adam and Christ. And on the representationalist rendering of Paul's argument, both Adam and Christ act as the 'federal' representatives of human kind. As Adam's sin affects human nature for the worse, so Christ's atoning act affects human nature for the better. But in both cases the act upon which this relation between humanity and these two representatives turns, has to do with this notion of a forensic fiction. On the one hand, God treats Adam's progeny as if they are guilty of Adam's sin (although, strictly speaking, they are not guilty of his sin), and punishes them accordingly. But on the other hand, Christ is treated as if he were the guilty party, being punished in my place for my sin, although strictly speaking, he has no personal guilt whatsoever. Let us call this sort of view *consistent representationalism*, because it stipulates that both in the matter of the imputation of sin and the atonement and imputation of Christ's righteousness, Adam and Christ act as the representatives of (certain) human beings. One example of just such a representationalist view of the imputation of Adam's sin is the twentieth century American Dutch Reformed theologian, Louis Berkhof. In his *Systematic Theology* says this:

> In his righteous judgment God imputes the guilt of the first sin, committed by the head of the covenant, to all those that are federally related to him. And as a result they are born in a depraved and sinful condition as well, and this inherent corruption also involves guilt.

Later in the same work, whilst admitting the difficulty attending a penal substitutionary understanding of the atonement regarding the fact that there does not seem to be an adequate human analogy to the notion of a penal substitute, he nevertheless maintains that,

> This does not mean that our sinfulness was transferred to Him – something that is in itself utterly impossible – but that the guilt of our sins was imputed to Him.... Strictly speaking, then, the guilt of sin as liability to punishment [*reatus poenae*] was imputed to Christ; and this could be transferred, because it did not inhere in the person of the sinner, but was something objective.[1]

Whatever we make of Berkhof's interpretation of penal substitution, it should be clear from the foregoing that this is not the only way in which the doctrine of the 'two Adams' found in Pauline theology, might be taken. Consider, for example, the Augustinian realist view. There are two ways in which the Augustinian might construe the 'two Adams'.[2] Both of these ways of thinking about Augustinian realism share the idea that the imputation of Adam's sin to his progeny depends upon Adam and his progeny being one metaphysical entity. The motivation behind this view is a desire to safeguard the doctrine of the imputation of original sin from the charge of injustice. For, so the Augustinian realist claims, it seems unjust that I am treated as if I were guilty of Adam's sin, and have the penal consequences of Adam's sin imputed to me by God. Yet this is what the representationalist alternative entails. However, if Adam's sin really is my sin because somehow Adam and I are really one metaphysical entity, then this problem may be evaded. If such an argument were forthcoming, then Adam's sin and guilt would be my sin and guilt, and God would be perfectly just in treating Adam and me as one entity for the purposes of the imputation of sin.[3]

The question then is what we are to make of the relation between Christ and his elect, that is, between Christ and those his atonement saves.[4] Here there are two possible answers. The first is to say that there are reasons why Christ's atoning work is not like Adam's sinful act, and that these reasons are sufficiently serious to warrant a different way of thinking about the relation that

---

[1] Louis Berkhof, *Systematic Theology*, pp. 242-243 and 377, respectively.

[2] By this I mean there are two live options for Augustinian realists on the matter of the relationship between the 'two Adams' of Pauline theology. I do not claim they are the only logically possible alternatives; clearly they are not. But I know of no theologian who claims that (a) the imputation of Adam's sin involves a mere representationalism, whereas (b) the relation between Christ and the elect is a realist one. Yet this is a position that might be taken. Theologians like Pelagius have argued that neither Adam's sin, not Christ's righteousness, are imputed to human beings at all. But this view is, I take it, not a live option for orthodox Christian theologians.

[3] As was pointed out in Chapter Two, there are several ways for an Augustinian realist to make sense of his or her realism.

[4] I presume that Christ's atonement does actually bring about the salvation of a certain number of human beings, who come to realise that they are saved through the secret work of the Holy Spirit in regeneration. We shall not deal with those who claim Christ's atoning work merely makes the salvation of fallen human beings possible, but is not sufficient to save any fallen human being without a the significantly free choice of a fallen human being, required for Christ's atoning work to have purchase.

obtains between Christ and the elect. For Augustinian realists sympathetic to this line of reasoning, the obvious alternative is a version of representationalism with respect to Christ's work. So, on this first version of Augustinian realism, there is an asymmetry between the work of the first and second Adam (of Paul's thinking in Romans 5). The first Adam is so united with his progeny that they are somehow one metaphysical entity, and Adam's sin passes to the later stages or phases of the life of this same entity, that is, humanity. But Christ's union with his elect is not such an intimate relationship. Christ acts as the representative of the elect and dies in their place, taking upon himself their sin and guilt, which God the Father is happy to impute to Christ's account. So there is, on this view, a forensic fiction in the atonement that there is not in the imputation of Adam's sin. Let us designate this view, *the mediating position*, since defenders of this view claim realism is true with respect to the imputation of Adam's sin, and representationalism is true with respect to Christ's atoning work.[5] As we shall see presently, a classic example of this mediating position is William Shedd.

But there is a second way in which the Augustinian realist argument could go. On this view, Christ, like Adam is really united with his elect, just as Adam is really united with his fallen descendents. Christ is somehow part of one metaphysical entity with the elect, just as Adam is somehow part of one metaphysical entity comprising Adam and his progeny. It should be clear that on this way of thinking there is an important symmetry between the two Adam's of Pauline theology, which extends to the metaphysics of the imputation of Adam's sin and Christ's righteousness, respectively. This last view we shall refer to as *consistent realism*. For according to this view, the mechanism by which both the imputation of Adam's sin and Christ's righteousness is brought about, is a realist one. However, this view is not one that, to my knowledge, has ever been systematically set forth in the Christian tradition. Having said that, there are some theologians who, in the context of discussion of the nature of the atonement say things that sound rather realist, or could be taken in a realist direction. Take, for example, the Puritan theologian, John Owen. In his *Dissertation on Divine Justice* he says that God,

> might punish the elect either in their own persons, or in their surety standing in their room and stead; and when he is punished, they also are punished: for in this point of view the federal head and those represented by him are not considered as distinct, but as one; for although they are not one in respect of personal unity, they

---

[5] This should not be taken to imply that the mediating view is a third sort of view in-between, but not exactly the same as, either Augustinian realism or representationalism. That would be inaccurate. Rather, this mediating view is a species of realism, but one modified on the question of the atonement, by representationalism. Therefore, it is mediating only in the sense that, on the matter of the imputation of sin this view is realist, whereas on the matter of the atoning work of Christ, this view is representationalist.

are, however, one, - that is, one body in mystical union, yea, *one mystical Christ* – namely, the surety is the head, those represented by him the members; and when the head is punished, the members also are punished.[6]

Although Owen retains the language of representationalism here, there is also material that sounds realist. And he is not the only thinker in the tradition to use such ambiguous language about the nature of the atonement.[7] Naturally, consistent realism would require more than realist-*sounding* language. But, at the very least this shows that even a theologian like John Owen, often taken to be a paradigm of consistent representationalism, is not unambiguously representationalist on the matter of the atonement. It may be that consistent realism is not such a theologically outlandish idea, after all.

Situating William Shedd's Views on these Matters

William Shedd wrestled with these issues and achieved a remarkable synthesis between aspects of the realist and representational ways of thinking, which, as I have already mentioned, corresponds to the first of our two ways of construing

---

[6] See John Owen, *A Dissertation on Divine Justice*, in *The Works of John Owen, Vol. X*, ed. William H. Goold (Edinburgh: Banner of Truth, 1967 [1850-1853]), p. 598. Similar sentiments can be found in James I. Packer's important essay, 'What Did The Cross Achieve? The Logic of Penal Substitution' originally published in *Tyndale Bulletin* 25 (1974): 3-46, reprinted as an RTSF Booklet (Leicester: UCCF, 2002). Like Owen, Packer denies that penal substitution involves a legal fiction, 'a form of words to which no reality corresponds' viz. Christ being treated by God the Father 'as if' he were guilty of my sin, and being punished in my stead as a consequence of this. Rather, Christ's death for us is an 'objective fact', a mystery 'that is "there" whether we grasp it or not'. He goes on to argue that '[w]e who believe have died – painlessly and invisibly, we might say – in solidarity with him because he died painfully and publically, in substitution for us', pp.41-42 respectively.

[7] Compare the language of Eusebius of Caesarea: 'And how can He make our sins His own, and be said to bear our iniquities, except by our being regarded as His body, according to the apostle, who says: "Now ye are the body of Christ, and severally members?"' in *Demonstratio Evangelica X. 1*, in *The Proof of The Gospel*, ed. and trans. W. J. Ferrar, Vol. 2 (Eugene, OR.: Wipf & Stock, 2001), p. 195. I owe this and the Owen reference to Dr Garry Williams, who pointed out to me in conversation that there are several instances of such ambiguous language in the tradition (another is St. Cyril of Alexandria in *De adoratione et culta in spiritu et veritate*, III. 100-102, PG 68: 293 and 296). See Williams' very helpful paper, 'God, The Individual, and Systematic Solipsism: Contemporary Anglo-American Criticism of Penal Substitution' (forthcoming). There is at least one Protestant theologian whose work does seem to be a version of consistent realism. I refer to the seventeeth century puritan, Tobias Crisp. See his posthumously published work, *Christ Alone Exalted*, especially sermons 18 and 19, based on Isaiah 53: 6, which can be found on the internet located at <www.gospeldefense.com/christ_alone_exalted.html>.

the Augustinian realist account of Paul's 'two Adams', that is, the mediating view. In his *Dogmatic Theology*, he set out an argument for this particular realist position.[8] In the remainder of this chapter, I want to consider his argument in some detail since it sheds light on some difficult matters to do with the nature of the atonement, and its relationship to the doctrine of sin. We will see that Shedd offers several interesting reasons for taking the realist-representationalist position over the consistent representationalist alternative. But he does not really address the consistently realist alternative in any systematic fashion, although it seems clear from comments he does make that Shedd was not sympathetic to consistent realism - see, for instance, DT: 461. After giving a critical account of Shedd's position on this matter, I shall offer some comments on the success of his view. It seems to me that there are some important shortcomings with his account that Shedd does not tackle adequately. Finally, in third section of the chapter, I shall offer some reflections on consistent realism as a possible alternative to Shedd's mediating position.

Shedd*ing* Light on the Atonement

That Shedd defends the doctrine of penal substitution is not in doubt. He devoted a whole chapter of his *Dogmatic Theology* (Part 6, Chapter 2) to the vicariousness of Christ's atonement. There he says things about the nature of the atonement like this:

> The sufferings of Christ the mediator were vicariously penal or atoning because the intention, both on the part of the Father and the Son, was that they should satisfy justice for the sin of man.... Scripture plainly teaches that our Lord's sufferings were vicariously retributive; that is, they were endured for the purpose of satisfying justice in the place of the actual transgressor: "Christ has once suffered for sins, the just for the unjust" (Gal. 3: 13). (DT: 716-717)

Although some theologians writing around the same time as Shedd, such as John McLeod Campbell, argued that the atonement might be substitutionary but not penal, so that a vicarious atonement need not imply the doctrine of *penal* substitution, it is clear from this and the whole tenor of Shedd's discussion that he is not sympathetic to non-penal arguments for a substitutionary atonement.[9] His is a staunch defence of penal substitution.[10]

---

[8] Shedd deals with his Augustinian realism elsewhere in his work, but often reproducing aspects of the argument he develops more fully in his *Dogmatic Theology*. See, for instance, his comments in his essay, 'The Doctrine of Original Sin' in DE, pp. 259 ff. See also his sermon 'On the Sinfulness of Original Sin' in SNM: 272, n. 1.
[9] See John McLeod Campbell, *The Nature of the Atonement*, 6th Edition (London: Macmillan, 1895 [1856]).
[10] Compare Shedd, DT: 735, where he says that Christ's sufferings, 'were a judicial infliction voluntarily endured by Christ for the purposes of satisfying the claims of law

Yet, as we have seen, Shedd was also an advocate of Augustinian realism with respect to the imputation of Adam's sin. In discussing original sin and Romans 5: 12-19, Shedd says that this passage teaches that, 'the death which came upon all men as a punishment came because of one sin and only one'. Moreover, 'this sin was the one committed by Adam and his posterity as a unity' (DT: 558). Later in the same discussion on the imputation of Adam's sin, Shedd states that,

> The first sin of Adam, being a common, not an individual sin, is deservedly and justly imputed to the posterity of Adam upon the same principle upon which all sin is deservedly and justly imputed, namely, that it was committed by those to whom it is imputed (DT: 561).

We have also seen that Shedd's argument for Augustinian realism depends upon a version of traducianism, the doctrine that the souls of human beings are passed down from parents to children, just as our genetic make-up is inherited from our parents. To re-cap, Shedd says this: Adam and Eve both share an undifferentiated 'human nature' including a 'psychical' part, or soul. This human nature is differentiated as it is passed down from one generation to the next. So, Adam's offspring had his genes and a 'part' of his soul, which became the soul of the particular individual member of Adam's offspring.

He goes on to argue that the imputation of either Adam's sin or Christ's righteousness must 'rest upon a union of some kind.' (DT: 561) But the union involved in each of these cases is quite different. The imputation of Adam's sin depends upon a 'natural union', that is, a version of realism, whereas the imputation of Christ's righteousness depends upon a union 'of constitutional nature and substance' (DT: 562). By this he seems to mean some version of representationalism applies to the atonement and imputation of Christ's righteousness.

The upshot of all this is that Shedd does not favour either a consistently representationalist, nor a consistently realist position on the relationship between the imputation of Adam's sin and of Christ's righteousness. He opts for realism with respect to the former, and representationalism with respect to the latter.

Shedd's Historico-Theological Argument Against Consistent Representationalism

What, then, are Shedd's reasons for opting for this way of understanding the imputation of Adam's sin and Christ's righteousness, respectively? There are several strands to his response. The first involves a historical-theological argument. In the context of his discussion and defence of traducianism in DT:

---

due from man; and this purpose makes them penal.' We shall analyse Shedd's understanding of the nature of the atonement in the next chapter.

451, Shedd claims that the 'elder Calvinists', that is, Calvin and his immediate successors in the post-Reformation period, say nothing about representation on the matter of the imputation of Adam's sin. 'The term', he opines, 'is foreign to their thought' (DT: 452). In the same context, he argues that the transition from the 'elder' to the 'later' Calvinism on this particular cluster of issues can be traced to Francis Turretin, whose view could be seen as a kind of mediating position between the elder and later Calvinists.[11] Like the 'elder Calvinists,' Turretin maintained that there is a real union between Adam and his progeny (usually, it has to be said, in the context of discussing the nature of the imputation of Adam's sin). But he also speaks in terms of representationalism as well, particularly when comparing the 'two Adams'.[12] This, according to Shedd, is to 'combine iron with clay'. 'For', he says, 'the two ideas of natural union and representation are incongruous and exclude each other. The natural or substantial union of two things implies the presence of both. But vicarious representation implies the absence of one of them.' (DT: 449 cf. 458-459)[13] According to Shedd, one must either opt for realism or representationalism with respect to the imputation of Adam's sin, but not both, or some combination thereof.

There is a good reason for Shedd's reluctance to cede ground to a representationalistic account of the imputation of Adam's sin. This reason, although not exactly the same as the objection - alluded to earlier - that imputing Adam's sin to me is unjust, is in the same neighbourhood as this reasoning. Shedd maintains that Adam's sin must be both *culpable* and *punishable* in his posterity. It is not sufficient to claim that Adam's progeny are punishable for Adam's sin, if they are not culpable for it. For that would be unjust. But, according to Shedd, this is just what the representationalist account of the imputation of sin does state. It claims that Adam acts on my behalf, and sins as my representative. Adam's sin is then attributed to me so that I am punishable for Adam's sin, although, on the basis of representationalism, I am not, strictly speaking, culpable for Adam's sin. God simply treats me as if I were guilty of that sin (the forensic fiction at the heart of representationalism, mentioned earlier - see DT: 457-459 for Shedd's argument). Turretin appears to

---

[11] 'Turretin marks the transition from the elder to the later Calvinism, from the theory of the Adamic union to that of the Adamic representation. Both theories are found in his system and are found in conflict.' DT: 448.

[12] Compare Francis Turretin, *Institutes of Elenctic Theology, Vol. I,* 9. 9. 16 on the 'two Adams' and Turretin's language of consistent representationalism, and 9. 9. 24-25 for Turretin's realist-sounding language with respect to the imputation of Adam's sin. Both are cited in Shedd, DT: 448-449.

[13] Although, according to Shedd, representationalism and realism logically exclude one another, these two views on the imputation of Adam's sin can be seen side-by-side in the work of a number of other post-Reformation theologians after Turretin, such as De Moor-Marck, Witsius, and, as we noted in the dogmatic preamble to this chapter, John Owen. See DT: 449-450.

have seen this problem, and, according to Shedd at least, it is because he recognised this shortcoming in representationalism with respect to the imputation of Adam's sin, that he attempts to hold culpability and punishability together in a cobbled version of realism regarding the imputation of sin (DT: 459).[14]

This places the consistent representationalist in something of a quandary. For if Shedd is correct, then consistent representationalism imputes injustice to God at the very point at which it attempts to demonstrate the rightness of divine justice, namely, in the imputation of Adam's sin. And, if Shedd's historico-theological reasoning is right, the problems that representationalism (with respect to the imputation of sin) throws up for Reformed theology, is an invention of later Calvinism. Or, to put it another way, it is a problem generated by theological innovation. What Shedd seems to be saying is this: if Calvinists had remained consistent with their own tradition, that is with the elder Calvinists and Augustinians more generally, they would have avoided speaking of the imputation of Adam's sin in terms of representation, expressing themselves in the language of Augustinian realism instead. But they did not do so, and as a result, confused theological thinking crept into Reformed theology.

This leads us from the first, historical-theological strand of Shedd's argument, directed against consistent representationalists, to a second strand of reasoning where Shedd argues for the dissimilarity between the 'two unions' (of Adam and his progeny in original sin, and of Christ and the elect in the atonement – hereinafter, simply 'the two unions'). The objective here seems to be to offer some reason for thinking that his mediating position is preferable to consistent representationalism.

Shedd on the 'Two Unions'

The first thing Shedd says on this matter picks up where we left off discussion in the previous section. He says, contrary to the later Calvinists after Turretin that 'culpability and punishment stand in the relation of cause and effect and hence, like these, are inseparable' (DT: 457). Against the representationalist account of the imputation of Adam's sin, this objection has purchase. But the same cannot be said against the representationalist account of Christ's atonement. Indeed, a consistent representationalist might reply to Shedd in the following fashion: 'the theological principle you are enunciating means that where there is no culpability, there can be no just punishment (in the case of the imputation of Adam's sin). Yet you affirm that Christ is punished for human sin, despite the fact that he is without sin, and is therefore neither culpable for

---

[14] Interestingly, Shedd notes that Jonathan Edwards comes to similar conclusions in his magisterial treatise, *Original Sin*, for similar reasons. See Edwards, *Original Sin, The Works of Jonathan Edwards Vol. 3*, ed. Clyde Holbrook (New Haven, CN: Yale University Press, 1970).

human sin, nor, strictly speaking, punishable for it.'[15] Thus, Shedd appears to be guilty of theological doublespeak.

However, in the same passage, Shedd responds to this potential counterargument to his own position with five reasons in favour of the dissimilarity between the 'two unions' (of Adam + progeny and Christ + elect). In the first of these, he claims that there is a significant difference between Christ's voluntary consent to atone for human sin, and the fact that Adam's progeny cannot consent to Adam's sin, and that this dissimilarity between the two cases is sufficient to account for the disparity between culpability and punishment. Both are required for the imputation of Adam's sin to be just. But only the latter is required for the atonement, since Christ consents to this arrangement, and, according to Shedd,

> If an innocent person, having the proper qualifications and the right to do so, agrees to suffer judicial infliction for another's culpability, of course no injustice is done to him by the infliction; but if he is compelled to do so, it is the height of injustice. (DT: 457, cf. DT: 461)

There is, then, on Shedd's way of thinking, a penal or forensic asymmetry between Christ and Adam's progeny, that means it would be unjust for representationalism to obtain in the case of the imputation of Adam's sin because I am not culpable for Adam's sin (according to the representationalist view). But it would not be unjust in the case of Christ's atonement, because Christ volunteers to act as a vicar.

Shedd is right to point out the difference between the voluntary nature of Christ's atoning work, and the involuntary nature of imputed sin. It is, in fact, a feature common to all accounts of the 'two unions' that hold to a robust doctrine of original sin and its imputation and a penal substitutionary account of the atonement, whether consistently representationalist or of the mediating persuasion. But, as he rightly points out, consistent representationalism has a problem explaining how it is just for Adam's progeny to be treated as if they were guilty of a sin committed on their behalf by their federal representative. A representationalist doctrine of the atonement (that aspect of representationalism Shedd shares with his opponents) does not face the same problem, says Shedd, because Christ consents to become a penal substitute for human sin.

But it seems entirely specious to claim that because an innocent person volunteers to undergo a certain act of punishment on behalf of another, this involves no injustice. It might very well be a quite unjust punishment, and unjustly imputed to the innocent party, whether or not he or she volunteers for the task. That is to say, the fact Christ consents to act on behalf of fallen human beings in the atonement does not, in and of itself, render his being punished in the place of human sinners a just action. Consider just one example that will

---

[15] Compare Shedd's comments at the top of DT: 461.

make the point, concerning Bill, a man who volunteers to undergo the just punishment for murder allotted to his friend, Ben. Now, suppose Ben is entirely culpable and owns up to this. Would the fact that Bill consents to take Ben's punishment upon himself render his vicarious act a just one? I think it would not, and I fancy most people would have similar intuitions about Bill, and other, similar cases of vicarious punishment. So, even if a penal substitute consents to becoming the vicar for another, this act is not, in and of itself, sufficient to ensure that no injustice is perpetrated against the person of the vicar in his or her act of substitution for the sinner. Consequently, on this particular point, Shedd's reasoning appears wide of the mark.

What, then, of his other reasons for affirming the dissimilarity between the 'two unions'? Do they fair any better? His second point is that Christ suffers undeservedly, whereas Adam and his progeny suffer deservedly (DT: 461). Christ has no personal guilt – he is not a sinner. So the fact that the connection between culpability and punishment is severed in the case of Christ is perfectly just. But the same would not be true of Adam and his progeny. In the case of Adam and his progeny, sin may only be justly imputed if they are all culpable for Adam's sin otherwise I am punished for someone else's sin, for which I am not culpable. (And, although he does not say so in this particular context, it is clear from the overall thrust of his thinking that the Sheddian solution to this problem is of a piece with his Augustinian realism.)

But even if we are minded to grant Shedd's realism in the case of the imputation of sin, this fails to address the fundamental problem this raises for any representational view of the atonement, which we have just touched upon. (I mean the objection that it is unjust for anyone to suffer the punishment due another in matters where serious sin is involved.) If anything, this point only plays into the hands of Shedd's opponents. For if Christ has no personal guilt, then it seems unjust that he is punished for the sin of another at all.

The remaining three reasons Shedd offers can be given a little more briefly. I shall pass comment only after mentioning all of them.

Third, Shedd says Christ is a substitute for sin, whereas Adam and his progeny are the principals involved in an act of sin (DT: 461). Christ suffers vicariously, but Adam's progeny do not. Fourth, Christ's suffering is expiatory; that of Adam's progeny is retributive. Christ endures suffering for the remission of sin, but Adam's progeny suffer to satisfy divine justice. Fifthly, unlike Adam's progeny, Christ does not possess original guilt (for Adam's sin). As a consequence, Christ could consent to undergo suffering as a penal substitute; he was under no obligation to suffer, as Adam's progeny are, because satisfaction is required in payment of their sin.

The third, fourth and fifth of these reasons for the dissimilarity between the 'two unions' do not seem to do much more by way of persuading putative interlocutors than the first two reasons did. The third point is clearly an important difference between the 'two unions' – provided Shedd's view, or something very like it, is assumed at the outset. But the theologian unwilling to concede the point at issue between Shedd and his opponents, without some reason for doing so, will find little in what Shedd says here to persuade him or her. For according to consistent representationalism, Adam's progeny are not the principals involved in original sin, but those to whom the sin of the principal, that is, Adam, is imputed.

Shedd's fourth point tells a rather one-sided story, weighting it in favour of Shedd's position. It is true, as he suggests, that Christ's suffering is expiatory whereas that of Adam's progeny is retributive. It is also true that Christ endures suffering for the remission of sin, but Adam's progeny suffer to satisfy divine justice. However, according to Shedd's doctrine of penal substitution, it would be perfectly correct to say that Christ suffers the divine retributive punishment I should suffer (but do not – because he acts as my vicar), and that Christ suffers to satisfy divine justice for the debt I owe because of my sin. Put like this, the dialectical force of Shedd's point is somewhat blunted. Yet, it might be thought, all Shedd is really trying to convey here is that Christ does these things voluntarily, as my penal substitute, whereas Adam's progeny do not. Well, perhaps that is right. But the consistent representationalist can say exactly the same thing, albeit for different reasons. So this does not do enough to distinguish Shedd's view from that of the consistent representationalist.

Similar problems beset Shedd's fifth point. This, the reader will recall, was that Christ is without original guilt, and has no obligation to suffer for sin, as Adam's progeny do, because Adam's progeny all bear original sin for which they are punishable. But, in at least one important respect, this is a theological notion Shedd shares with the consistent representationalist. On both views Adam's progeny all bear original sin and are punishable for it. And the idea that Christ is guiltless in a way that Adam's progeny cannot be, is not at issue between Shedd's mediating position and the consistent representationalist view. The representationalist understanding of the imputation of sin does entail that Adam's progeny are punishable without being culpable for Adam's sin. That much does distinguish the two views, as Shedd has already pointed out. But, with respect to the atonement, the representationalist position is that Christ is guiltless and therefore not liable for punishment, yet takes on the punishment of (some number of) fallen human beings. The same cannot be said, on a representationalist scheme, of Adam and his progeny. So, although there is a difference between Shedd and the consistent representationalists on the matter of the culpability and punishability of Adam and his progeny, on the one hand, and Christ in place of the elect on the other, both affirm Christ's guiltlessness and innocence. And both affirm that Adam's progeny should be punished for Adam's sin. The difference lies in the nature of what is imputed from Adam to his progeny. Both parties agree that, unlike Christ, Adam's progeny are punishable for Adam's sin.

At the culmination of these reasons for the dissimilarity between the 'two unions', Shedd has this to say:

The obvious fallacy in this argument from the parallel between Christ and Adam lies in the assumption that because there may be vicarious penal suffering there may be vicarious sinning and that because there may be gratuitous justification without any merit on the part of the justified there may be gratuitous condemnation without any ill desert on the part of the condemned. The former is conceivable, but the latter is not. One person may obey in the place of others in order to save them; but one person may not disobey in the place of others in order to save them. (DT: 462)

This, I suggest, goes to the heart of Shedd's mediating position. Let us call it, *the representationalist fallacy*. It amounts to this: there are good (theological) reasons for thinking that vicarious penal suffering is viable (in the case of Christ and the elect). From this we may infer that there are good (theological) reasons for thinking that vicarious sinning is also a viable notion (in the case of Adam and his progeny).[16] But, Shedd points out, these two issues are distinct, and one does not imply the other. The nature of these two unions, between Adam and his progeny on the one hand and between Christ and his elect on the other, is different in important respects. For one thing, righteousness may be imputed to a person meritoriously, or non-meritoriously. But sin cannot be imputed non-meritoriously (DT: 462). For another (and here, once again, Shedd turns to Francis Turretin for assistance), the two unions are different with respect to the ground and reason for the imputation in each case (DT: 463[17]). The ground and reason for the imputation of sin is inherent and personal, viz. Adam and his progeny. But the ground and reason for the imputation of righteousness is judicial and forensic, viz. Christ's penal substitution.[18] For this reason, Shedd feels able to conclude his discussion of the 'two unions' by suggesting that God 'can pronounce a man innocent when he is guilty because Christ has obeyed for him; but he cannot pronounce a man guilty when he is innocent because Adam disobeyed for him. These are self-evident propositions and intuitive convictions', (DT: 464) which, Shedd believes, concur with Scripture.

---

[16] I think it is unjust to characterize consistent representationalists as saying the union between Adam and his progeny depends upon Adam's vicarious sinning. For there is surely a difference between Adam sinning for me (because I have authorized him to do so), and Adam acting as my representative, and committing a sin in his capacity as my representative (without my specific authorization). Shedd's language suggests the former is true of representationalism. But of course, it is not. For representationalists (at least, those who are Augustinians) both Adam and Christ act on my behalf, but without my specific authorization to do so.

[17] Compare Turretin, *Institutes*, Vol. II, 16. 2. 19.

[18] 'The formed imputation [viz. original sin] rests upon something propagated, inherent, and subjective in the posterity; the latter [viz. the atonement] rests upon something wholly objective – namely, the sovereign decision and judicial declaration of God.' DT: 464.

There are several things that can be said in response to this. The first is that Shedd is right to point out that the 'two unions' of Adam and Christ with (some number of) humanity present different problems for the theologian. An explanation of one does not necessarily imply an explanation of the other. And to the extent that Shedd's discussion makes this clear, his contribution is a welcome one. However, Shedd's intuitions about these differences, particularly his claim that Christ may act as a representative of human beings whereas Adam cannot, is, as I have already suggested, wrongheaded. But then, to be fair to Shedd, these matters are very difficult to make sense of; the metaphysical issues are complicated and do not admit of easy resolution. It is no wonder, then, that different theologians have such different intuitions about these matters.

That said, it seems to me Shedd does not do enough to establish the nature or metaphysical description under which the two unions are dissimilar. And the central problem, around which he organizes much of what he has to say on the subject, is that Adam and his progeny must be culpable as well as punishable for Adam's sin in order for the imputation of sin to be just. But the same reasoning does not apply to the atonement. For in the case of Christ, he may be punishable for a sin he did not commit, and for which he cannot be culpable. But, despite the fact that Shedd sets out a clear case for his mediating position which has much to recommend it, it seems to me that he does not do enough to deflect the consistent representationalist criticism that his realism should apply to both the imputation of sin and the atonement. He does raise some serious problems for consistent representationalists over the imputation of Adam's sin. But his doctrine of the atonement is as liable to claims of injustice as the consistent representationalist's way of thinking about imputing Adam's sin, albeit for slightly different reasons. In short, it seems to me that Shedd's achievement is rather mixed. He has taken the fight to the consistent representationalists over the imputation of sin, and does, in the present author's opinion, have the better of that aspect of the argument. But, in siding with the representationalists over the atonement he has not done enough to show, despite considerable efforts, that representationalism in this particular matter, fairs any better than it does regarding the imputation of sin. And in that respect he is in the same metaphysical boat as the consistent representationalists.

Shedd and Consistent Realism

But finally, what of the consistent realist? Has Shedd any good reason for thinking that those who believe both the imputation of Adam's sin and of Christ's righteousness depends on a form of realism are wrong about the latter? As we have seen Shedd's energies were directed against consistent representationalist arguments and in favour of his own mediating position. He has almost nothing to say about the possibility of consistent realism, although at one point Shedd does reiterate a representationalistic objection to traducianism that may be applied in a realist account of the atonement. This is that 'believers are inherently and personally meritorious through their union with Christ, that participation in Adam's disobedience carries with it participation in Christ's obedience.' (DT: 461)[19]

In fact, there are two objections here. The first is that a realist union with Christ through his atoning work means that believers are themselves inherently, and personally, meritorious. Shedd conflates this with the further claim that participation in Adam's disobedience might, via some sort of transitivity relation, involve participation in Christ's atoning work. But, of course, the former claim need not include the latter.[20] The domain comprising Christ and his elect does not necessarily contain all the same members as the domain comprising Adam and his progeny.

Still, it would appear that commitment to consistent realism ends up with the first of these problems. It is one thing to claim, with Shedd and other Augustinian realists, that Adam and his progeny are (somehow) one metaphysical entity, such that Adam's sin is really my sin (I am culpable and therefore punishable for it). But it is quite another to say that the relation between Christ and the elect is similarly realist. For how can Christ and his elect be one metaphysical entity, such that, with certain important qualifications, Christ's righteousness is my righteousness, and my original sin is taken up by Christ in his atoning work, without this also involving some much stronger metaphysical arrangement, whereby I have Christ's merits inherently and personally, whilst Christ has my demerits in a similar manner? Even more damaging: a realist doctrine of the atonement would appear to mean I am (somehow) one with the God-Man. But does this make me a *part* of the God-Man (whether in terms of metaphysical proper parts, or parts in some attenuated sense)?[21] Are you and I somehow parts of God Incarnate?[22]

---

[19] The context of these comment is the claim, made by consistent representationalists, that the 'two unions' of Adam and his progeny and Christ and the elect are so alike that, were the traducianist to be consistent, he or she would have to argue that, as Adam's posterity are inherently and personally culpable because of their union with Adam, so the elect must be inherently and personally meritorious through union with Christ.

[20] A transitivity relation obtains where A entails B and B entails C. Where this is the case, A entails C. Applied to the sinner and Christ, and assuming a version of consistent realism, it could be argued that (a) I am somehow united with Adam (b) Adam is somehow united with Christ, so (c) I am somehow united with Christ.

[21] Language of 'proper parts' applied to the person of the God-Man is, for some traditional theologians, problematic, if one holds to a doctrine of divine simplicity. But I cannot go into these matters here. See Brian Leftow, 'A Timeless God Incarnate' in *The Incarnation* eds., Stephen T. Davis, Daniel Kendall and Gerald O'Collins (Oxford: Oxford University Press, 2002), for useful discussion of these issues.

[22] While we are on the subject, here are a few more problems a realist doctrine of the atonement faces: How can Christ be part of one entity that contains sinners like you and I, when Christ is without sin? Does this mean that I am divine if I am a member of the

These are thorny questions, at least as problematic as those posed by the representationalist account of the atonement. Even though Shedd was probably not aware of a serious contender for consistent realism, it might, at first glance, seem strange that he does not take the position more seriously than he does, especially since there is evidence that theologians like John Owen, whom Shedd admired and whose work is often cited by Shedd with approbation, sounds, at times, disconcertingly like an realist when speaking about the atonement. But, I suspect, Shedd is not alone in disregarding the consistently realist option. A number of classical theologians happy to endorse realism on the question of the imputation of Adam's sin have not been quite unwilling to carry over this realism into their soteriology. (Jonathan Edwards is a case in point. Perhaps a realist in the matter of original sin - although I am not sure he was a realist of the standard sort – his views on the nature of the atonement were much more in keeping with Anselmian satisfaction theory, with smatterings of the governmental view of the atonement thrown in.[23]) Nevertheless, it seems to me that there is much more to be said on this matter than is often thought.[24] Shedd's account is admirable for its clarity, although not, I think, conclusive in his arguments against consistent representationalism, as I have tried to suggest. (That said, I think he makes an interesting case for his use of realism). But if a consistently realist argument could be given that is able to overcome the considerable problems just canvassed, this would solve two important theological problems. The first has to do with the injustice of imputing Adam's sin to my account, a problem Shedd saw, and sought to address with his realist alternative. But, secondly, a consistent realism would also be able to deal with certain problems that beset penal substitution, to do with the justice of imputing my sin and guilt to the sinless and guiltless Son of God. And this is a problem which a purely representationalist doctrine of penal substitution is, it seems to me, quite unfit to offer.

Although Shedd would almost certainly disapprove of a realist argument for the atonement, he would surely applaud an Augustinian realism that showed how the deficiencies of representationalism might be attended to, without departure from the witness of Scripture. For my part, I think a realist argument for the atonement is intriguing, despite the not inconsiderable obstacles it faces.

---

elect and joined in this intimate way with Christ, the God-Man? Does it mean that Christ is literally a sinner, although God cannot sin?

[23] See Jonathan Edwards, *Original Sin,* IV: III, and Edwards, 'Miscellaneous Remarks on the Satisfaction for Sin' in *The Works of Jonathan Edwards, Vol. II*, ed. Edward Hickman (Edinburgh: Banner of Truth, 1974 [1834]). Edwards' doctrine of the imputation of sin is treated at length in Oliver Crisp, *Jonathan Edwards and The Metaphysics of Sin* (Aldershot: Ashgate, 2005).

[24] The sketch of how one realist account of the atonement might go, using the contemporary metaphysical doctrine of temporal parts, can be found in an appendix to Crisp, *Jonathan Edwards*. See also the chapters on temporal parts and inherited guilt in the same volume.

Such an argument, as part of a consistent realism, would, I think, have the metaphysical resources available to solve the problems of injustice that apply to both the imputation of Adam's sin and the penal substitutionary doctrine of the atonement.[25] But setting out such a view will have to wait until another day.

---

[25] In *Jonathan Edwards and the Metaphysics of Sin,* I intimate that the doctrine of temporal parts - a metaphysical idea that says entities that persist through time (like humans, horses and hackney cabs) are composed of temporal parts, just as they are composed of physical parts - might offer the basis upon which to argue for realism with respect to the atonement (or a temporal parts doctrine consistent with realism). This raises the problems associated with the fallacy of composition, alluded to earlier, to wit: properties of parts do not necessarily distribute to wholes, nor properties of wholes to their parts. For instance, Tibbles the cat is made up of colourless subatomic particles. But this does not mean that Tibbles the cat is colourless. Nor, if Tibbles is a ginger cat, does this mean all his parts are ginger – clearly parts of him, like his bones, are not ginger. This sort of reasoning may count against a realist argument for the atonement (am I 'part' of the God-Man?). But it may also be used in defending such a view: the God-Man may be one part of an entity including the elect, but this, in and of itself, does not necessarily mean that all the properties of the Christ-part of this entity are had by all the other 'parts' of the same entity. Nor, does it follow that if the whole entity has certain properties, all the parts of the entity in question have the properties of the whole – just as with the example of Tibbles.

CHAPTER 6

The Nature of the Atonement

Having considered the question of Shedd's doctrine of the atonement in relation to both representationalist and realist understandings of the imputation of original sin, we come to two chapters on his doctrine of the atonement proper. This chapter considers Shedd's doctrine of the nature of the atonement. The next chapter deals with his doctrine of the extent of the atonement and its connection to the question of the number of those saved, referred to by Shedd as the 'larger hope'.

We have already had cause to note that Shedd defends a version of penal substitution. To recapitulate, this is the theory of the atonement according to which Christ elects to take upon himself the penal consequences of the sins of human beings in order to expiate them. Advocates of penal substitution claim that Christ is able to act as a vicar for fallen humanity and pay the price that the sin of fallen humanity requires. This price is set by the divine justice, which demands, amongst other things, that a satisfaction is offered for the sin of fallen human beings either in the person of the fallen human, or in the person of some equivalent substitute. Christ, as the God-Man, is able to act as vicar to fallen human beings, and his death pays the penal debt owed by humanity to God. This arrangement is acceptable to the creditor (God), even though it does not directly involve the debtor (fallen human beings) in the process.[1]

This sketch of penal substitution needs some tweaking. As it stands it is not applicable to *all* those who have advocated this view. In fact, as J. I. Packer observes, it is difficult to locate one paradigm case of penal substitution in the

---

[1] Richard Swinburne points this out in his book, *Responsibility and Atonement* (Oxford: Oxford University Press, 1989), p. 151. Swinburne allows that God, as the divine arbiter of justice, may accept either a vicar to act on behalf of the sinner, taking upon himself the penal consequences of that sin, or some lesser penalty (cf. Chapter Six of the same volume). The first point depends upon one person being able to act as a vicar in situations where *penal* substitution is at issue, and this is by no means uncontroversial. The second point touches upon the matter of acceptation. This is the view that God can substitute a penalty of inferior value to that which justice demands. Shedd holds the first of these views (for reasons somewhat different to Swinburne) but denies the second (although, as Gomes points out, Shedd wrongly denominates acceptation as 'acceptilation' – see DT: 733, n. 123).

literature.[2] For this reason it is perhaps better to describe this as one approach to the atonement shared by a number of theologians, who differ in points of detail, rather than a theory of atonement as such.

There are several places in Shedd's work where he discusses the nature of the atonement. The most sustained treatment can be found in DT. But his essay 'The Doctrine of the Atonement' that originally appeared in the second edition of DE, and subsequently reappeared in TE, is an important treatment of the same issues. And Shedd's discussion of the development of soteriology in HCD2 is also a useful resource, although it does not offer a sustained defence of Shedd's own position. As with previous chapters, the main focus of what follows is Shedd's discussion in DT, which is the place where his mature position is set forth.

Of course, the doctrine of penal substitution is not merely of historical interest. There has been considerable discussion on and around this particular understanding of the atonement in recent times, although sometimes this has generated more heat than light. With this in mind, and having set out the main issues in Shedd's account of penal substitution, we shall consider some criticisms of the penal substitution theory that have been raised in the recent literature by the Dutch-Afrikaner philosophical theologian, Vincent Brümmer. Whilst Shedd's doctrine has the resources to rebut most of Brümmer's objections to penal substitution, there is one issue in particular, to do with the morality of the doctrine, which appears to present a real problem for Shedd's account as it stands. However, although Shedd's account does not resolve this difficulty, it turns out that, given certain considerations about natural justice, this is a problem that Brümmer's way of thinking shares with Shedd.

An Outline of Shedd's Doctrine of Atonement

Shedd, in common with most Reformed theologians, sets his discussion of the work of Christ within the context of the so-called *munus triplex*, outlined by John Calvin. In his *Institutes*, Calvin sets forth three offices that Christ fulfils, comprising his prophetic, priestly, and kingly roles. All these are aspects of Christ's mediatorial work.[3] But it is his priestly work in vicarious atonement that is of particular interest here. The main issues in Shedd's version of the doctrine are these:

---

[2] James I. Packer, 'What did the Cross Achieve? The Logic of Penal Substitution' first published in *Tyndale Bulletin* 25 (1974): 3-46. Reprinted under the same title as an RTSF monograph (Leicester: UCCF, 2002). I cite from this later edition of the paper, p. 36.
[3] See John Calvin, *Institutes of the Christian Religion*, trans. Ford Lewis Battles, ed. John T. McNeill (Philadelphia, PA: Wesminster Press, 1960), II. XV, pp. 494-503.

1. Divine justice requires atonement or condemnation for sin.
2. The atonement is essentially vicarious, substitutionary and penal in nature.
3. The nature of Christ's sufferings are infinite in value but do not affect his divine nature.
4. Atonement is fundamentally objective, but has a subjective aspect.

Let us consider each of these in turn.

1. Divine justice requires atonement or condemnation for sin. According to Shedd, divine justice 'is that phase of God's holiness which is seen in his treatment of the obedient and the disobedient subjects of his government. It is that attribute where he gives to everyone what is due him' (DT:292). Holiness is the perfect rectitude of God's will, in perfect harmony with other aspects of the divine nature that is supremely expressed in the moral law of God (DT: 290-291). Justice is one 'phase' or aspect of this divine holiness. There are several components to Shedd's understanding of divine justice. First, there is rectoral justice, which relates to the divine rule of the created order, and in particular, to the imposition of divine law. Then, there is distributive justice, which has two aspects, (a) renumerative justice, and (b) retributive justice. These distinctions are common amongst Reformed divines.[4] Renumerative justice has to do with the expression of divine love to created beings, whereas divine retribution has to do with the expression of divine wrath (DT: 293). It is this latter, retributive aspect of divine justice that is particularly important in connection with Shedd's doctrine of the atonement.

Like a number of classical divines who hold some version of either the satisfaction or penal substitution doctrine, Shedd maintains that divine retributive justice is an essential divine attribute that is inexorable, whereas divine mercy is not. Thus Shedd,

> For whatever else God may be, or may not be, he must be just. It is not optional with him to exercise this attribute, or not to exercise it, as it is in the instance of that class of attributes which are antithetic to it. We can say: "God may be merciful or not, as he pleases;" but we cannot say: "God may be just or not, as he pleases." It cannot be asserted that God is inexorably obligated to show pity; but it can be categorically affirmed that God is inexorably obligated to do justly. (DE: 292)

The reason he offers for this is that necessary exaction, as he puts it, is a characteristic of divine justice, whereas mercy is known only by a divine declaration or promise: we would have no certain hope of divine mercy were it

---

[4] See, for example, Louis Berkhof, *Systematic Theology* (Edinburgh: Banner of Truth, 1958 [1939]), p. 75.

not for the fact that God promises it in revelation (DE: 292-293). In this regard, Shedd is in good company, and he cites the Puritan John Owen as someone whose work reflects just this way of thinking about the relationship between divine justice and mercy.[5]

But this does raise a wider question about the nature of divine justice. Why must God exact a penalty for sins committed? Why may he not overlook sin, or just forgive it without punishment? This is precisely the sort of objection the Socinians raised against penal substitution in the post-Reformation period.[6] Some Reformed theologians sought to counter this by conceding that God may, in all justice, relax the demand that the moral law be satisfied, and forgive sin, although there may be good reasons why God does punish sin – its fittingness, perhaps, or the fact that, in punishing sin God's divine justice is seen to be vindicated. This, in turn, was connected with the distinction between God's absolute and ordained power. God's absolute power is, roughly, his power all things considered. His ordained power consists of what God has ordained he will do, and the parameters this sets upon the exercise of his divine power. So, for instance, if God has ordained that he will create and sustain the world, he cannot then annihilate or destroy the world once this decree is given, because he has ordained that this will be the case. Prior to the giving of this decree, God was free to create and then to annihilate the world, but once he has said he will create *and sustain it*, he has placed restrictions upon the exercise of his own power. Reformed theologians like William Twisse, Prolocutor to the Westminster Assembly, or the early John Owen, were concerned to uphold the absolute power of God in being able to forgive sin, though, according to his ordained power, sin must be punished. For, they maintained that failure to uphold this distinction meant the denial of divine omnipotence.[7]

Shedd does not favour this position (see DT: 300-301). And, from a Sheddian point of view, there are good reasons to be suspicious of such gerrymandering of the divine attributes. For one thing, if God may lay aside the exercise of his retributive justice, all things considered (even if he cannot do so once he has ordained to create the sort of world he does create), then this particular aspect of divine justice ceases to be *inexorable.*[8] But this Shedd

---

[5] Shedd cites Owen's *Dissertation on Divine Justice,* ch. II in DE: 292.

[6] Shedd discusses the Socinian soteriology in HCD2: 376-386 and makes a number of references to it in DT, e.g. pp.292, 299-300. An accessible and informative recent treatment of Socinian soteriology can be found in Alan Gomes's essay, '*De Jesu Christo Servatore:* Faustus Socinus on the Satisfaction of Christ' in *Westminster Theological Journal* 55 (1993): 209-231.

[7] This issue is also connected with the question of the necessity of the atonement, which we shall come to presently.

[8] But might it not be that divine retribution is inexorable only relative to the divine decree to ordain that its exercise should be inexorable (viz. the distinction between God's absolute and ordained power, perhaps)? If this is right, it still undercuts the Sheddian claim that divine justice is absolutely inexorable. This divine attribute *must be*

cannot allow. Indeed, it appears that the conception of divine justice that informs the work of theologians like Twisse and, perhaps, the early John Owen, is quite different from that Shedd has in mind. Shedd speaks at times as if divine justice is a 'central' and 'ultimate' divine attribute (DE: 292),[9] and affirms that God *must* be propitiated for sin (DE: 272); indeed, his divine nature requires this (DE: 274; DT: 300) – it is not a matter contingent on the precise arrangement of the divine power. This is not to deny that God may satisfy the demands of justice in more than one way. He may demand satisfaction from the transgressor, in punishment. Or he may provide some substitute to whom the penalty due for sin may be meted out. God 'has a choice of methods', says Shedd, but 'one or other' of punishment or provision of a substitute, he 'must do' (DT: 299). Shedd does not favour the idea that the punishment for sin in the transgressor or a substitute is 'relatively' necessary, rather than 'absolutely' necessary (DT: 300). Here, the relative necessity of retributive justice has to do with the absolute power of God, just mentioned. Once God ordained he would punish sin, it is necessary that sin be punished. But he was free to withhold the punishment of sin prior to his decree, according to his absolute power. Shedd denies this scholastic doctrine, although he grants that, in the case of Twisse and the early Owen, 'the motive' (viz. fear of limiting divine omnipotence) was 'a good one' (DT: 300). In place of this doctrine, Shedd affirms that divine retribution is absolutely necessary. God cannot withhold the exercise of his justice; it is in his nature to act thus, just as we might think it is in the nature of a human to think, or a songbird to sing. Behind this, is the idea that privileging any one divine attribute above the others, as in the case of divine power in the relative-absolute necessity of divine retributive justice, is mistaken and leads to a skewed conception of the divine attributes, and divine nature. Shedd is clear that 'it is impossible and inconceivable for divine power to act in isolation from all the other attributes, as it is for divine omniscience or for divine benevolence to do so.... This theory resolves the deity into mere blind force' (DT: 300). No single divine characteristic 'controls' or 'organises' the whole, for Shedd. Rather, the whole character of God is brought to bear upon any given particular circumstance or issue.

---

exercised, according to Shedd. And this means there is a clear difference on the nature of divine justice between Shedd and theologians like Twisse.

[9] Earlier in his essay on the atonement in DE Shedd says that it is the divine essence that provides the unity between different attributes, not the specific attribute of love (DE: 280, n). This appears to conflict with his later comments, although this may be some sort of rhetorical infelicity on Shedds' part. More importantly, he speaks in DE as if God has an emotional life, including distinct emotional states (DE: 277; see also DT: 723). But this does not sit well with his declared allegiance to the doctrine of divine simplicity in DT: 276-277, according to which God has no distinct states at all.

2. *The atonement is essentially vicarious, substitutionary and penal in nature.* On the matter of the mode of the atonement, Shedd claims several things. First, that the biblical view of the atonement is a substitutionary, or vicarious one (DT: 690). He supplies a wealth of New Testament passages in support of this, including Matt. 20: 28, Mark 10: 45, John 15: 13, Rom. 5: 6-8. 2 Cor. 5: 14-15, Gal. 3: 13 and 1 Tim. 2: 5-6. Second, he maintains that the notion of vicariousness implies substitution and that this is 'vital to a correct theory of Christ's priestly office' (DT: 692).[10] The idea here is that one who acts on behalf of another acts vicariously, and to act vicariously is to act as a substitute for another, much as a substitute who is brought on in a football game because his colleague is injured acts in place of, and in a sense, on behalf of, his injured team-mate. Third, Shedd thinks that there is an important distinction to be made between personal and vicarious atonement that is pertinent in this regard (DT: 693). Personal atonement is offered by the offender in order to satisfy justice, whereas vicarious atonement is offered by the offended party. Justice must be satisfied one way or another, according to Shedd. Either the offending party offers satisfaction for sin, in which case that person is condemned to hell, or Christ offers it on behalf of the sinner. And the result is the salvation of the sinner.

Later in DT Shedd elaborates upon the correlation between divine justice and atonement, explaining that there must be a fit between crime and punishment (as per retributive justice) and that if 'a criminal suffers the penalty affixed to his crime, he owes nothing more in the way of penalty to the law. He cannot be punished a second time' (DT: 724). We might think of it like this. Once the penalty fixed for a crime is met, the penal consequences for that crime are satisfied. It remains true that the person who sinned is guilty of that crime, in the sense that it was that particular person who committed that crime, but the penalty attending guilt has been dealt with, so that there is no further need for punishment. As far as Shedd is concerned sin is dealt with either by the sinner being punished or Christ being punished in the sinner's stead. But once Christ has paid the penalty due for sin, the divine moral law has been satisfied and no further punishment is due from the sinner or his vicar. Of course, the same does not apply to the sinner, inasmuch as the sinner who suffers for his own sin (the punishment for whose sin is not met by Christ as vicar) suffers an infinite punishment, which, according to Shedd, is everlasting, in hell.[11]

---

[10] Shedd's language suggests that he thinks of the atonement as essentially vicarious, and that penal substitution (not a term he uses much) captures that which is at the heart of Christ's atoning act. There is no evidence that he would have acceded to the modern notion that penal substitution is one amongst several 'metaphors' of the atonement. Perhaps the most influential exponent of the 'metaphor' view is Colin E. Gunton in *The Actuality of Atonement* (Grand Rapids, MI: Eerdmans, 1989).

[11] Shedd does not distinguish between an infinite and an everlasting punishment in the way that some ceontemporary philosophical theologians have. Here I am thinking of

But what of the conditions for substituting a vicar in place of the sinner, for the penalty due for sin - what might these be? Earlier in DT, when discussing the divine attributes, Shedd sets out two conditions that must be met by any penal substitution. The first of these is that 'the substituted penalty must be a strict and full equivalent'. The second is that 'the person substituted be able to render complete satisfaction and be himself no debtor to law and justice' (DT: 299). God does not relax the requirements of divine justice in penal substitution; nor does he waive them. He cannot do so because of the absolute (metaphysical) necessity of the nature of divine retribution. The same issues crop up again in Shedd's discussion of the possibility of a substitutionary atonement in DT: 732-739, but with important qualifications. The first of these qualifications has to do with the administration of divine justice, which we have already mentioned. In keeping with Reformed theologians like John Owen, Shedd is willing to allow that God may choose the manner in which his justice is administered. This means that, although divine justice *must* be administered, *the way in which this is worked out* is a matter for God to decide. He says, 'God may vary the mode of administering justice, provided the mode adopted really satisfies justice and there be no special reason in his [i.e. God's] own mind why in a particular instance the variation may not be permitted.' (DT: 732-733)

This constitutes a 'relaxation' of divine justice with respect to the person enduring punishment, but not with respect to the penalty demanded by divine justice. The full force of that penalty must still be met, but the person upon whom it is visited may be either the guilty party, or some suitable substitute (i.e. Christ). Shedd is at pains to distance this sort of legal 'relaxation' from that proposed by theologians like Duns Scotus and (according to Shedd at least) Hugo Grotius.[12] Such theologians claim that God may relax the full force of the penalty due for sin, as well as relaxing who suffers this penalty. Scotus is well known as an advocate of the view called 'acceptation', according to which God may have accepted some satisfaction for sin that was inferior to the punishment due. As Richard Cross puts it, 'on Scotus's account, an act is meritorious if and only if God assigns a reward to it'.[13] This could be taken in a rather extreme direction: satisfaction for sin concerns divine justice being satisfied by some act that balances out the scales of justice. Christ's atoning act is of sufficient merit

---

Peter Geach's argument that a punishment might be infinite and yet last for only a finite period of time, where time itself is a densely ordered continuum.

[12] Whether Grotius actually held to the doctrine of relaxation Shedd imputes to him is moot. See, for example, Garry Williams 1999 Oxford DPhil Thesis 'A Critical Exposition of Hugo Grotius' Doctrine of the Atonement in *De Satisfactione Christi.*'

[13] Richard Cross, *Duns Scotus* (Oxford: Oxford University Press, 1999), p. 130. It should be noted that Cross believes Scotus's doctrine of the atonement combines elements of a satisfaction and a merit theory. In this respect he departs from those interpreters of Scotus who think the Scotist position is simply a merit theory. Cross does concede that piecing together the satisfaction component of Scotus's view is 'difficult', ibid.

to balance off the demerit incurred by human sin. But God could have accepted some alternative act of atonement for human sin that was of insufficient merit to balance off the demerit of human sin (according to the value assigned these things by divine justice). He did not do so; but he might have done so. Which is to say, it was within God's power to do so, all things considered, and it was possible for God to do so – there was no moral constraint on God (viz. the nature of divine justice) to prevent this outcome. Whether Scotus or any other theologian actually held this view, it is this sort of idea that Shedd is set against. His notion of legal relaxation is not the same as the sort of legal relaxation in view in this acceptation theory.

Shedd also states that, in the case of human sin, the suffering endured by Christ on behalf of the those for whose sins his work is an atonement, 'must be penal in nature and purpose' as well as being of equal value to the 'original penalty' (DT: 733). A substituted penalty cannot be identical to the original penalty due for the crime. By its very nature a substitution cannot be identical with what is substituted. But it may be of the same moral value as that which is substituted. Shedd thinks that, provided this is the case, no violence is done to divine justice in the acceptance of a vicarious penal substitution.

Shedd also rehearses a number of issues common to the Anselmian tradition concerning the mode of atonement. For instance, he says that the person who acts as a substitute cannot already be a debtor to divine justice – he must be without sin in order to be able to act vicariously. Fallen human beings are incapable of performing this sort of action on account of the fact that we already owe our whole lives as a debt incurred for sin (DT: 735). So God must provide an alternative substitute himself, one who is without sin. For only someone who is without sin may act vicariously for those who are sinners, because such a person would not already owe their lives to God as penalty for their sin. And only a divine person can supply a substitute whose death would be of sufficient worth to clear the debt owed by fallen human beings (which Shedd, in common with Anselm, thinks is an infinite debt). So God provides the God-Man as a vicar for (some number of) fallen human beings.

3. The nature of Christ's sufferings are infinite in value but do not affect his divine nature. Turning to the matter of the suffering inflicted on Christ as a substitute for sin, Shedd claims that it is permissible 'to denominate Christ's suffering a vicarious punishment' because this is synonymous with denominating it 'a vicarious atonement'. If it makes sense to speak of the work of Christ on the cross in this last fashion, as a vicarious atoning act, then it should be perfectly acceptable to speak of Christ's work on the cross in the former manner, as a vicarious punishment. The reason for this, according to Shedd, is that the terms 'atonement' and 'punishment' are equivalent in meaning:

> No objection is made to calling Christ's suffering an atonement. But atonement

and punishment are kindred in meaning. Both alike denote judicial suffering. There is, consequently, no more reason for insisting that the term *punishment* be restricted to personal endurance of suffering for personal transgression than there would be in insisting that the term *atonement* be restricted to personal satisfaction for personal sin.... No one asserts that they were "personal" punishment. (DT: 736-737, emphasis original)

Shedd thinks this despite the fact (pointed out by other theologians) that Christ is not personally guilty for the sin that he atones for. This looks odd, to say the least; we shall return to it presently.

The other matter he touches upon in this connection is the question of the value of Christ's sufferings. Shedd believes that the value of Christ's suffering lies in the nature of the one suffering, not in the particular act of suffering, nor its duration.

Whatever a man suffers in either of his natures [sic], body or mind, gets its value from his personality. Measured by this, it is limited suffering. But when a human nature suffers in a theanthropic person, the suffering is divine and infinite because of the divinity and infinity of such a person. The suffering of the human nature, in this instance, is elevated and dignified by the union of the human nature with the divine (DT: 737).

Christ's suffering, unlike that of those condemned to hell, is not endless. Yet, according to Shedd, it has a value greater than any length of suffering a human being may endure on account of the fact that the person suffering is infinite, being the God-Man (DT: 738). Shedd thinks that the suffering of any human for an endless period is never actually infinite, but only potentially infinite, or 'relatively infinite' as he has it (DT:738). The same is not true of the suffering of the theanthropic person of Christ because the divine nature of Christ is truly and actually infinite and eternal.[14] Shedd is careful not to say that the divine nature of Christ suffers – although earlier in DT he does say that although God cannot be made to suffer by any created being, he may cause himself suffering, and does so, at the cross (DT: 695). Yet in commenting on the act of atoning suffering the human nature of God Incarnate endures, Shedd reasons that somehow Christ's human nature is elevated by being in hypostatic union with the divine nature of the Son, which conveys to the human nature a dignity that means the suffering of Christ's human nature has an infinite value, and that it is the human nature alone that suffers. Thus Shedd:

---

[14] It is strange that Shedd does not address the question of whether any suffering endured by the God-Man, however trivial, has infinite value because it is the God-Man who suffers. If Shedd grants this, then it is difficult to see why the crucifixion, or even the death of Christ, is necessary for salvation. But perhaps a defender of Shedd could concede that the crucifixion is the most fitting means of salvation. This is in keeping with what he does say about the necessity of salvation for human sin coupled with the idea that the mode of atonement might have been different.

The suffering of a mere man is human; but the suffering of a God-man is divine. Yet the divine nature is not the *sensorium* or seat of the suffering in the instance of the God-man, any more than the rational nature is the *sensorium* or seat of the suffering in the instance of physical suffering in man. A man's immaterial soul is not burned when he suffers human agony in martyrdom, and the impassible essence of God was not bruised and wounded when Jesus Christ suffered the divine agony. Hence it is said that Christ "suffered in the flesh," that is, in his human nature (1 Pet. 4: 1). (DT: 737)

Earlier, in his discussion of the divine attributes, Shedd endorses a classical notion of divine impassibility with respect to the Incarnation: 'Incarnation makes no change in God. Divine essence was not transmuted into a human nature but assumed a human nature into union with itself.' (DT: 285)

It would seem that Shedd says different things about divine impassibility and the bearing this divine attribute has on the suffering of Christ, in different contexts within his *Dogmatic Theology*. These different statements of his view appear to be inconsistent with each other. A closer inspection of what Shedd does say shows that there are two different ways of construing what Shedd thinks about this issue, depending on the divine attribute (or predicate) under consideration. It is fairly clear that Shedd endorses a traditional doctrine of the Incarnation, according to which the impassible suffers according to his human- but not according to his divine nature. In which case, Shedd is merely reiterating a standard way of thinking about this matter.[15] Things are rather different if we consider his comments about God being able to inflict suffering upon himself, and the Incarnation being an instance of such pain. But these two things, the impassible suffering in his human nature, and God being able to inflict suffering upon himself, are not necessarily inconsistent. Shedd may simply define divine impassibility as the doctrine that God may not be changed or affected by anything outside himself. In fact, what he says suggests this way of thinking about the matter. In which case what he says about the suffering of Christ and divine self-inflicted suffering may be compatible. What is more, there is precedent for such a way of thinking in the tradition.[16]

But one could construe impassibility in a stronger way, to mean God cannot suffer any emotional change whatsoever.[17] Given Shedd's stated allegiance to

---

[15] This sort of traditional view has been set forth with admirable clarity in recent times by Thomas Weinandy in his monograph, *Does God Suffer?* (Edinburgh: T&T Clark, 2000), ch. 8.

[16] For example, Leonard Prestige, in his treatment of the Patristic understanding of this doctrine states at one point, 'It is clear that impassibility means not that God is inactive or uninterested, not that he surveys existence with Epicurean impassivity from the shelter of a metaphysical insulation, but that his will is determined from within instead of being swayed from without.' *God in Patristic Thought* (London: SPCK, 1952), p. 7.

[17] In fact, as Richard Creel points out, one of the problems with the concept of divine impassibility is that there are several different ways in which it is used in the tradition,

the traditional notion of divine simplicity (DT: 276-277), according to which God is without parts and potentiality, and cannot, not merely may not, change, one might be forgiven for thinking that Shedd's view must be that God is incapable of any change whatsoever, even change he inflicts upon himself. For how could a simple being change its own mind about something, or exchange one belief for another – indeed, what would it mean to say such a being *had* beliefs? To suffer, even if that suffering is self-inflicted, is (at least) to undergo emotional change, and can hardly be said to be consistent with impassibility taken in this strong sense of the term, a sense that seems, at face value, to sit better with Shedd's commitment to divine simplicity. Yet Shedd remains adamantly of the view that, although nothing in the created universe can make God suffer, nevertheless,

> it does not follow that God cannot himself do an act which he feels to be a sacrifice of feeling and affection and insofar an inward suffering. When God gave up to humiliation and death his only begotten Son, he was not utterly indifferent and unaffected by the act. It was truly a sacrifice for the Father to surrender the beloved Son as it was for the Son to surrender himself. (DT: 695)

If this does represent his considered view of the matter, then Shedd must make a straightforward choice: retain his doctrine of divine impassibility and forego the classical doctrine of divine simplicity, or retain divine simplicity and opt for a stronger doctrine of divine impassibility. As it is, there appears to be a conflict of interests in the position he actually adopts, which is not sustainable. A traditional doctrine of divine simplicity does not appear to be consistent with any change whatsoever, apart from merely relational (or Cambridge) changes, expressed by sentences such as 'my brother was shorter than me, but now he is taller'. Such relational change predicates no real change in the person concerned. But Shedd's stated view requires much more than this sort of relational change. In which case, his doctrine of divine impassibility appears caught on the horns of a dilemma.

4. Atonement is fundamentally objective, but has a subjective aspect. According to Shedd's way of thinking, the atonement is fundamentally, or essentially, an objective work, but also has a subjective component. However, it cannot be essentially subjective, because this, says Shedd, is a contradiction. 'Atoning to oneself is like lifting oneself' (DT: 699). The biblical idea is that of propitiation (*hilasmos*) and reconciliation (*katallage*), and these terms are irreducibly objective in signification. They imply that one party is reconciled to another, and that one party is propiated by the action of another. Even biblical language of a 'ransom' (*lutron*, as in Matt. 20: 28) should not be thought of as

---

and some writers oscillate between two or more conceptions of the doctrine. See Creel, *Divine Impassibility* (Eugene, OR: Wipf & Stock, 2005 [1986]), ch. 1.

God paying off the Devil, as some Patristic authors thought, but as terminating upon God as the object of the atoning act (see DT: 701-702). 'A merely subjective reference' says Shedd, 'would find all the meaning of them [these biblical terms] within the soul of man' and 'requires a forced and violent exegesis of Scripture and a self-contradictory use of the word *atonement*' (DT: 702, emphasis original).

In constrast to the purely subjective account of the atonement, Shedd thinks that Christ's work is about God propitiating *himself,* providing the means for the satisfaction of sin in Christ. God is the 'agent and the patient' (DT: 702). In the essay on the atonement in DE, he even goes as far as saying the divine nature 'requires this' (DE: 274). In DT he puts it like this, '[t]he propitiation is no oblation *ab extra*: no device of a third party or even of sinful man himself to render God placable toward man. It is wholly *ab intra:* a self-oblation upon the part of the deity himself, in the exercise of his benevolence toward the guilty' (DT: 704).

This means that divine justice and compassion are both at work in the act of atonement. Divine justice demands satisfaction for sin. But the provision of satisfaction in the person of Christ is an act of sheer compassion for fallen humanity. Shedd makes much of this insight (see DT: 702, 704-706). Nevertheless, this does not preclude a subjective aspect to the atonement. For,

> While Christ's atonement has primarily this objective relation to the divine nature, it has also a secondary subjective relation to the nature of the guilty creature for whom it is made. The objective atonement is intended to be subjectively appropriated by the act of faith in it. (DT: 708)

There is a sense in which Christ's work pacifies the human conscience. (This is a theme Shedd also discusses in his earlier essay on the atonement in DE: 276.) By this he means that the objective work of Christ finds a corollary in the subjective sense of peace wrought in the soul of the sinner who comes to faith. Shedd also states that the subjective appropriation of Christ's benefits is evidence of genuine repentance (DT: 709). True penitence can be distinguished from remorse, which is false penitence, because remorse is ultimately a selfish affection, that includes no desire to suffer and make amends for what has been done (DT: 710). By contrast, genuine repentance includes just such a desire to make amends, which is met in the atoning work of Christ who alone is able to offer genuine reconciliation between God and humanity.

So, Shedd thinks that the subjective component to the atonement is wholly to do with the appropriation of Christ's work by faith, and what that entails, and nothing to do with the nature of the act of atonement itself. It is for this reason that he conceives of the act of atonement as wholly objective. And in this fashion he is following closely in the footsteps of those defenders of penal substitution who look back to aspects of Anselm's satisfaction theory to make sense of the objective nature of Christ's work on the cross.

Brümmer's Critique of Penal Substitution

There has been a renewed interest in the doctrine of penal substitution in recent theology, amongst both systematic and philosophical theologians.[18] Some of this literature has been positive; but much has been critical of the doctrine. One recent critic of the doctrine is the Utrecht philosophical theologian, Vincent Brümmer. In a monograph on central Christian doctrines including the Incarnation, Brümmer offers six objections to penal substitution. These are:

a. Penal substitution is immoral because it entails that God punishes the innocent (Christ) for the transgressions of the guilty (fallen human beings).
b. This view of the atonement implies that God values my satisfying his honour more than he values me. For on this view, what matters is that divine honour is satisfied, not that *I* satisfy the divine honour.
c. This view of the atonement has a defective understanding of divine forgiveness because it confuses divine forgiveness with condonation.
d. Penal substitution does not do justice to the unity of the work of the divine Trinity in salvation.
e. It also denies the Patristic intuition that atonement is something done by God and not to God.
f. Finally, although penal substitution can account for the satisfaction of sin, it cannot give an adequate explanation of the restoration of fellowship with God. Hence, penal substitution is not a theory about atonement (i.e. at-one-ment) at all.[19]

Let us consider each of these in turn, in dialogue with what we have already

---

[18] Representative samples of recent favourable accounts of penal substitution include Christina Baxter, 'The Cursed Beloved: A Reconsideration of Penal Substitution' in John Goldingay, ed., *Atonement Today* (London: SPCK, 1995); Stephen R. Holmes, 'Can Punishment Bring Peace? Penal Substitution Revisited' in *Scottish Journal of Theology* 58 (2005): 104-123; ' James I. Packer, 'What Did The Cross Achieve? The Logic of Penal Substitution', originally published in *Tyndale Bulletin* 25 (1974): 3-46; and the collected essays in *The Glory of the Atonement*, eds. Chalres E. Hill and Frank A. James III (Downers Grove, IL: IVP, 2004). Amongst philosophical theologians, Steven Porter offers a defence of a modified version of penal substitution in 'Rethinking The Logic of Penal Substitution' in *Philosophy of Religion, A Reader and Guide* (ed) William Lane Craig (Edinburgh: Edinburgh University Press, 2002). Richard Swinburne is critical of this doctrine, and offers an important version of satisfaction theory in its place in *Responsibility and Atonement* (Oxford: Oxford University Press, 1989). For a response to the view that the atonement should be non violent, see Hans Boersma, *Violence, Hospitality, and the Cross* (Grand Rapids, MI: Baker Acadeemic, 2004).

[19] See Vincent Brümmer, *Atonement, Christology and The Trinity, Making Sense of Christian Doctrine* (Aldershot: Ashgate, 2005), pp. 75-77.

seen of Shedd's way of conceiving the doctrine.

First, is Shedd's doctrine of penal substitution immoral? Some recent objectors to penal substitution have claimed that the doctrine is immoral because it is inherently violent, or because it involves some notion of cosmic child-abuse (Christ, as the Son Incarnate, being 'punished' by his heavenly Father). But neither of these criticisms is in view here. Nor do they seem to be very serious objections to the doctrine.[20] Brümmer's initial problem with the doctrine seems to be that it is unjust for God to 'punish' the innocent in place of the guilty. If a principle of natural justice is that punishment may only be visited upon those who are the guilty parties, then Shedd's doctrine does violate this principle. Shedd, of course, must deny that such a principle obtains in the case of the atonement. As we have seen, he says that divine justice must be exercised – it is inexorable in that respect. But God may be satisfied by the punishment due for sin being meted out to a suitable substitute. In this respect, Shedd allows a certain legal relaxation with respect to the person upon whom the punishment due for sin is visited. The severity of the 'punishment' does not vary. So there is no legal relaxation envisaged that is comparable to the Scotist notion of acceptation. Nevertheless, despite the fact that Shedd's account is careful to avoid the Scotist position, it does mean that it is just for God to punish an innocent substitute in the place of a guilty perpetrator. And, as Brümmer suggests, this seems immoral.

Often, defenders of penal substitution presented with this sort of objection make much of the fact that there are circumstances in which human justice does allow for penal substitution of a sort. For instance, in the case of fines, what is important is that the fine is paid, not that I pay the fine. Someone else can pay it for me, thereby acting as a penal substitute. This is the case even where serious fines are imposed for considerable offences, such as fraud. Such penalties are hardly trivial when they run to thousands or millions of pounds. This has not gone unnoticed in the contemporary literature. For instance, the philosopher David Lewis reasons that the fact human justice recognises that there are certain circumstances where pecuniary penal substitution is permissible, and yet we register no problem with this legal double-think, means the defender of penal substitution has a ready-made *tu quoque* argument against the objector. Admittedly, penal substitution in the case of the atonement looks odd. But why is this more odd than allowing penal substitution in the case of crimes for which fines are payable, and not for crimes where custodial sentences are required? Lewis comments,

> A *tu quoque* is not a rejoinder on behalf of penal substitution. Yet neither is it

---

[20] For one thing, crucifixion is an inherently violent act. So talk of a non-violent atonement is nonsense. Secondly, the atonement cannot be an act of child abuse because Christ is not the child of God but God Incarnate. So this objection can only go through if the doctrine of the Trinity is false.

intellectually weightless. It indicates that both sides agree that penal substitution sometimes makes sense after all, even if none can say how it makes sense. And if both sides agree to that, that is some evidence that somehow they might both be right.[21]

Critics like Brümmer may still point out that even if our intuitions on such matters are not as clear as we would like, there are cases where a merely pecuniary penal substitution would not be sufficient, such as first degree murder. No fine imposed upon the perpetrator of such a crime would be just. And traditional accounts of the atonement such as Shedd endorses rely on a robust doctrine of sin, satisfaction for which is arguably far more serious than that applicable for first-degree murder. This is surely right. But it does not explain why our intuitions are ordered in this way. Why is it morally acceptable to punish the corporate fraudster with a massive fine, and not the murderer? Where do we draw the line between what we might call pecuniary- and non-pecuniary penal substitution? Such matters are not easily discerned. So Lewis's *tu quoque* on behalf of those theologians who hold to penal substitution - like Shedd - has weight as he says it does. Brümmer is right that there is a moral issue here, and one that is unresolved. But this is a difficulty that a critic of the doctrine, such as Brümmer, has in common with the defender of penal substitution, provided the objector allows pecuniary penal substitution for certain sorts of crime.[22]

Secondly, does the penal substitution view of the atonement imply that God values my satisfying his honour more than he values me, as Brümmer suggests it does? There are several things to be said here. To begin with, Brümmer's use of the notion of divine 'honour', familiar from discussions of Anselm's satisfaction theory of the atonement, seems to sit rather ill with the penal element of penal substitution. Satisfaction does not entail penal substitution: the two theories are distinct, though overlapping. In penal substitution, as Shedd is at pains to point out, it is the relation of the sinner to the divine law that is the primary focus, not the divine honour, as with Anselm's *Cur Deus Homo*. The atonement is made in order to satisfy divine justice in its retributive aspect, not to appease and restore the offended divine honour. So it is not clear that this objection is actually to the point. Nevertheless, perhaps the idea behind what Brümmer says here may still have something to be said for it. What he seems to be getting at is that the penal substitutionary view makes human sinners merely

---

[21] See David Lewis, 'Do We Believe in Penal Substitution?' in *Philosophical Papers* 26 (1997): 209.

[22] Brümmer thinks that the only way to avoid the problem of immorality he raises for penal substitution is to borrow capital from an Anselmian satisfaction theory, whereby what is at stake in the atonement is the divine honour, with God as the feudal lord whose honour has been violated by the sin of his creatures. His only objection to taking penal substitution in this direction is that we find it difficult to see God in these terms today, which is hardly a knock-down, drag-out argument against penal substitution.

instrumental in the satisfaction of sin. What is important on the penal substitutionary view, one might think, is that divine justice is satisfied one way or another. Who does the satisfying is a matter of secondary importance. But, it might be thought, such an arrangement fails to treat human beings with sufficient value. For, though fallen humans have committed a crime against God, if God's objective in reconciling human beings to himself is to bring some number of humanity back into fellowship with himself, God would surely treat those who are the objects of his compassion as ends in themselves, rather than merely as means to the end of satisfying divine justice. As Brümmer puts it: 'To put it crudely: God values my serving his honour more than he values me.'[23]

It is true that Shedd, in common with a number of advocates for penal substitution, conceives of the act of atonement as essentially concerned with divine self-propitiation. But Shedd thinks this is because human beings are incapable of saving themselves in the absence of such an act. So it is divine compassion that makes God act in this way. It does not follow from the fact that God brings about the salvation of some large number of human beings via an act of self-propitiation that God does not value each person that he thereby saves. Consider an analogy: a liner is sinking and the captain sees that there are a certain number of passengers still aboard who need to be saved, all of whom are members of his own family. The only means of saving them is via the last lifeboat. So the captain uses a load-hailer to direct the whole group to jump into the lifeboat and pushes them out and away to safety. It might be thought that the captain's action in dealing with the group as a whole, rather than each as individuals somehow devalues them. He does not speak to each individual and offer each one a place on the lifeboat. He simply deals with them as a whole group, and directs them all with one command over the loudhailer. But why would such an action devalue the persons concerned? This is surely to confuse the manner or mode of the saving act with the intention of the saviour. God intends the salvation of all those whose sin is atoned for by Christ. There is nothing in the logic of Shedd's position that requires that God's intention is not to save every individual in that group, but merely the group as a whole, as opposed to some other group, or no group whatsoever. So this objection does not seem to have purchase.

We come to the third issue. This was that the penal substitution view of the atonement has a defective understanding of divine forgiveness because it confuses divine forgiveness with condonation. Elsewhere in his monograph, Brümmer has more to say about this matter. To begin with, he states that there are two necessary conditions for reconciliation. These are forgiveness on the part of the offended party, and repentance and a change of heart on the part of

---

[23] Brümmer, *Atonement, Christology and the Trinity,* p. 76.

the offending party.²⁴ Forgiveness alone is not enough. But it is a necessary condition of reconciliation. Brümmer states,

> By forgiving you I fully acknowledge the pain you did to me, but declare that I would rather give up the pain and give up my right to satisfaction than to abandon the fellowship with you.... The one who forgives is the one who pays the price. To pay the price is not to trivialize it.²⁵

But without repentance and a change of heart on the part of the offending party, the forgiveness of the offended party is just a matter of condoning the disruption of the relationship. No reconciliation is thereby effected. So, if I sin against you and seek reconciliation, I must ask for your forgiveness. Such an act is itself a turning away from my sin in penitence and expresses a change of heart.²⁶ Applying this to the case of the divine-human relationship, Brümmer says this:

> Sin is not primarily a state of corruption calling for a divine manipulative cure, nor guilt to be wiped out through punishment or satisfaction, but estrangement from God requiring reconciliation. As in the case of damaged human fellowship, the necessary and sufficient conditions for reconciliation with God are not punishment or satisfaction or condonation, but repentance and forgiveness.... Nothing more than this is required.²⁷

The point is that penal substitution, like satisfaction theories of the atonement, sets up a false dichotomy between punishment for sin that satisfies divine justice on the one hand, and forgiving sin without punishment, which amounts to condoning sin, on the other. These, says Brümmer, are not the only alternatives open to God. For a God of love would seek restorative justice in his relations with us, rather than retribution.²⁸

Here, as before, a response to this objection must begin by clarifying some confusion. It is perfectly consistent with a doctrine of penal substitution to claim that God might have forgiven sin without punishment, but that he did not do so because, say, it was more fitting for him to punish sin than not to, all things considered. This, as we have already seen, was a view taken by several prominent Reformed divines, including Twisse and Owen (in his earlier work). Although Shedd distances himself from this view, he does acknowledge that there are reasons for taking this sort of view, to do with the nature of divine power. If God is omnipotent, then, one might think, it is within his absolute power to forgive sin without punishment, but not within his ordained power

---

²⁴ *Atonement, Christology and the Trinity*, p. 41.
²⁵ Ibid., p. 46.
²⁶ Ibid.
²⁷ Ibid., p.49.
²⁸ Ibid., p. 77.

(given what we know of God through revelation). And, for all we know, God has good reason for bringing about this state of affairs. So, it is simply not true to say *all* defenders of penal substitution set up a false dichotomy between forgiveness and punishment, as Brümmer suggests.[29]

However, Shedd's doctrine might be thought liable to this objection because he denies that God could have forgiven sin without punishment. Divine justice is, he says, inexorable, unlike divine mercy. But even here, what is at stake is not whether or not Shedd is in thrall to a false dichotomy about forgiveness and punishment, but something more fundamental. The difference between Shedd and Brümmer on this matter has to do with the intuitions that inform the arguments each adopts on the matter of divine justice and reconciliation. Shedd is convinced that divine justice is necessarily retributive and that this is of the divine essence. Brümmer is convinced that divine justice is essentially restorative. Neither denies that God is essentially good. What is at issue is the weight given to different aspects of, or, perhaps, different conceptions of, divine justice. Shedd maintains that no single divine attribute governs the rest, and that justice is as essential to the divine nature as love. So God must act in a way consistent with both his justice and his love, which he does in the atonement for some and the condemnation of others. Brümmer, on the other hand, is convinced that the nature of divine love is such that divine justice cannot be essentially retributive. It must be restorative. Adjudicating between these two conceptions of the divine nature in general, and the relationship between divine love and justice in particular, is no easy matter. Much depends on making certain value judgements about what God is like that leads to different conceptions of God, and of the relation between the deity and his creatures. Seen in this light, it does not seem at all *obvious* that Shedd's doctrine of penal substitution is false because he holds to the particular view of the divine nature that he does. That contention would have to be argued for. But I cannot see such an argument in what Brümmer offers.[30]

The fourth problem is that penal substitution does not do justice to the unity of the work of the divine Trinity in salvation. Following Bernard of Clairvaux, Brümmer observes that in the doctrine of the Trinity there must be a unity of will, not merely a union of wills. Yet penal substitution demands only a union of wills. 'Unlike the union of love [between the creator and the creature], the unity of the Father and the Son involves an identity of will and essence. This entails that their purpose and attitude towards us should be similarly identical: the purpose and attitude of the Son should be a direct expression of that of the

---

[29] To be fair to Brümmer, he does seem to be following Gustav Aulen at this point in his discussion, from whom he takes this objection. Nevertheless, it is surprising that he adopts Aulen's mistaken view without qualification.

[30] And another thing: Shedd's discussion of these matters is thoroughly grounded in Scripture. It might be objected that the same cannot always be said of Brümmer's discussion, and that this is a weakness in Brümmer's approach to the doctrine.

Father.'[31]

But this doctrine of the Trinity is contentious, and it is not clear why this is a problem peculiar to the doctrine of penal substitution. Some contemporary theologians who defend a social model of the Trinity would deny that the persons of the Trinity have a single will. In fact, social-Trinity theologians often claim that the idea of three distinct divine persons sharing only one will between them looks very odd indeed, and does not adequately capture important doctrinal themes about the divine life, such as divine perichoresis (the mutual 'indwelling' or circumincession of the persons of the Trinity 'in' one another). On this way of thinking it is more fitting to think of a unity of wills in the divine life, rather than a union of will. I am not concerned to defend this model of the Trinity. My point is merely that (a) some contemporary theologians take such a view, (b) many who do so are not committed to penal substitution, and (c) there are good theological reasons for doubting that a unity of will is a requirement for a doctrine of the Trinity.

But what about whether defenders of penal substitution are committed to the notion that God has a unity of wills rather than a union of will? Does that hold water? Well, for one thing, a defender of penal substitution might also hold to a social view of the Trinity like that just sketched. In which case, they may doubt that Brümmer has got things right on the matter of the unity of will in the divine essence. But some defenders of penal substitution might opt for a more Latin view of the Trinity, according to which God has a union of will, as Brümmer suggests. For such theologians, the issue is whether God can be said to have a unity of will on the one hand, and yet for the first and second persons of the Trinity to compact together to bring about the reconciliation of some number of fallen humans through the atonement, on the other. Traditionally, this latter idea is known as the *pactum salutis,* or the covenant of redemption between the Father and the Son. Does it require a social model of the Trinity? Not necessarily. Brümmer's criticism only has bite if the conjunction of

1. God has a unity of will in the divine essence, and
2. The Father and Son compact together to bring about reconciliation

yield a contradiction. The problem is, in order to generate a contradiction here, one would have to show how it is that having a unity of will is not compatible with thinking that the Triune God is able to make covenants with himself, viz. the Father compacting with the Son to bring about the atonement in the *pactum salutis.* One difficulty with this objection, though not, to be sure, a difficulty of logic, but of history, is that many post-Reformation Reformed theologians have thought that (1) and (2) are perfectly consistent. That is, many theologians have

---

[31] Brümmer, *Atonement, Christology and the Trinity,* p. 76.

held to the *pactum salutis* and a Latin view of the Trinity.[32] Still, conceivably, such theologians were mistaken in this belief. The question is a logical, not an historical one, after all. Well then, does the conjunction of (1) and (2) yield a contradiction? Not obviously. It is notoriously difficult to demonstrate that (1) and (2) yield a contradiction because it is not clear what the necessary and sufficient conditions for divinity are – let alone the necessary and sufficient conditions for the divine Trinity! This is a mystery, after all. As Shedd observes, 'The great mystery of the Trinity is that one and the very same substance can subsist as an undivided whole in three persons simultaneously.... that a substance without any division or distribution can at the same instant constitute three distinct divine persons baffles the human understanding.' (DT: 248) If Brümmer is to make good on his claim of contradiction, he is faced with the not inconsiderable task of demonstrating that (1) and (2) are incompatible with the necessary and sufficient conditions for the Trinity (whatever they might be). But nothing he says provides an *argument* for this conclusion.

Shedd, like the post-Reformation Reformed Orthodox theologians, affirms the traditional Reformed doctrine of the *pactum salutis* (e.g. DT: 350) and a Latin model of the Trinity (DT: 249 ff.). He also offers a reason for thinking that the unity of essence (including, I think, a unity of will) in the deity is consistent with the different operations of the persons of the Trinity in creation, by application of the *opera trinitatis ad extra sunt indivisa* principle common in catholic theology:

> In every external operation of a person, the whole essence is in each person. The operation, consequently, while peculiar to a person, is at the same time essential, that is, is wrought by that one divine essence which is also and alike in the other persons. An official personal act cannot, therefore, be the exclusive act of a person in the sense that the others have no participation in it.... At the same time, an act like creation, for example, which is common to all the persons of the Trinity by virtue of a common participation in the essence, yet stands in a nearer relation to the essence as subsisting in the Father than it does to the essence as subsisting in the Son or the Spirit. *The same reasoning applies to redemption and the second person...*' (DT: 252-253, emphasis added.)

We could adapt this for present purposes in the following manner. Assume God has a unity of will (which, admittedly, Shedd does not make explicit in this passage) and that there is a certain class of divine act in the created world that is, in some sense, attributable to one of the persons of the Trinity, such as the atonement. Shedd is claiming that the whole divine essence is involved in any given divine act *ad extra* in the created world, that is attributable to one of the divine persons. Although he does not say so explicitly, this looks like a construal of the *opera trinitatis ad extra sunt indivisa* principle. Taken together

---

[32] See, for example, the works cited in Heinrich Heppe, *Reformed Dogmatics*, trans. G. T. Thomson (London: Collins, 1950).

with our initial assumptions, this would mean that the whole divine essence, including (for our purposes) the unity of will, is operative in each divine act attributable to a given divine person that is an act in the created order. This does not explain *how* the *pactum salutis* is consistent with a doctrine of the unity of will in the divine essence. Shedd does not seem to deal with this particular problem in detail. But what this does show is that Shedd's thinking is consistent with the notion that the *ad extra* acts of God may be related to one or other divine person, and yet be the act of the divine essence as a whole - which includes, one presumes, the divine will. Somehow the divine essence is wholly present in each divine act *ad extra*, just as each divine person coinheres with the other two persons, yet without confusion or mixture, and without dissolving the Trinity into bare monotheism, or separating the divine persons in tritheism.

Brümmer's fifth objection is that penal substitution denies the Patristic intuition that atonement is something done by God and not to God. He contends that, on penal substitution, 'the agent of the Atonement is Christ in his humanity.'[33] The idea is that *qua* human, Christ brings about atonement. In which case, it is not God, or God Incarnate, who atones, but the human nature of Christ. So Christ offers atonement to God as a man; atonement is not brought about by God on behalf of human beings. But this objection can only work if the human nature of Christ is not the human nature of the second person of the Trinity. No defender of penal substitution worth his salt, and certainly not Shedd, is going to concede this. Shedd, like Anselm, maintains that it is necessary that a person who is at once fully divine and fully human makes atonement, since a human nature without a divine nature is unable to perform an act that generates an infinite merit, and a divine person in abstraction from the Incarnation cannot offer a perfect human sacrifice, as required by the doctrine of satisfaction (DT: 617 ff.). So a God-Man is required. It is simply false to say that a doctrine of penal substitution means only the human nature of Christ atones for sin. The very logic of the doctrine militates against this objection.

Sixthly, and finally, Brümmer claims that though penal substitution can account for the satisfaction of sin, it cannot give an adequate explanation of the restoration of fellowship with God. Hence, penal substitution is not a theory about atonement (i.e. at-one-ment) at all. Here the idea seems to be that in satisfying the need for punishment due for sin, Christ is only able to restore the balance and remove the penal debt incurred by human sin. He is not able to reconcile God and man *through this paticular act*. Suppose a mediator is able to pay the debt owed by an offending party to one offended. In paying the debt, the mediator does not bring about reconciliation between the offender and the one offended against. He merely ensures justice is done. This seems to be what Brümmer has in mind with respect to the doctrine of penal substitution.

---

[33] *Atonement, Christology and the Trinity,* p. 77.

But this objection is a straw man. If Christ is the God-Man, and if God ordains that this act of atonement will bring about reconciliation via satisfying the requirements of the divine law, then Christ's act brings about reconciliation. If Christ is God Incarnate, as Shedd supposed, then he is able to reconcile human beings with God precisely because he is *both* fully divine *and* fully human at one and the same time. Only if the mediator between God and man is not himself divine can this objection begin to make headway. But no defender of penal substitution – indeed, no orthodox Christian theologian – will accede to this.

But perhaps Brümmer means something slightly different in raising this objection. He could mean that penal substitution has no mechanism for explaining the subjective, restorative component of atonement necessary for bringing about reconcilation with God. It is one thing to provide the means for reconciliation between two estranged parties. It is something quite different to be the catalyst that brings about reconciliation between these two parties. Brümmer might think that penal substitution is like the first of these examples, whereas his own alternative is like the second. In which case, penal substitution does not bring about reconciliation with God, it merely makes reconciliation possible, where previously it was not possible.

Interestingly, Shedd's way of conceiving the subjective aspect of the atonement involves helping himself to the notions of penitence and faith (DT: 708-709). There are other recent writers on the atonement who have done something similar (e.g. Richard Swinburne). But this may play into Brümmer's hands if it means assimilating aspects of a doctrine of regeneration to the doctrine of atonement. For, so it might be objected, atonement and regeneration are two distinct events. Whereas atonement makes possible reconciliation, regeneration is the appropriation of that atoning act in the life of an individual believer. In which case, Shedd's doctrine of atonement is wholly objective, and relies upon the subjectively orientated notion of regeneration to generate a doctrine of reconciliation.

But a defender of Shedd could supply what is missing in Shedd's account in order to avoid this consequence. This involves claiming that Christ's atoning death is effective for the elect, because Christ dies for all the sin of the elect, including the sin of unbelief. If the atonement includes satisfaction for the sin of unbelief, then there is a bridge between a wholly objective penal substitution and the subjective appropriation of that atonement by faith in regeneration. Faith is still requisite (although the next chapter offers a qualifier to this), but this faith is enabled by satisfaction for the sin of unbelief, amongst other sins atoned for by Christ.

Conclusion

It appears that Shedd's version of penal substitution is fairly robust. Although there is some inconsistency in his own exposition of the doctrine, when set alongside other things he says in his corpus about the divine nature, what he does say is invariably clear and represents an orderly account of the doctrine – bar his comments on divine suffering. We have also seen that Brümmer's criticisms of penal substitution, when brought into dialogue with what Shedd offers, are either wide of the mark, moot, or not problems peculiar to this particular theory of the atonement. Of the six objections canvassed, only the first offers a real problem for penal substitution as Shedd conceives it. Even though Shedd does not offer a compelling reason for thinking that God may allow Christ to act as a penal substitute, anyone who allows some notion of pecuniary penal substitution in their account of natural justice is open to the same sort of objection, the relevant changes having been made. For, as David Lewis contends, all those who think pecuniary penal substitution is permissible are in two minds about the viability of the doctrine, whether or not they are also Christian theologians who hold to a penal substitution theory of the atonement. In which case Shedd, and opponents of penal substitution like Brümmer who allow pecuniary penal substitution, are all in the same metaphysical boat. Both are without an adequate reason for thinking penal substitution applies in certain cases, but not in others.

CHAPTER 7

The Extent of the Atonement

In this chapter, we come to a consideration of Shedd's understanding of the scope, or extent, of the atonement. This involves thinking through several interrelated themes in Shedd's work, spanning his *Dogmatic Theology* and one of his last published pieces, *Calvinism: Pure and Mixed* (hereinafter, CPM).[1]

In DT Shedd argues for an unlimited atonement but limited application of that atonement, in redemption. This, he believes, is consistent with historic Calvinism, despite first appearances. He also deals with a number of terminological questions pertaining to the discussion of the extent of the atonement and the question of whether Christ's atonement is distributive, that is, effectively applied to all those for whom Christ atones, or conditional (upon the faith of the believer).[2]

In CPM he considers the scope of the atonement as it bears upon the question of the so-called 'larger hope'. This 'larger hope' is the belief, held by several prominent Calvinistic divines, that God will save the majority of humanity through the work of Christ, reprobating, or passing over only a small minority of the human race.[3] In the course of exploring this position, Shedd offers several reasons for thinking that the eschatologically sanguine vision presented in the 'larger hope' is true. These reasons include the salvation of

---

[1] Shedd also has a long and detailed account of the history of soteriology in HCD2. His essay, 'The Doctrine of the Atonement' in DE is concerned with the nature of the atonement, not its scope.

[2] For a useful recent treatment of the Reformed doctrine of particular redemption and its historical antecedents, see Raymond A. Blacketer, 'Definite Atonement in Historical Perspective' in *The Glory of the Atonement*, eds. Charles E. Hill and Frank A. James III (Downers Grove, IL: IVP, 2004).

[3] Shedd was not alone amongst nineteenth century Reformed theologians in embracing the idea that the atonement brings about the salvation of the majority of humankind. See, for example, Benjamin Warfield, *The Plan of Salvation* (Grand Rapids, MI: Eerdmans, 1975), ch. V, and Charles Hodge, *Systematic Theology, Vol. III*, (London: James Clarke, 1960), pp. 879-880. There Hodge states, 'the number of the finally lost in comparison with the whole number of the saved will be very inconsiderable.' For discussion of Warfield on this matter, see Paul Helm, 'Are There Few That Be Saved?' in *Universalism and The Doctrine of Hell*, ed. Nigel Cameron (Carlisle: Paternoster, 1992). There are also precedents in Reformed divines prior to the nineteenth century, like Augustus Toplady.

some large number of those who do not have a knowledge of Christ and therefore cannot consciously be related to him, and the question of the salvation of all children who die in infancy. Shedd also touches upon the millennial aspect of this theological issue - although I shall not consider this aspect of his thinking here. We shall see that he develops a careful and nuanced case for these positions.

Having spent some time laying out Shedd's arguments we shall then offer some objections to them. These comprise, whether Shedd's distinction between the extent and application of the atonement makes sense; why Shedd limits divine election to some (large) number of human beings less than the totality of humanity; and the problem of the necessity of regeneration that the logic of Shedd's position raises. In a closing section I offer some reflections on the success of Shedd's way of thinking about the scope of the atonement.

Shedd's Argument in *Dogmatic Theology*

Clearing up Some Terminological Problems

Shedd begins his treatment of this topic in DT by pointing out the ambiguity involved in speaking of the *extent* of the atonement. The English word 'extent' may connote the real value of a particular thing, as when we speak of the extent of the holdings of a particular bank. Applied to the doctrine of the atonement, this would mean that its 'extent' is infinite because the value of Christ's work is infinite. But this cannot be the sense of the word in controversy over the extent of the atonement, since, Shedd observes, no responsible theologian would gainsay the idea that the value of the atonement is infinite. (We might add, *sotto vocce:* if not an infinite value, then at least a value sufficient to atone for the sin of all humanity). So, the sense of 'extent' that is relevant to debate about the scope of the atonement has to do with who the benefits of the work of Christ are 'effectually extended' to (DT: 740). Thus Shedd,

> In modern English, the term extent is so generally employed in the passive signification of value that the active signification has become virtually obsolete and requires explanation. Writers upon the 'extent' of the atonement have sometimes neglected to consider the history of the word, and misunderstanding has arisen between disputants who were really in agreement with one another. Accordingly, in answering the question as to the 'extent' of Christ's atonement, it must first be settled whether 'extent' means it intended application or its intrinsic value, whether the active or passive signification of the word is in the mind of the inquirer. If the word means *value,* then the atonement is unlimited; if it means *applying,* then the atonement is limited. (DT: 741, emphasis added.)

He also observes that similar confusion arises with the use of the preposition 'for' in discussion of the scope of the atonement. Since, on Shedd's way of thinking, 'for' signifies intention ('I did it *for* you', 'the ball is *for* the dog', 'that is what it is *for*' etc.), the problem posed by the use of this connective must be to do with the intention that it is understood to imply. It might be thought to include the effectual application of the benefits of the atonement to the believer. In which case, according to Shedd, Christ did not die *for* all humanity, because this would imply (some version of) universalism, the doctrine that all human beings are redeemed through the work of Christ, which thereby saves all human beings. And, according to Shedd, someone who affirmed this way of thinking about Christ 'dying for humanity' would be in error, since universalism is unorthodox.

Alternatively, 'for' might signify merely the intention of God to offer the benefits of Christ's atonement to all humanity, leaving the matter of the appropriation of those benefits to the choice of the particular human being in question. This is a more restricted application of this soteriological application of 'for'. There is a third way that 'for' could be construed in this context, which, like the first deployment of 'extent' in discussion of the scope of the atonement, has to do with the value or sufficiency of the work of Christ. The idea would be that Christ's death is of sufficient value to atone for the sin of all human beings. But, although Shedd would not dissent from the notion that Christ's death does have a value sufficient to atone for all humanity,[4] he does not favour this construal of 'for' because it introduces a circumlocution in important scriptural passages like 1 Tim. 2: 16, 'Christ gave himself a ransom for all'. If 'for' has the meaning of 'value', then in this context, the passage means, 'Christ gave himself a ransom *that has the value of being sufficient* for all', whereas, if 'for' is taken to mean intention, then, says Shedd, it better accords with the noun 'ransom', meaning something like, 'Christ gave himself a ransom *intended* for all'. (See DT: 742.) This, as we shall see, is an important distinction for Shedd's way of thinking about the relationship between the scope of the atonement and its application.

Unlimited Atonement, Particular Redemption

We have just noted that Shedd affirms that Christ's death is sufficient to atone for all humanity. He also endorses the idea that Christ's death is efficacious for the elect only (where the elect is some number of humanity who are the objects of divine grace, usually thought to be less than the totality of humanity). This is

---

[4] Shedd's position is perfectly consistent with the medieval distinction, introduced into western theology by Peter Lombard, between the *sufficiency* and *efficiency* of Christ's work. Lombard maintained that Christ's work was sufficient to atone for all humanity, but efficient only for some number less than the total number of humanity (the elect). See *IV Libri Sententiarum* 3. 20. 3. This distinction has been somewhat controversial in Reformed theology. For discussion, see Herman Bavinck, *Reformed Dogmatics, Vol. 3, Sin and Salvation in Christ,* ed. John Bolt, trans. John Vriend (Grand Rapids, MI: Baker Academic, 2006), pp. 455 ff.

summed up in the ancient soteriological principle, cited by Shedd, *satisfactio Christi sufficienter pro omnibus, sed efficaciter tatum pro electis* (the atonement of Christ is sufficient for all, but efficient only for the elect).[5] However, Shedd distinguishes between 'atonement' and 'redemption'. Whereas atonement is the act by which Christ brings about the possibility of reconciliation with God, redemption is a richer expression than this, and includes the application of the atonement to the believer.[6] Thus atonement is unlimited, according to Shedd, but redemption is limited – to the particular number of the elect, to whom the benefits of Christ's atoning work are effectually applied. (As we shall see, this includes agents who are not 'believers' in the conventional sense, on Shedd's way of thinking.) Shedd believes that this distinction has scriptural warrant, citing passages like Heb 2: 17, Eph. 1: 14 and Luke 1: 68 in support of it (DT: 742-743), saying,

> Since redemption includes reconciliation with God and inheritance in the kingdom of heaven, it implies something subjective in the soul: an appropriation by faith of the benefits of Christ's objective work of atonement. (DT: 743.)

This leads him to suggest that it is the term 'redemption' that is used in 'controversial theology' to denote the application of Christ's benefits to the elect, so that it is perfectly just to say that the atonement 'is unlimited, and redemption is limited'. Moreover,

> He who asserts unlimited atonement and limited redemption cannot well be misconceived. He is understood to hold that the sacrifice of Christ is unlimited in its value, sufficiency, and publication, but limited in its effectual applications. (DT: 743.)

Interestingly, in DT Shedd offers this distinction between unlimited atonement and limited redemption as if it were a device of his own making. Yet in his earlier essay, 'The Doctrine of the Atonement', it appears that he found it ready-made in the work of Jonathan Edwards.[7] In that essay he cites Edwards'

---

[5] DT: 742. As an example of this distinction, Shedd cites John Owen's *Against Universal Redemption*, § 4. 1. Cf. Heinrich Heppe, *Reformed Dogmatics*, p. 475 ff., para. 28. Heppe gives ample evidence of its use amongst other post-Reformation Reformed theologians. As noted in the Introduction, this principle dates back to Peter Lombard.

[6] Earlier in DT: 726 he argued that this sufficiency of the atonement is worthless without faith: 'The assertion that because the atonement of Christ is sufficient for all men therefore no men are lost is as absurd as the assertion that because the grain produced in the year 1880 was sufficient to support the life of all men on the globe therefore no men died of starvation during that year.'

[7] See Shedd, 'The Doctrine of the Atonement' in DE, p. 321, n. The only citation Shedd gives is to the 'New York' edition of Edwards' Works, Vol. IV, p. 530 (p. 322 of Shedd's essay, the same footnote).

account of two distinct acts of divine sovereignty in order to bring about salvation. The first is the provision of a means of atonement, which is itself an entirely gratuitous act, since, according to both Edwards and Shedd God is under no obligation to make atonement for sin.[8] The second is the application of this atoning work to the individual 'elected sinner'. From this it is clear that Shedd's discussion of what we might call *the atonement-redemption distinction* (i.e. unlimited atonement but limited redemption) that is a key element of his way of construing the scope of the atonement, draws upon Edwards' expression of substantially the same point. And, of course, both Edwards and Shedd are merely setting forth a terminological variant on a much older notion, going back to the sufficiency-efficiency atonement distinction found in medieval theology.

Three Alternatives to Shedd's Position

Shedd contrasts his own (Edwardsian) view of the atonement-redemption distinction with those who advocate an unlimited atonement and deny a limited redemption. Such theologians could hold one of several different views. (And, although he does not say this explicitly, it seems Shedd thinks these are the only live options in theology. They are certainly not the only logically possible options.)

The first is a version of what today would be called necessary universalism: necessarily both the atonement and redemption are unlimited in scope (bringing about the salvation of all humanity), or, alternatively, the atonement is *potentially* unlimited so that it is possible for all humanity to be saved, but the redemption, in Sheddian language, is *necessarily* distributive to all humanity so that all human agents are inevitably saved.[9] The important thing here is that necessary universalism requires that Christ's death is (somehow) effectual for all humanity so that necessarily, all human beings are saved by Christ's work.[10]

---

[8] According to Shedd, Edwards does say that 'as it *now* stands, he [God] is obliged [to save some particular number of fallen human beings]; he cannot bestow salvation in one case, or refuse it in the other, without prejudice to the honor of his *truth*. But God exercised his sovereignty *in making these declarations*. God was not obliged to promise that he would save all who believe in Christ; nor was he obliged to declare that he who committed the sin against the Holy Ghost should never be forgiven. But *it pleased him so to declare*', DE, p. 322, n, emphasis original. But this is perfectly consistent with the claim that God is not obliged to offer salvation to fallen humanity, until such time as he places himself under such an obligation.

[9] Jonathan Kvanvig coined the term 'necessary universalism' in *The Problem of Hell* (New York: Oxford University Press, 1993), ch. 1.

[10] For a recent account of necessary universalism consistent with the tenets of Augustinian theology, see Oliver D. Crisp 'Augustinian Universalism' in *International Journal for Philosophy of Religion* 53 (2003): 127-145. As Shedd points out in CPM, the most celebrated example of this sort of universalism in the Reformed tradition is found in the work of F. D. E. Schleiermacher. See CPM: 51.

Second, one could, like the Arminian, hold to an unlimited atonement (possibly, all human beings could be saved on the basis of the work of Christ, which is sufficient for the salvation of all humanity), coupled with the requirement that faith is requisite for the application of this to the believer, and faith is an operation of the Holy Spirit in tandem with the will of the particular believer.[11] On this view, unlike necessary universalism, redemption is conditional, rather than distributive. That is, the effectiveness of redemption depends upon the concurrence of the suasive working of the Holy Spirit in the life of an individual fallen human with the free choice of that individual. Redemption is not applied universally and effectually, to all human beings. This means that, although redemption is potentially universal in effectiveness (possibly, all humanity could exercise faith and be saved), in practical terms it is limited to the number of human beings who do exercise faith in Christ, which, Arminians presume, is less than the totality of humanity. So on this view, although redemption is particular in the trivial sense that a certain number of fallen humanity is saved, is not particular in the non-trivial sense that Shedd's view requires, because it is dependent on the choices of individual fallen human beings working in tandem with the Holy Spirit (we might add: where those human choices are libertarian). Shedd attributes this 'confusion' on the part of the Arminians to the fact that they did not 'carefully distinguish, as the elder Calvinists did, between atonement and redemption' (DT: 758, n. 6.2.9).[12] Of the Arminian alternative to Shedd's Calvinistic particular redemption view, Shedd says this,

> It is not rational [consistent?] to suppose that God the Father merely determined that God the Son should die for the sin of the world, leaving it wholly or in part to the sinful world to determine all the result of this stupendous transaction.... Neither is it rational to suppose that the Son of God would lay down his life upon such a peradventure; for it might be that not a single human soul would trust in his sacrifice, and in this case he would have died in vain. (DT: 746)

---

[11] In CPM: 96, Shedd distinguishes the Calvinistic from the Arminian view of common and special grace thus: 'Calvinism asserts that common grace cannot be made successful by the *co-operation* of the unregenerate sinner with the Holy Spirit, and thereby be converted into special or saving grace: Arminianism asserts that it can be. The Arminian contends that the ordinary operations of the Divine Spirit which are experienced by all men indiscriminately will succeed, if the unrenewed man will cease to resist them and will yield to them.'

[12] There is a sophisticated literature on the relationship between human freedom and divine foreknowledge, which this problem touches upon. Here is not the place to pursue this matter. But representative treatments include William Hasker *God, Time and Knowledge* (Ithaca, NY: Cornell University Press, 1989); Paul Helm, *The Providence of God* (Leicester: IVP, 1993); Thomas P. Flint, *Divine Providence*; and Linda Trinkhaus Zagzebski, *The Divine Foreknowledge- Freedom Dilemma* (Oxford: Oxford University Press, 1998). See also *Divine Foreknowledge: Four Views*, eds. James Beilby and Paul Eddy (Downers Grove, IL: IVP, 2001).

The third alternative to his own view that Shedd highlights is hypothetical universalism, a position advocated by the French Reformed School of Saumur in the seventeenth century.[13] Earlier in DT, in discussing the Salmurian soteriology, Shedd observes that the Salmurians began 'with Arminianism' and ended 'with Calvinism' (DT: 350). They thought that God decrees to provide a redeemer to all humanity conditional upon the faith of fallen human beings. However, foreseeing that no fallen human being will turn to Christ for salvation without divine special grace, God elects some of fallen humanity, whom he effectually brings to salvation.

This hypothetical universalism is consistent with the claim, found in much of the Reformed tradition, that God must display his justice, which is inexorable, in the punishment of sin, and may display his mercy. (As we have already seen, Shedd himself makes a great deal of this in his discussion of the nature of the atonement.[14]) If this sort of assertion is coupled with hypothetical universalism it goes some way towards explaining why defenders of this view might think that an initial, and hypothetical universalism is superseded in the divine decrees by the redemption of a particular number of humanity.[15] As far as Shedd's taxonomy of different options open to defenders of unlimited atonement + the denial of limited redemption goes, the logic of the Salmurian position is clearly universal with respect to the extent of the atonement in the hypothetical decree, but does not necessarily deny that only a particular number of human beings are saved (although it does require a rather different notion of the theological concept of election). What is at stake for the Saumur theologians is the ordering of the divine decrees. It is the sequence of divine decrees that determines the Saumur way of thinking about the relation between a universal atonement and a hypothetically universal redemption. Benjamin Warfield, writing within a generation of Shedd, explains:

---

[13] The standard work on the theology of Saumur is still that of Brian Armstrong, *Calvinism and the Amyraut Heresy: Protestant Scholasticism and Humanism in Seventeenth Century France* (Madison, WI: University of Wisconsin Press, 1969). This book should be read alongside Richard Muller's recent cautionary words, to the effect that the Salmurian theology, though censured in the *Formula Consensus Helvetica,* was not identified as a heresy by the Reformed, but merely as a 'problematic teaching that troubled the confessional orthodoxy of the church'. See Muller, *Post-Reformation Reformed Dogmatics, Vol. I, Prolegomena to Theology, Second Edition* (Grand Rapids, MI: Baker Academic, 2003), p. 77. For an interesting recent treatment of Amyraldianism, see G. Michael Thomas, *The Extent of the Atonement, A Dilemma for Reformed Theology from Calvin to the Consensus* (Carlisle: Paternoster, 1997), Part 3.

[14] See DT: 726 and Shedd's essay, 'The Doctrine of The Atonement' in DE, pp. 292-293, and 298.

[15] Of course, the claim that God's justice is inexorable and his mercy a matter of the divine will does raise further, deeper theological questions about the divine nature that we cannot enter into here. For this reason I say this claim only goes *some way* towards understanding the doctrine of hypothetical universalism.

> They [the Saumur theologians] propose therefore to think of the provision of salvation in Christ as universal in its intent; but to represent it as given effect in its application to individuals by the Holy Spirit only particularistically. That is to say, they suppose that some, not all, of the divine operations looking to the salvation of men are universalistic in their reference, whereas salvation is not actually experienced unless not some but all of them are operative.

This means that,

> As the particular saving operation to which they ascribe a universalistic reference is the redemption of Christ, their scheme is expressed by saying that it introduces the decree of election, in the order of thought, at a point subsequent to the decree of redemption in Christ. They may therefore be appropriately called Post-redemptionists, that is, those who conceive that the decree of election is logically postponed to the decree of redemption.[16]

To put it crudely, the Saumur theologians maintained that God first decrees creation, then decrees to permit the Fall, followed by the decree putting in place the atonement, which is sufficient for the salvation of all humanity. But foreseeing that no fallen human will avail him- or herself of this redemption, God then decrees the election of a limited number of fallen humanity. (The reader should bear in mind that the ordering of decrees here is not a temporal series, but only a logical one – God decrees what he does timelessly, according to the Salmurians, and Shedd.)

The difficulty for the Saumur theologians is what Shedd calls the matter of redemption or the application of the atoning work of Christ. In his discussion of the divine decrees, Shedd points out that there are three principle objections to the Salmurian scheme. These are (a) that it makes the decree of redemption (the first, hypothetical decree) dependent on human action, (b) that it implies a divine decree can fail, and (c) that the net result of the Salmurian theory is not inclusive of all fallen humanity, but only of those who are elect and, as a result, come to saving faith in Christ.

It would certainly seem odd, if not downright immoral, to think God decrees universal redemption, in the full knowledge that no fallen human being is morally capable of availing him- or herself of this proffered salvation. This would be like offering a full pardon to all prisoners who avail themselves of this offer, by turning up at midday in the local town hall. How could someone who is incarcerated avail him- or herself of such a proposal? In fact, it seems entirely disingenuous to make this offer, knowing none of those to whom it is

---

[16] Warfield, *The Plan of Salvation*, pp. 89-90. Warfield does not have a high view of this 'Post-redemptionist' view of the atonement, calling it a 'reduced' form of Calvinism (p. 92).

offered are able to avail themselves of the promised benefit. And it certainly runs against the grain of Reformed thinking to conceive of a divine decree as something that may fail, as is the case with the Salmurian hypothetical universalistic decree. How can a decree issued by an omnipotent God fail? Given that this universalism remains hypothetical, and that the consequent decree of election includes only those who have saving faith in Christ (not, in addition, some number of 'righteous pagans', as Shedd believes), Shedd rejects this alternative. On a Sheddian way of thinking, Salmurian soteriology is not an advance on the traditional, Reformed theory. And, contrary to first appearances, it does not offer greater hope concerning the scope of salvation.

In contrasting his own position to these three alternatives, Shedd states that the doctrine of limited redemption rests upon the doctrine of election, which in turn depends upon the inability of fallen human beings to free themselves from the effects of sin. Thus, 'Soteriology here runs back to theology [i.e. the doctrine of God], and theology runs back to anthropology. Everything in the series finally recurs to the state and condition of fallen man' (DT: 744). For Shedd, it is impossible for fallen human beings to freely exercise saving faith apart from the prevenient work of the Holy Spirit, who grants faith to the unbelieving soul and applies the benefits of Christ's atoning work to the human individual ('atonement in and by itself, separate from faith, saves no soul' DT: 747; compare CPM: 92-101). And it is a constituent of Shedd's view, in common with the majority of his Reformed Orthodox forebears, that this work of the Holy Spirit is a particular work, the salvific effects of which are enjoyed only by an elect number (less that the total number of fallen human beings), chosen by divine fiat.

The Extent of the Atonement and the 'Larger Hope' in *Calvinism: Pure and Mixed*

We turn now to Shedd's discussion of the 'larger hope' in CPM. There are two distinct issues to be considered here. These are whether the number of elect human beings will be greater than the damned, and if they are, what reasons there might be for thinking this is true.

The Number of those who are Saved

We take these two issues in turn. First, let us consider the question of the number of those who will be saved. Shedd's thinking on this matter can be further sub-divided into considerations drawn from Scripture, the tradition, and reason. He firmly believed that Scripture teaches the number of elect humans will greatly outnumber those who are reprobate, or damned:

> The kingdom of the Redeemer in this fallen world is always described [in Scripture] as far greater and grander than that of Satan. The operation of grace on

earth is uniformly represented as mightier than that of sin. 'Where sin abounded, grace did much more abound'. And the final number of the redeemed is said to be 'a multitude which no man can number', but that of the lost is not so magnified and emphasized. (CPM: 81)

This is touched upon elsewhere by Shedd (e.g. CPM: 116), although (perhaps significantly) without any detailed exegetical support.

In the second place, he adverts to the Augustinian-Calvinist tradition. The 'Elder Calvinists', he remarks, took 'a wide and large view of the *possible extent* of election' (CPM: 67). This is reflected, so Shedd thinks, in the *Westminster Confession*, his own denominational symbol, whose standards he had set out to defend in CPM. The most interesting remarks Shedd makes in this regard arise in connection with his discussion of the *Westminster Confession* and the doctrine of the divine decrees. He maintains that the Confession teaches God elects whom he wills, according to an infralapsarian way of thinking about the ordering of the divine decrees (CPM: 35). The supralapsarian scheme asserts that in the logical ordering of the divine decrees the decree to elect and reprobate certain men is before the decree to create them, whereas infralapsarianism says that election and reprobation come after, or are logically subsequent to, the decree to create (CPM: 35). The problem that Shedd detects in the supralapsarian scheme is that it means God creates some human beings to damn them, because creation is subsequent to damnation in the logical ordering of the divine decrees. Such a difficulty does not obtain in the case of infralapsarianism because the decree to create the world logically precedes the decree to reprobate some number of humanity. Moreover, the nature of reprobation is not so much a positive *decretum absolutum* (absolute decree) as a divine permission to allow sin to take place, and punish the consequences of that sin in the person of the sinner (or a vicar).

Shedd, like many defenders of classical Reformed theology, thinks this notion of a 'permissive decree' is important in explaining how it is that sin is not a chance occurrence, but takes place according to God's appointment (though not his positive ordination).[17] In this connection, Shedd introduces the concept of divine preterition. This, as Shedd defines it, is 'God's passing by a sinner in the bestowment of *regenerating*, not of common grace' (CPM: 42; compare DT: 335-336).[18] Preterition has to do with the divine decree to

---

[17] Compare, for example, Lorraine Boettner, whose work in this area is a digest of classical Reformed thinking on the matter: 'The good acts of men then are rendered certain by the positive decree of God, and the sinful acts occur only by His permission. Yet it is more than a bare permission by which the sinful acts occur, for that would leave it uncertain whether or not they would be done.' *The Reformed Doctrine of Predestination* (Philadelphia, PA: Presbyterian and Reformed, 1963), p. 242.

[18] See also *The Westminster Confession of Faith*, III. VII: 'The rest of mankind God was pleased, according to the unsearchable counsel of His own will, whereby He extends or withholds mercy, as He pleases, for the glory of His sovereign power over His creatures,

reprobate some number of humanity. In fact, on the infralapsarian scheme Shedd aligns himself with, preterition is usually thought of as that aspect of the divine decree of reprobation that is generated by the sovereign will of God. Damnation is distinct from preterition, in that it is grounded in the action of the sinner. Whereas God elects or reprobates, it is in the case of the reprobate, and in view of God's will to pass him or her by, the sinner who damns him- or herself. Those infralapsarians, like Shedd, who held this view thought it shielded the divine nature from any aspersions of injustice in the act of damning some number of sinners. The reasoning seems to be this:

1. God elects some and brings about their salvation by supplying them with the requisite grace for reconciliation.
2. God passes by the rest of humanity, withholding this special grace (preterition).
3. Human beings that are not the objects of God's election, but of his preterition, are damned because they are culpable for being in a state of sin.
4. But the act of damning those who are not the objects of God's decree to elect is not a sovereign act of God, but a consequence of human sin.
5. So God is not morally responsible for the damnation of human sinners, although he is responsible for withholding the divine grace that is a necessary condition for salvation.

The difference in view here is something like that used in contemporary medical ethics, when distinguishing between killing and letting die. A doctor who lets his patient die by withholding treatment that may keep him alive is not thereby guilty of killing the patient, as he would be if he smothered the patient with a pillow. Similarly, God is not the author of damnation, but he does withhold the saving grace requisite for salvation in the decree of preterition – although, of course, unlike the physician, God decrees the whole matter from beginning to end.[19]

This is important for Shedd. He maintains that if 'God could permissively decree the fall of Adam and his posterity without being the cause and author of it, he can also permissively decree the eternal death of an individual sinner without being the cause and author of it.' Moreover, in preterition 'God repeats, in respect to an individual, the act which he performed in respect to the race.'

---

to pass by; and to ordain them to dishonour and wrath for their sin, to the praised of His glorious justice.' Hereinafter cited as *WCF*, followed by chapter and section.

[19] For discussion of the post-Reformation Reformed doctrine of preterition and its relation to reprobation, see Richard Muller, *Dictionary of Latin and Greek Theological Terms* (Grand Rapids, MI: Baker Books, 1985), entry '*reprobatio*', p. 263, and Heinrich Heppe, *Reformed Dogmatics,* pp. 180 ff.

(CPM: 37) In other words, God permits the fall of humanity 'in' or 'through' the primal sin of Adam (which, for Shedd, is understood in terms of Augustinian realism), and he permits each individual who is not elect to remain in a state of sin and suffer the penal consequences attending that state.

Shedd mentions two standard objections to this view of divine preterition. First, that it is inconsistent with divine compassion. This he denies. Apart from the fact that the doctrine is taught in Scripture, Shedd argues that God is not obliged to offer the same degree of mercy and compassion to every particular human sinner (CPM: 44). God does show common grace to all fallen human beings, which act is itself a manifestation of divine compassion upon his creatures. But he is not obliged to go beyond this and regenerate all humanity because salvation is not a right but a gift.[20]

However, this raises a second objection. If God may provide salvation to human sinners, though he is not obliged to, why does he not save all humanity? In other words, why include a doctrine of preterition in the divine decrees? Why not simply do away with reprobation altogether and elect all fallen human beings instead, guaranteeing their salvation through the work of Christ? This objection has been taken up in recent theology under the guise of the so-called 'scandal of particularity', the view that it is scandalous to think God only saves a certain number of humanity comprising those who hear and respond to the gospel, damning those who through no fault of their own fail to hear the gospel message and are therefore not in a position to trust in Christ.

Shedd's answer to this problem, like his response to the previous difficulty, is nothing if not conventionally Calvinist. Preterition is partial; it applies to some number of humanity less than the total number of fallen humans. This is perfectly just because sinful human beings have no claims upon God with respect to salvation, given what has previously been said about the nature of salvation as an act of sheer grace. God has no duty to save any human being, so it is just that he withholds salvation from some and allow them to perish in their sins. Later in CPM, Shedd also claims that the denial of divine preterition, which he calls, 'a lopsided view of the Divine decree' is 'founded upon an erroneous view of the nature of retributive justice' (CPM: 78). Whereas those Shedd is concerned with who deny preterition assert that the exercise of divine retribution is not in accordance with the nature or glory of God, Shedd upholds

---

[20] Later in CPM Shedd claims that God offers salvation to all, but that only the elect are the recipients of regenerating grace (CPM: 93). This is more problematic because it appears to make God's universal offer of salvation insincere. Shedd thinks this is not the case because all fallen humans are obliged to respond to divine grace, even though they are disposed not to do so, through the morally debilitating effects of sin. It is rather like a drug addict being commanded to give up his habit by a judge. The addict is legally obliged to obey the judge's command, although his physical and psychological addiction to the drug militates against his obedience. Unfortunately, this example only underlines the fact that Shedd's way of thinking about this does make God's universal offer of salvation disingenuous.

the position of the *Westminster Confession* and the majority voice in the Reformed tradition, that the exercise of divine retribution is a manifestation of divine self-glorification, and that this manifestation of divine glory in the created order includes both the decree to elect, and its consequences, and the decree to reprobate, with its consequences (see CPM:76-80).[21]

But there is a third, more fundamental criticism often mounted against the distinction between divine ordination and divine permission that is pertinent to his discussion of infralapsarianism, preterition and the 'larger hope' in the *Westminster Confession*. This is that it is difficult to sustain a distinction between divine ordination and permission, or election and preterition, on the one hand, and damnation on the other, if God's action is a necessary and sufficient condition for bringing about any given creaturely action. For suppose that God is an absolute sovereign who ordains all that comes to pass, as the *Westminster Confession* affirms. Then, no event occurs in the created universe without God's ordination. Yet, without qualification, this would make God the author of sin, and the one solely responsible for the number of human beings who are saved.

Is this commensurate with Shedd's position? He certainly affirms a Calvinistic view of the absolute sovereignty of God:

> Nothing comes to pass contrary to his decree. Nothing happens by chance. Even moral evil, which he abhors and forbids, occurs by 'the determinate counsel and foreknowledge of God'; and yet occurs through the agency of the unforced and self-determining will of man as the efficient. (CPM: 37)[22]

---

[21] Cf. *WCF* III. III. One reason sometimes supplied in defence of reprobation and preterition in classical theology, both Medieval and post-Reformation, is that divine self-glorification requires that God display the wealth of his attributes in the created order. The idea behind this line of thought is that God would not be seen to be truly just if he did not display that justice in the punishment of sinners, and that he would not be seen to be merciful and loving if he did not display these attributes in his gracious work of redemption. So his grace and mercy are displayed in the elect, whereas his justice and wrath against sin are displayed in reprobation. Shedd hints at this sort of reasoning in CPM, ch. 7. He explicitly endorses it in DT: 328, where he makes the startling claim that sin is necessary to the best possible world, because such a world would be best adapted to manifest divine attributes like retributive justice that would not otherwise be made manifest in the creation. This sounds like a very strong version of a *felix culpa* (happy fault) version of theodicy, which has a long pedigree in Augustinian thought. For more on the classical-theological argument (independent of Shedd), see Oliver D. Crisp, 'Divine Retribution: A Defence' in *Sophia* 42 (2003): 35-52. A more nuanced and careful version of the *felix culpa* argument is given by Alvin Plantinga in 'Supralapsarianism, Or 'O Felix Culpa'' in *Christian Faith and the Problem of Evil*, ed. Peter van Inwagen (Grand Rapids, MI: Eerdmans, 2004).

[22] Cf. *WCF*, III. I: 'God from all eternity, did, by the most wise and holy counsel of His own will, freely and unchangeably ordain whatsoever comes to pass: yet so, as thereby

Elsewhere, he points out that even divine permissive decrees are such that they 'render the event infallibly certain, but not by immediately acting upon and in the finite will.' Moreover, 'by reason of his permissive decree, God has absolute control over moral evil, while yet he is not the author of it and forbids it.' (DT: 318 and 319 respectively.)

There are two classes of action under consideration here. Those ordained by God which will necessarily come to pass, including the salvation of a certain number of human beings. And those which are permitted by God, where divine permission is a necessary condition of their coming to pass, but where God is the ultimate but not the proximate cause of such actions. Although Shedd does not explicitly mention it in this context, the notion here seems to be that of divine *concursus* with secondary causes, whereby any secondary cause, including human volition, can only occur where God concurs with it. Shedd, like a number of other Augustinians, believes that this distinction preserves the moral integrity of the divine character in the face of sinful creaturely actions. God causes the creature to act in such and such a way; but it is the creature that freely chooses to act in that way. To which we may add: yet any creaturely action only takes place providing God concurs with it. Nevertheless, it is the creature that is responsible for his- or her actions, though God is the ultimate cause of all that takes place.

In a similar way, Shedd argues that preterition does not bring about damnation, but is a necessary condition for the bringing about of damnation, just as the withdrawal of medication is not the cause of the patient's death, but it is a necessary condition for bringing about the patient's death. Nevertheless, it is the human sinner, not God, who, through his- or her own deliberate fault, damns him- or herself.

However, it is just at this point that Shedd's argument runs into difficulties. There seem to be at least three alternatives here. The first affirms that God ordains all things, including sinful actions. But then, God is the author of sin. Shedd in his *Dogmatics* rejects this option because it is contrary to Scriptures like James 1: 3; 1 John 1: 5 (DT: 321-322).

The second is that God ordains all non-sinful things, and is a necessary, but not sufficient condition for sinful acts. Fallen human beings must choose to

---

neither is God the author of sin, nor is violence offered to the will of the creatures; nor is the liberty or contingency of second causes taken away, but rather established.' In his commentary on this section of the *Confession*, A. A. Hodge comments 'this plan comprehends and determines all things and events of every kind that come to pass'. See Hodge, *The Confession of Faith* (Edinburgh: Banner of Truth, 1958 [1869]), p. 63. There has been some discussion amongst Calvinistic commentators on this particular passage as to whether it entails a doctrine of divine concurrence with secondary causes, or some species of libertarianism. Hodge and most Calvinists favour something like the former. For a discussion favouring the latter, see William Cunningham's essay, 'Calvinism and the doctrine of Philosophical Necessity' in *The Reformers and The Theology of The Reformation*.

perform sinful actions for those actions to take place. God does not determine that they do so, but he permits this. On this option, God somehow provides the 'space' in which sin may take place, although he does not ordain that it takes place. But, even if sense can be made of such a notion, it is hardly consistent with God ordaining *all* events that take place. And, in any case, it is not clear why, on this view, sin is 'infallibly certain' as Shedd has it, if God has not ordained it. Were I to permit an alcoholic to take a sip from my hip flask, it would not necessarily follow from this that he would inevitably take a sip, even if he were an alcoholic. There may be all kinds of reasons that dispose the alcoholic to refuse my offer. For instance, he might want to preserve an appearance of being sober.[23] And, as Paul Helm has pointed out in the contemporary literature on this matter, it is not sufficient for the purposes of Augustinians like Shedd to say that some notion of general permission is involved here, where God leaves 'space' in which sin may take place. For the Augustinian who believes God ordains all things, a specific sort of permitting must be involved in any given act of sin.[24] Shedd is aware of the drawbacks to this option, and rejects it too (DT: 322).[25]

A third option, involves arguing that somehow God knowingly and willingly brings it about that a particular fallen human creature knowingly and willing brings about some sinful action, and yet that this does not implicate God in the action of his creature. Shedd seems to imply something like this sort of explanation when he speaks of God causing the matter, but not the form, of sin. And here he does make explicit use of the notion of divine concurrence with

---

[23] But perhaps God can arrange things so that, in any given act of sin, his permission involves a complex series of barriers that channel the sinner in a particular direction, although the sinner herself makes the choice to sin. The 'space' in which divine permission operates on this sort of conception would be rather like the way a barrier on a roadside 'channels' the car away from the side, and down the lane to its destination. Perhaps God has a series of such sophisticated 'barriers' that channel sinners in the direction of their sin, and permits the sin in this fashion. But, without also providing some careful safeguards that enable the sinner to avoid this outcome, it is difficult to see how this idea of divine permission is materially different from straightforward divine ordination. In which case, we still have the original problem: there is the very real possibility that the sinner will not commit the sin permitted by God.

[24] Paul Helm, *The Providence of God*, p. 172. Helm suggests that God might ordain the circumstances of the sin, but not approve of the sin itself, which sounds rather like the third option discussed here.

[25] To be sure, there are significant disanalogies between this example and divine permission of event x. Presumably God foresees all events that take place, and this is part of the reason why Shedd says divinely permitted events are 'infallibly' certain. But, we might ask, if God knows a future contingent event will take place, how can the human agent freely choose it? Does it make sense to think that God infallibly foreknows x will occur at tn, and that x is a contingent event that is brought about by the uncoerced action of S at tn (uncoerced in the compatibilist sense)? This, or something like it, is behind Shedd's objection to this view.

secondary causes: 'God concurs with the act and causes it, but not with the intent or viciousness of the act. But the form or "viciousness" of the act is the whole of the sin; and God's concursus does not extend to this.' (DT: 322.)

This seems to be the most promising way of thinking about the problem posed by permissive divine decrees. But Shedd places it amongst unsatisfactory attempts to make sense of this problem (although he does note with seeming approval that the Puritan Stephen Charnock thinks it is a viable way of making sense of this problem – DT: 322). There is good reason to be wary of this response. It depends on driving a wedge between the notion of *God being causally responsible for x* and *God being morally responsible for x*. But this is a very difficult distinction to substantiate, if it can be substantiated at all.[26] To extrapolate a little: on this view, God is causally responsible for what is causally necessary for x to take place. But God is not causally sufficient for the bringing about of x (where x is the action of some human agent). What is necessary, in addition, is that the action have some moral deficiency, which God cannot be the cause of, according to this way of thinking. But then, we may legitimately ask, whence this moral deficiency if God is causally responsible for all things that come to pass?[27]

Shedd's considered view is that there is no solution to this problem to which we currently have access:[28] 'How the permissive decree can make the origin of sin a certainty is an inscrutable mystery. God is not the author of sin, and hence, if its origination is a certainty for him, it must be by a method that does not involve his causation.' (DT: 321. Compare DT: 327, 343)[29]

So, although Shedd believes the distinction between divine ordination and permission obtains (because, in his estimation, it is a biblical principle), he has no argument that makes sense of this distinction.[30] How some of humanity is

---

[26] I deal with this problem as it arises in the context of Jonathan Edwards's theology in *Jonathan Edwards and the Metaphysics of Sin,* chs. 3 and 4. The reader is directed there for more detailed discussion.

[27] Paul Helm pointed out to me in private correspondence that this way of trying to solve the problem under consideration was common in the seventeenth century, and can be found, for example, in the work of Theophilus Gale.

[28] He offers several other attempts to make sense of divine permission without implicating God in DT: 322, both of which he considers inadequate. These are: God somehow non-culpably presents the human will with a motive to sin; and God passes over sinners allowing them to continue in sin. The first of these collapses into the causal- vs. moral responsibility distinction discussed above. The second appears to beg the question.

[29] To be fair to Shedd, he is not alone in admitting defeat at this point. Compare another nineteenth century Calvinist, A. A. Hodge, 'The problem of the permission of sin is to us insoluble, because unexplained.' *The Confession of Faith,* p. 68.

[30] There are two further things to say in Shedd's defence here. First, causation is a vexed philosophical issue. There are competing views on what exactly causation consists in, and it is at least possible that there is some notion of causation at work in divine

reprobate without implicating the divine character is a mystery. However, it might be thought that the relevant distinction Shedd skates over in placing this problem amongst those matters that are theological mysteries is between an account of this theological conundrum that is coherent and one that is not. Appealing to divine mystery is only appropriate where the conditions under which the purported example of mystery arises do not themselves yield a contradiction – in other words, where we have conditions that are not obviously incoherent when conjoined, or do not necessarily admit of contradiction, although it is unclear how they might be conjoined without raising serious intellectual difficulties pertaining to the consistence of what is being affirmed *in the absence of further information.* Does Shedd's position run aground at this point? Not necessarily: much depends on the plausibility of the claim – admittedly unsubstantiated by an argument in its defence - that God can be causally but not morally responsible for sinful creaturely acts he permits. To be fair to Shedd, this is a theological Gordian knot that theologians of all stripes approach with trepidation, and which most theologians admit has yet to receive a completely satisfactory resolution, if it can be resolved at all. Nevertheless, placing a particular problem within the pale of 'the mysterious' can be an unprincipled way of simply avoiding difficult questions that require answers, rather like a medieval cartographer's characterisation of unknown lands with the legend, 'here be dragons'. Although Shedd is not an unprincipled theologian, it is difficult to see how Shedd can turn back the objections of a determined opponent on this particular issue.[31]

This brings us to the third sub-division in Shedd's thinking on the 'larger hope', drawing on arguments from reason. On this matter Shedd states that although election is particular and restricted to some number less than the whole of humanity, there is nothing about the logic of the Calvinistic doctrine of the double decree (to election and reprobation respectively), which dictates the number of those elect. This seems to be firmer theological ground upon which to stand. Thus Shedd:

---

causation that we are simply not aware of. Which leads to the second point: there are philosophers who think that the problems surrounding the mind-body debate, and the problem of free will, are insoluble – even that we humans simply do not have the hardware required to make sense of these issues (e.g. Colin McGinn and Peter van Inwagen, respectively). Like these philosophers, perhaps Shedd could be seen to be taking what is often called a 'mysterion' position on the matter of ordination and permission (of sin).

[31] Here I am thinking of the following sort of objection: 'the reason you do not have a satisfactory solution to this theological conundrum is that one of the premises from which you are working is false. It is simply not the case that God is the cause of all that takes place. Remove this premise, and it become much easier to explain how it is that God is not the author of sin.' However, on these terms it also becomes much more difficult to explain how evil originates, and God still looks like an accessory to evil, which is hardly a better position to be in.

there is nothing in the nature of either election or preterition, that determines the number of each; nothing that implies that the elect must be the minority, and the non-elect the majority, or the converse. The size of each circle depends upon the will of him who draws it. God, conceivably, might have elected the whole human family without an exception, as [Friedrich] Schleiermacher says he did. Or, conceivably, he might have reprobated the whole human family, because he was not in justice obliged to save it.

Moreover,

God may elect and regenerate a heathen if he please, or he may leave him in the sin which he loves. And the same is true of the ideas of election and preterition as related to dying infants. Since everything in this matter depends wholly upon the sovereign will of God, he may regulate his choice as he pleases.... We cannot, therefore, determine from the mere idea of election how many are elected, or from that of preterition how many are passed by. (CPM: 58-59; Compare CPM: 81.)

Before exploring the issues these passages raise for the question of the 'larger hope', it is worth pausing to note a distinction Shedd makes later in CPM, concerning the nature of the regenerating work of the Holy Spirit. There is the matter of the period in which regeneration occurs, and the range of this operation (CPM: 118). As to the first of these, Scripture is clear, says Shedd, that the scope of God's regenerating work is restricted to this life. There is no possibility of salvation post-mortem. This has become a popular way of overcoming the problem posed by the 'horrendous evil' of everlasting damnation, in contemporary philosophical discussion of the problem of hell.[32] But Shedd is convinced that such thinking is mistaken. He cites various scriptures that teach or imply that salvation is restricted to this life only, such as Prov. 11: 7; Ezek. 33: 9; Ps. 6: 5; and John 8: 21, 24. (CPM: 130.) If Shedd is right about this, then the argument for post-mortem salvation fails to get off the ground.

On the question of the extent or scope of regeneration (in this life), Shedd begins by stating that it appears 'utterly improbable' on *a priori* grounds, to conceive of the 'stupendous miracle' of the work of Christ as yielding a 'small and insignificant result' (CPM: 125). It would be like committing vast resources and astronomical costs to a project that yielded pitiful results. Quite apart from the issues this raises for divine power (is God not able to bring about

---

[32] See, for example Jonathan Kvanvig, *The Problem of Hell;* Thomas Talbot, *"The Doctrine of Everlasting Punishment"* in, *Faith and Philosophy* 7 (1) 1990: 19-40; Jerry L. Walls, *Hell: The Logic of Damnation,* (Notre Dame, IN: University of Notre Dame Press, 1994); *Universal Salvation? The Current Debate,* eds. Robin Parry and Chris Partridge (Carlisle: Paternoster, 2003); and Gregory MacDonald's provocative study, *The Evangelical Universalist* (Eugene, OR: Cascade Books, 2006).

a better resolution that this?) it raises important moral questions concerning the scope of salvation: Would God commit himself to the salvation of some small fraction of humanity when he has the power to bring about a much greater salvation that this, assuming there is no moral impediment to him doing so?[33] Shedd thinks the answer to this is clear, and clearly negative.

And so, to the reasons Shedd supplies for thinking there is a 'larger hope', with respect to the scope of the atonement. These include, the salvation of all children who die in infancy; the salvation of a large number of 'heathen'; and the scriptural 'promise' of a great 'outpouring' of God's Holy Spirit in the "last days', that will far exceed in sweeping and irresistible energy anything in the past history of the Church' (CPM: 129).[34]

Reasons for Holding to the 'Larger Hope'

Let us focus on the first two of these reasons, since they have been important in recent theological discussion.

The first reason Shedd gives is that all children who die in infancy are regenerate through the work of the Holy Spirit without any outward call or need for common grace (CPM: 63). Although there was considerable discussion amongst the post-Reformation Reformed Orthodox divines about this matter, and some disagreement about whether all such infants are amongst the elect or not, this is the position Shedd believes can be found in the *Westminster Confession,* and it is the position he wishes to defend (CPM: 66).[35]

The reason why *all* who die in infancy are amongst those redeemed by the work of Christ is that all such infants are elected by God as a class, rather than individually. Clearly, infants are incapable of responding to an outward call to become Christians (e.g. through preaching) or to common grace. So, if they are

---

[33] Of course, this reasoning could be applied to the case for universalism: if God has the power to save all, and there is no moral impediment to him doing so, why does he not save all humanity? Shedd thinks the reason God does not do so is because sin is necessary for the manifestation of certain divine attributes in the created order, such as divine retribution, that would not otherwise be displayed. And he thinks that the display of these divine attributes in addition to those that would be displayed in creation absent sin brings greater glory to God. See DT: 328 ff. We will return to this matter presently.

[34] Shedd is tapping into a long tradition in North American Reformed thinking, which tends towards an eschatological optimism about the number of the elect. For discussion of this, see Mark Noll, *America's God: From Jonathan Edwards to Abraham Lincoln* (New York: Oxford University Press, 2004). See also Shedd's remarks on eschatology in HCD2, pp. 389-419.

[35] It is interesting that on this issue, Shedd departs from the teaching of the 'elder Calvinists', most of whom taught that only the infants of Christians were amongst the elect. Shedd aligns himself with those amongst the 'later Calvinists' who take the view that all infants who perish before reaching maturity are amongst the elect. See CPM: 112.

elect at all, the manner of their election must be different from human beings who have reached maturity, and are capable of responding to the outward call and common grace:

> The only form of grace that is possible to the dying infant is regenerating grace, and the only call possible is the effectual call. If therefore God manifests any grace at all to the dying infant, it must be special and saving; and if he call him at all, he must call him effectually. (CPM: 64.) [36]

This, says Shedd, is perfectly consistent with a robust doctrine of sin. The original sin possessed by children dying in infancy is atoned for by the work of Christ, just as the sin of any mature fallen human is (CPM: 109). It is only the means by which the benefits of Christ's atoning work are applied to the dying infant that is different.[37]

Yet, curiously, Shedd does not extend this mode of election to those who are mentally handicapped or otherwise psychologically incapable (whom he refers to, rather unhelpfully – but not untypically for a Victorian – as 'idiots and maniacs', CPM: 59.) Those who are in this class of fallen human being are not moral agents, and therefore are neither damnable nor salvable.

Clearly, there are certain sorts of individuals whose mental or psychological limitation is such that they are incapable of making rational decisions. Such individuals are in a parallel condition to children dying in infancy, who, one might think, are not capable of rational thought. So it is difficult to see why Shedd believes on the one hand that children in this condition are salvable as a class, whereas on the other hand those adults who are mentally or psychologically incapable of rational thought are not salvable. Nor is it much of a response to this objection to say that the boundary cases of a child dying in infancy are clearer than those distinguishing individuals who are psychologically incapable in some fashion from those who are 'in their right mind'. It looks to me like both classes of individuals are inherently 'vague' at the boundaries. Is a one year old infant incapable of exercising faith? A two year old? A three year old? Are all children capable of exercising faith at the same age, to the same extent? And so forth. It would be more consistent to think that both these groups of humans are saved as a class, due to the fact that neither group can respond to the outward call or to common grace – Shedd's

---

[36] Shedd thinks the fact the *Westminster Confession* fails to apply a doctrine of preterition to any children dying in infancy is evidence that the Assembly did not intend to discriminate between elect and non-elect children dying in infancy. See CPM: 65.

[37] Naturally, Shedd thinks this doctrine of the salvation of dying infants is perfectly in accord with Scripture. See, for example, 2 Samuel 12: 23; Jonah 4: 11; Matthew 18: 10, 14; Luke 18: 15-16; Acts 2: 38-39; Romans 11: 16; 1 Corinthians 7: 14. It should be pointed out that none of these passages explicitly teach the doctrine, although they might be thought to imply it. See CPM: 126-127.

two conditions for believing that children dying in infancy are regenerated by Christ through the Spirit in some immediate and secret fashion.

But what of those who have never heard of Christ or the gospel, and that are the subjects of the 'scandal of particularity'? Shedd maintains that there may be what, in DT, he calls 'natural preterition' in conjunction with 'individual election' (DT: 337). In other words, there are those who do not hear the gospel or have any knowledge of Christ (natural 'preterition' – having been 'passed over' in this respect) and yet are numbered amongst the elect. For the sake of brevity, I shall refer to this group of humanity as *elect pagans* in what follows ('pagan' carries no pejorative overtones in this connection; it serves merely to demarcate those fallen human beings who are not believers). Shedd finds several divines who support this view, including Augustine and Jerome Zanchius (1516-1590). From Zanchius, Shedd takes the notion that elect pagans have a *habitus* or inward disposition towards the gospel (DT: 338).[38] Says Shedd, 'it is evident that the Holy Spirit by an immediate operation can, if he please, produce such a disposition and frame of mind in a pagan without employing as he commonly does the preaching of the written word.' There is scriptural precedent for this view (e.g. John 9: 36-38; Acts 8: 27-28), although Shedd concedes that 'from the nature of the case, the data are not numerous' (DT: 338). He even goes as far as to say that the universality of the gospel taught to both Abraham and Isaiah, 'makes it probable that the divine Spirit does not invariably and without any exceptions wait for the tardy action of the unfaithful church in preaching the written word, before he exerts his omnipotent grace in regeneration.' (DT: 339.)[39]

But Shedd is careful to note that an elect pagan is not saved through anything other than the regenerating work of the Holy Spirit in applying the benefits of Christ's work to the individual concerned. As with other members of the elect, God chooses to save these elect pagans for no other reason than his own good pleasure. They are not elect on the basis of foreseen merit (DT: 339).

The subtlety of Shedd's position should not be overlooked. We might put it like this: regeneration is necessary to salvation, but, in the case of elect pagans this can be cashed out as a solely dispositional faith in Christ, which is brought

---

[38]Zanchius says, 'it is not indeed improbable, that some individuals in these unenlightened countries [i.e. countries where the gospel has not been preached] may belong to the secret election of grace, and the habit of faith may be wrought in them.' In Zanchius, *Absolute Predestination,* located at <www.straitgate.com/books/zanchius/doctrine.htm>, p. 20, cited in Daniel Strange, *The Possibility of Salvation Among the Unevangelised* (Carlisle: Paternoster, 2002), p. 313. Strange also picks up on a similar discussion that has been had about Jonathan Edwards's notion of an 'infused habit of grace', although this is more controversial. See, e.g., Anri Morimoto, *Jonathan Edwards and The Catholic Vision of Salvation* (Pittsburgh: Penn State University Press, 1995).

[39] Shedd is more cautious in CPM. There he says 'That this work is extensive, and the number of saved unevangelized adults is great, cannot be affirmed. But that all the adult heathen are lost is not the teaching of the Bible or of the Westminster Standards' (p. 61).

about by the internal work of the Holy Spirit:

> This felt need of mercy and desire ... is potentially and virtually faith in the Redeemer. For although the Redeemer has not been presented to him historically and personally as the object of faith, yet the Divine Spirit by the new birth has wrought in him the sincere and longing *disposition* to believe in him. (CPM: 128-129.)

This sounds rather like a doctrine of 'anonymous Christians', popularised in modern theology the Roman Catholic thinker, Karl Rahner, who states:

> If, however, he [i.e. the elect pagan] has experienced the grace of God - if, in certain circumstances, he has already accepted this grace as the ultimate, unfathomable entelechy [realisation of what was previously only potential] of his existence by accepting the immeasurableness of his dying existence as opening out into infinity - then he has already been given revelation in a true sense even before he has been affected by missionary preaching from without.[40]

If Trevor has the dispositional property 'being able to run like a cheetah' but is addicted to the sin of sloth and refuses to exercise in any fashion, especially physically, then this property will remain unrealised. Shedd's use of the language of dispositions or a *habitus*, as he calls it, looks like a disposition to act in a certain way that may not be realised in this life. It is what we might call a condition or state of faith but not faith that is exercised.[41]

Rahner makes a similar distinction between what may be apprehended 'unconsciously' and what may be known 'consciously'. The elect pagan may have the disposition to trust in Christ, though he has no knowledge of Christ. This disposition is brought about by the internal work of the Holy Spirit. Conceivably, such a person might be among the elect, although she does not know that she is among the elect, having no epistemic access to such theological notions. But more importantly, such a person may not be aware of being amongst the elect, or being saved through the work of Christ, though they are. Although Shedd's doctrine states that dispositional faith in Christ is requisite to salvation, it is difficult to see how this is different from claiming that there may be elect pagans for whose salvation the work of Christ is ontologically, but not always epistemically, necessary. On such a view Christ's work would be the means by which such elect pagans are saved, although these individuals would not (indeed, could not, in the nature of the case) know anything concerning Christ's work.

Shedd's views about elect pagans are not unique in the Reformed tradition,

---

[40] Cited in William Hasker, et. al., *Philosophy of Religion, Selected Readings* (New York: Oxford University Press, 1998), p. 511.
[41] This is how Helm speaks of Shedd's position in 'Are There Few That Be Saved?', p. 275.

but they are certainly unusual, and more pronounced than those amongst his peers who were sympathetic to the doctrine of the 'larger hope', like the Princetonian theologian, Benjamin Warfield.[42] His position could be not characterised as outside the bounds of orthodox thinking. But it does place him amongst a small band of Reformed theologians willing to speculate in detail about the possibility of election amongst pagans, and the mode of their salvation. In the parlance adopted by much recent discussion of these issues, Shedd's position is a version of 'inclusivism', rather than 'restrictivism'. That is, his position is consistent with the idea that God 'includes' more people in the scope of salvation, and ensures the salvation of more, than have access to the gospel – at least, as it is proclaimed. The stronger view, often popularly thought to be synonymous with the Calvinistic position, is that God only saves those who hear and respond to the outward call of the Gospel as it is proclaimed, often referred to as *fides ex auditu* (faith come via hearing [the message of salvation]). It is this 'restrictivism' that Shedd dissents from.[43]

Objections to Shedd's Account

Having set out Shedd's position on the extent of the atonement and the 'larger hope', we will consider three objections to his view. These are, (a) whether Shedd's distinction between the extent and application of the atonement makes sense, (b) why Shedd thinks God limits divine election to some (large) number of human beings less than the totality of humanity, and (c) the problem of the necessity of regeneration that the logic of Shedd's position raises.

Let us begin by considering (a) and (c) together. This will lead into some observations concerning (b). It would appear that Shedd's atonement-redemption distinction is perfectly defensible, within the parameters of Reformed orthodoxy. But, problems arise for Shedd's account when we conjoin this with what he says about regeneration apart from the *fides ex auditu* condition of restrictivism. To see this, consider a parallel with the work of one

---

[42] Strange, in *The Possibility of Salvation Amongst the Unevangelised*, confirms this: 'There seems to be no consensus on what represents an 'historic orthodox' evangelical position on the question of the unevangelised.' (p. 21.)

[43] See Strange, Ibid., ch. 1 and Appendix 1. Strange speaks of Shedd's view as a 'soft-restrictivism', by which he means that salvation normally requires a response to the Word preached, but may, in certain extraordinary circumstances, include salvation without a knowledge of Christ, via a dispositional faith (pp. 312-313). The problem with this characterisation of Shedd's position is that it fails to take seriously enough what he says about dispositional faith, which is, I take it, a notion difficult to square with traditional notions of 'restrictivism' where God saves only those who hear and respond to the outward call of the preaching of the gospel. Strange's distinction between Shedd's 'soft-restrictivism' and 'inclusivism' does sound rather like a distinction without a difference.

of Shedd's great heroes, the puritan divine John Owen. On this question of the requirement of faith as a necessary condition for salvation, Owen has this to say:

> That unbelief, is it a sin, or is it not? If it be not, how can it be a cause of damnation? If it be, Christ died for it, or he did not. If he did not, then he died not for the sins of all men. If he did, why is this an obstacle to their salvation? Is there any new shift to be invented for this? Or must we be contented with the old, namely, because they do not believe? That is, Christ did not die for their unbelief, or rather, did not by his death remove their unbelief, because they would not believe, or because they would not themselves remove their unbelief; or he died for their unbelief conditionally, that they were not unbelievers. These do not seem to me to be sober assertions.[44]

This passage is rather compressed, so I shall unpack it a little in order to make its structure clear. First, Owen's reasoning depends on the claim that unbelief is a sin and is a cause of damnation. It is a sin because it involves not giving due honour and regard to God. Presumably, unbelief is not the only cause of damnation. Possession of a corrupt moral nature supplied by original sin would be another cause, in fact the very thing that gives rise to unbelief in the first place.

Secondly, either Christ died for the sinful unbelief of all humanity, or he did not. If, according to Owen, Christ did not die for the sinful unbelief of all humanity, then he did not die for all the sins of all humanity and all are not saved. The reason for this is that if Christ had died for the sinful unbelief of all humanity, he would have atoned for the unbelief of all humanity as one of the sins of all human beings, and all humanity would have been saved. But, says Owen, the evidence of scripture and experience show that not all are saved. So Christ did not atone for the sinful unbelief of all humanity. (Indeed, if Christ does not die to atone for the unbelief of any of humanity – that is, the unbelief of any particular individual human being - then no sinful humans are saved because one sort of sin all sinful humans exhibit, namely unbelief, is not atoned for by Christ.)

Alternatively, if Christ did die for the sinful unbelief of all humanity, then all humanity would be saved because he would have atoned for all the sin of humanity, unbelief included. For suppose Christ dies for the sin of all humanity apart from the sin of unbelief. Then no member of the human race would be saved because one class of sin – the sin of unbelief - would not have been atoned for. But clearly, Christ has atoned for all sin, including the unbelief of those for whom his death procures salvation, if his death really is an act that brings about atonement for human sin. Now, reasons Owen, unbelief would not be an obstacle to salvation if Christ's atonement was made for all humanity.

---

[44] John Owen, *The Death of Death in the Death of Christ* in *The Works of John Owen, Vol. X*, ed. William H. Goold (Edinburgh: Banner of Truth, 1967 [1850-53]), p. 249.

For then, presumably, all would be saved irrespective of their unbelief and whether they continued in their unbelief during this life. But of course, Owen has already said that all are not saved according to Scripture and experience. So it cannot be that Christ died for the sinful unbelief of all humanity, irrespective of whether or not all human beings are aware of this fact.

Owen thinks that this counts against the sort of reasoning mounted by his Arminian opponents.[45] But it might also be applied to Shedd's thinking in the following way. First, Owen's argument makes sense on the basis of Shedd's atonement-redemption distinction. Christ's atonement is sufficient for the salvation of all humanity, but redemption is limited, or particular, as applied to the elect. In this respect Shedd's account is simply a particular construal of the Lombardian notion of the sufficiency-efficiency contrast adopted by many Reformed theologians. This is certainly consistent with Owen's thinking in the passage just cited. In fact, Owen's argument could be thought of (somewhat anachronistically, perhaps) as a clarification of the distinction between atonement and redemption that Shedd offers, construed in a certain way.

We might put it like this. Christ's work is of infinite merit, and therefore has the potential to save all humanity – it is an atoning act of such worth as to be able to bring about the salvation of all human sinners. But, as a matter of fact, God has so ordained matters that Christ's death actually atones only for those who are amongst the elect, which is some number less than the whole of humanity. The crucial clarification offered by Owen concerns the means by which this distinction between atonement and redemption might be sustained. If Christ's work atones for the sin of unbelief, then either all are saved (the sinful unbelief of all humanity is atoned for and all are reconciled to God), or only some are saved (that number whose sinful unbelief Christ's work atones for).

Clearly, Owen and Shedd believed the latter (as, of course, did Edwards, from whom Shedd poached the idea in the first place). Shedd cashes this distinction out without Owen's explanation of why it is that Christ's death atones only for the elect. But there is an important difference between what Owen has to say about the atoning for unbelief and what Shedd says. For, as we have seen, on Shedd's way of thinking regeneration is not necessarily tied to the *fides ex auditu* principle. Some are regenerate without anything more than a *habitus,* or dispositional faith. So, Shedd seems to think that Christ's atoning

---

[45] The problem for Arminianism as Owen sees it is that if unbelief is a sin (as Arminians would suppose), Christ must atone for it. But then, his atonement is effective for all he came to save. There is not metaphysical room, so to speak, for the Arminians to say that Christ's death is potentially but not actually effective, because this equivocates on whether or not Christ has actually died for the sin of unbelief or not. If he has died for unbelief as well as all the other sin of those for whom he came to die, then either all are saved (irrespective of whether they believe or not), or only some are saved – and this is brought about by faith. So faith is a necessary condition for salvation according to Owen, and Christ's work atones only for a limited number of humanity.

work redeems a much greater number than Owen does. And he denies that the *fides ex auditu* principle upheld by Owen is a requirement for salvation. Put simply: Christ's atoning work may redeem me even if I am unaware of who Christ is or what he has done on my behalf, and (adapting Owen's thinking to Shedd's purposes) this means that Christ atones for my unbelief even though I am unaware of that. Shedd, unlike Owen, decouples the atonement for unbelief from the requirement for faith exercised in response to that atoning work. However, it is worth pointing out, on Shedd's behalf, that a person who does not believe in Christ because she is ignorant of the person and work of Christ in some respect is not the same as the person who knowingly and willingly rejects Christ on the basis of some understanding of the gospel that would be sufficient to render such a person culpable for failing to respond to the message of salvation. So, on Shedd's way of thinking, someone can be a *non-believer,* and yet not be an *unbeliever*.

Is this a problem for Shedd? That depends on what one thinks about the necessary and sufficient conditions by which salvation is appropriated by those who are elect. For Shedd, faith that is exercised is simply not a requirement for the salvation of some of humanity. What he does not offer is a complete account of what it would mean for a person to be amongst the elect on the basis of a mere *habitus*.[46] Followers of Owen will undoubtedly be suspicious of such thinking. But the gulf between Shedd and Owen may appear to be greater than it is. Owen and other classical Reformed theologians want to affirm that faith in Christ is itself a gift of God. It is not some work performed by the sinner in response to divine grace that brings about the salvation of the sinner. Were this the case, salvation would not be *sola gratia* (solely by grace), but partially an act of divine grace and partially an act of human response to that grace - what is often called synergism (compare DT: 769). In one sense, of course, faith is a

---

[46] Shedd does have some interesting things to say about the nature of regeneration that would chime with his advocacy of the *habitus* doctrine. For instance, although he admits that the operation of the Holy Spirit upon the human will in regeneration is 'inexplicable' (DT: 767), he goes on to say that 'regeneration is a work of God in the human soul that is below consciousness' Moreover, this fact 'places the infant and the adult upon the same footing and make infant regeneration as possible as that of adults'. Furthermore, 'regeneration is not effected by the use of means, in the strict signification of the term *means'*. Although the context here is the normative means of bringing about regeneration, that is, response to the Word preached, Shedd can say that nothing 'of the nature of means or instruments can come between the Holy Spirit and the soul that is to be made alive.' (DT: 669-770). However, he is clear that the preaching of the Word is the normal means of bringing about regeneration (DT: 780). There is a tension in Shedd's thinking here, because he does say that conversion, and saving faith follows regeneration and 'always presupposes it' (DT: 788), although there may be an interval of time between regeneration and conversion as in the case of infant regeneration and subsequent conversion (DT: 771, n. 27). One wonders how this might be squared with the *habitus* doctrine appealed to elsewhere.

human response to grace according to Owen (and Shedd). But it is generated not by the human agent, but by a secret work of the Holy Spirit. Once this much is clear, Shedd's departure from the *fides ex auditu* tradition seems less pronounced than it might appear at first glance. Both Owen and Shedd claim salvation is entirely a work of divine grace, through faith, which is itself a gift of God. But Shedd thinks that this means the Holy Spirit might work in extraordinary ways amongst those who have not heard the gospel, whereas Owen does not. Nevertheless, for both theologians, the issue is the sovereignty of God in bringing about the salvation of his elect. Shedd simply has a more generous notion of election because he is convinced that the work of Christ cannot save a mere remnant of humanity, but must bring about the salvation of a great host, including some who are what I have been calling 'elect pagans'. The task for someone wanting to defend Shedd's views would be to provide a more comprehensive account of the nature of dispositional faith than Shedd himself offers. In the current intellectual climate, such an offering might make a constructive contribution to the discussion of the so-called 'scandal of particularity' associated with classical Christian theology.[47]

This brings us to the matter of (b), which was to do with why Shedd thinks God elects the majority, but not the totality, of humanity. Shedd's view could be taken in a universalist direction. If one grants that faith that is exercised is not a requirement for salvation, then possibly, atonement and redemption are co-extensive. That is, possibly, Christ's atonement brings about the salvation of all humanity. Shedd would no doubt have strenuously resisted this line of thinking, on the grounds that divine justice must be exercised in preterition and damnation.[48] But this alone is not sufficient to rebut universalism. For if the idea here is that somehow divine retributive justice is inexorable (as, indeed, we have already seen Shedd does maintain), this requirement of divine justice

---

[47] A sketch of one such way: Aratus, cited by the Apostle Paul in Acts 17, might have been referring to God when he (Aratus) thought he was referring to Zeus – which is surely how Paul takes Aratus when he cites the passage about 'in him we live and move and have our being...'. We could take this in a certain way so that Aratus, say, or pagans like him, might have a faith that is dispositional, or if exercised (as with Aratus) is uninformed about the nature and identity of the Deity. Such a pagan might successfully refer to God without knowing it, just as a foreign journalist might unknowingly but successfully refer to the Prime Minister when he speaks of 'that man at the front there with the silly grin'. It is interesting in this connection that Shedd does not in fact make more of the concept of union with Christ that others like Calvin had. Then, like Calvin, Shedd could have allowed for a union with Christ that does not issue in justification and sanctification. These are interesting matters that must be pursued elsewhere. I am grateful to Paul Helm for drawing my attention to them.

[48] 'Hence, in every instance of transgression, the penalty of law *must* be inflicted either personally or vicariously, either upon the transgressor or upon his substitute' (DT: 297, emphasis added). The reader will recall that Shedd maintains divine justice is absolute and may not be laid aside or abrogated (DT: 300).

(if it is a requirement) could be satisfied in the damnation of one individual. Such an individual might be a non-human sinner, such as the devil. Or it might be a human sinner; or the substitute for human sinners, that is, Christ. Such notions, or notions very similar to these, have been mooted in the recent philosophical-theological literature on hell, as well as in earlier twentieth century theology, particularly that associated with Karl Barth. Shedd does not appear to address these issues directly in his dogmatic theology.[49] Yet we might offer a partial defence of Shedd that takes what he does say in a particularistic direction. It might be that part of the way in which divine retribution is distributed in the preterition and damnation of the reprobate has to do with a certain 'fit' in the divine mind between the number of those that are elect and those that are reprobate. In which case, perhaps God ordains that some minority of humanity is reprobate, displaying his divine justice in his work of creation, whilst shewing the redemptive power of the atonement in the redemption of the vast majority of humanity. This seems consistent with what we have seen of Shedd's stated views. But it does raise the following question, not easily answered by Shedd (and other Reformed thinkers who are inclined to the *habitus* doctrine he espouses). Why would God bring about the reprobation of even one more sinner than was strictly necessary for the display of his retributive justice? Surely he would not. Yet if one of Satan, a single human sinner, or Christ, is sufficient to demonstrate or display the inexorable divine justice, why need God reprobate a single sinner more than this? The logic of Shedd's position, independent of his appeals to the particularism of Scripture, is such that we are left wondering whether his optimism with respect to the number of those who will be saved is sanguine enough, all things considered.

---

[49] Although, see my earlier comments about the created order and the *felix cupla* tradition Shedd endorses.

CONCLUSION

An Augustinian Vision of Sin and Salvation

Christian theology is sometimes characterised as 'thinking God's thoughts after him', or, alternatively, as ectypal theology reflecting and original, archetypal theology in the divine mind.[1] There is truth in this. Theology is human reflection upon the deposit of divine revelation. It is concerned with probing this revelation, making senses of it, expounding it, and applying it. As Wolfhart Pannenberg observes, 'whether inside the Christian church or outside it, and even in the so-called natural knowledge of God, no knowledge of God and no theology are conceivable that do not proceed from God and are not due to the working of his Spirit.'[2] But to this should be added the caveat, shared with Pannenberg, amongst others: theology is always provisional in nature. No merely human reflection upon divine revelation can ever hope to achieve complete fidelity to the divine original, or even to circumscribe the whole of what is revealed in Scripture. We do, after all, see in a glass darkly.

In his treatise, *On The Orthodox Faith* (*de fide orthodoxa 3. 24*), the great systematiser of Patristic theology, John of Damascus, makes the point that theology cannot be a science, properly speaking, because it is not possible to say what God is – he is ineffable, and beyond the scope of human understanding. Thomas Aquinas, reflecting on the same issues some centuries after the Damascene, countered that the qualities and relations of an object are the subject matter of any science. Hence it is meaningful to speak of theology as the science of God, where this connotes the study of the qualities and relations of this object. No creature may fathom the depths of the divine essence. But creatures may make sense of what has been revealed to us about God from the relations he has with his creation, and supremely, as revealed in the person and work of God Incarnate. Thus Thomas:

> Although we cannot know in what consists the essence of God, nevertheless in

---

[1] For discussion of archetypal and ectypal theology, see Richard A. Muller, *Post-Reformation Reformed Dogmatics Vol. 3, The Divine Essence and Attributes* (Grand Rapids: Baker Academic, 2003), pp. 159 ff. and Willem van Asselt, 'The Fundamental Meaning of Theology: Archetypal and Ectypal Theology in Seventeenth-Century Reformed Thought' in *Westminster Theological Journal* 64 (2002): 319-335.

[2] Wolfhart Pannenberg, *Systematic Theology, Vol. I,* trans. Geoffrey W. Bromiley (Grand Rapids: Eerdmans, 1991), p. 2.

this science we make use of His effects, either of nature or of grace, in place of a definition, in regard to whatever is treated of in this science concerning God; even as in some philosophical sciences we demonstrate something about a cause from its effect, by taking the effect in place of a definition of the cause.[3]

Shedd was in entire agreement with Thomas over and against the Damascene on this matter, declaring 'there is no science of matter any more than of God, if by science be meant a knowledge that excludes all mystery. The ultimate elements in chemistry are as much beyond complete apprehension as the divine attributes.' (DT: 53.) For Shedd, theology is a positive science, rightly understood. It is an ordered body of knowledge that has to do with its divine object. Today when the word 'science' is invoked, most readers think of the natural sciences as the paradigm case of an ordered body of knowledge. But the sense of 'science' Shedd uses is an older, and traditional theological use of the term. His work represents an attempt to pursue this 'positive' science in a rigorous and careful fashion, with an eye to the chorus of voices that make up the Christian tradition, whilst remaining attentive to the nature and character of divine revelation.

Nevertheless, Shedd's work, like all theology, betrays its provisionality at various points along the way. In this volume we have examined a cluster of central issues in his dogmatics. Some of these have yielded original and unusual conclusions, such as the idea that Christ's human nature needed to be cleansed from the effects of original sin inherited from the Virgin, on account of traducianism. Others have been found to be incomplete – as with his account of Christ's impeccability. Still others help to make sense of long-standing theological distinctions often left out of other works of theology. For instance, Shedd's distinction between realism with respect to the transference of original sin from Adam to his progeny on the one hand, and a representationalist account of Christ's work on the cross, on the other. Some of what he has to say may seem quaint to modern ears. But what is interesting in light of this study is just how much of what Shedd does say on the related matters of sin and salvation remains pertinent to contemporary theological discussion of these doctrines.

However, there is something more that this study points to. In addition to the interesting arguments Shedd mounts for the particular conclusions he holds on a range of different doctrines pertaining to sin and salvation, there is what we might call a 'dogmatic theme' that runs through his remarks on these different topics. This dogmatic theme is not an organising principle as such that, once understood, unlocks all of his work. The quest for such a dogmatic holy grail, which may be found with lamentable frequency in secondary works concerned with the theology of great doctors of the Church, is, it seems to me, an

---

[3] *Summa Theologica* 1. 1. 7.

unhelpful attempt at reducing the fluency and creativity of a theological mind to a single concept. Almost always, it fails to do justice to the whole body of thought concerned by ironing out the intricacies of theological reflection, or making the complexity of a person's thought fit some procrustean bed. The dogmatic theme I have in mind is not like this. Instead, it is rather like the key phrase, or *leitmotif*, of a symphony, which appears, with variations, at different 'moments' in the work, as it unfolds. It is not all there is to the piece of music, which is far more complex than a single musical phrase, but it is a signature that appears, and reappears (with adaptations), picking out something important, to which the hearer's attention is drawn. In Shedd's work, this theme is Augustinian realism.[4] This can be traced through his dogmatic theology, into various *loci*, as has been attempted in this volume. It can be seen in his treatment of traducianism in his anthropology, as well as in his doctrine of sin. But it is also apparent in his Christology, and is reprised, with surprisingly sanguine results, in his soteriology, where he tells his readers that most of humanity will be part of the whole that God redeems – only a remnant will be damned, and that by their own action.

There are other theologians who have been committed to similar theological principles. Indeed, as has already been indicated in this work, there was at least one theological contemporary of Shedd who thought along rather similar lines with respect to Augustinian realism in theology, namely, Augustus Strong.[5] But what is interesting in Shedd's work is the way in which he pursues this theme in a variety of different, and sometimes, unexpected places, with a relentless energy and unfaltering desire to present an internally coherent body of divinity. The fact that he was not entirely successful in this last respect is hardly unexpected. No Christian theologian of any prominence can be said to have left an entirely self-consistent legacy. Such is the provisional nature of theology (to which we might add: and such are the noetic effects of sin upon the human intellect). But what Shedd has left posterity is a body of work that, like other great systems of theology, gives his readers a particular perspective on the gospel.

Shedd's thinking is also interesting as a case study in how Augustinianism can be taken in directions often neglected by textbooks of Christian theology. As we have seen, he thought of his own work as of a piece with the

---

[4] Shedd thought of traducianism as of a piece with his Augustinian realism. But, as I have already indicated, I do not think the two must go together.

[5] There are other American theologians of the same period whose work is important here. Here I am thinking of the likes of Robert Dabney as well as John Williamson Nevin and the Mercersburg School of thought. For an illuminating discussion of these matters, see Mark Horne's on-line essay 'Real Union or Legal Fiction? John Williamson Nevin's Controvery with Charles Hodge Over the Imputation of Adam's Sin (with a Comparison to Robert L. Dabney', which can be found located at: http://www.hornes.org/theologia/content/mark_horne/real_union-or-legal-fiction.htm.

Augustinian tradition, but distinct from the 'later Calvinism' that is often mistakenly identified with Calvinism *per se*. As a sub-group of Augustinianism, Calvinism comprises a hard core of ideas that can be construed in quite different ways. Shedd's work is an example of this when compared with, say, the Princetonian Calvinism of his own day. He saw no tension in holding to both the Westminster Standards and his views about realism, traducianism and the 'larger hope' of the atonement (not to mention his adherence to philosophical idealism in the teeth of Princetonian common-sense realism). And in this respect he was merely following in the footsteps of many other Augustinians whose views do not fit into a neat theological pigeonhole, yet whose work is deeply indebted to the tradition from which they sprang (here I think of theologians as diverse as St. Anselm of Canterbury, John Owen and Huldrych Zwingli).

We might think of the great systems of Christian theology as cathedrals. Each is built with a complexity and detail that can at times seem breathtaking when viewed as a whole. Each has a family resemblance: the architectural style is applied in a unique fashion to each edifice, but is echoed, and reworked in different ways in numerous different instances. Each building has its own majesty and beauty, and each, in its own way, has its failings. In fact, the most ambitious of these constructions, and there are only a handful on such a scale, are often left incomplete, like Antoni Gaudi's Cathedral of the Holy Family in Barcelona, Spain. Shedd's work is, I suggest, a cathedral of doctrine that points to the glory of God. It is a complete work unlike, say, Thomas's *Summa Theologiae*, Edwards's *History of the Work of Redemption*, or Barth's *Church Dogmatics*. But it is also more modest than these other great systems of doctrine. Yet, like these other cathedrals of Christian theology, it is beautiful in its own particular, though flawed, way.

All systematic theologies are there to be enjoyed by the student of divinity. Shedd's *Dogmatics* is no different. But some theological cathedrals, like their stone counterparts, attract more attention than others. Shedd's work has been neglected until now, a largely forgotten work from a bygone age. It is time that this particular dogmatic edifice was given the place of dignity it deserves among other, similar, works of theology that yield new and exciting ways of thinking about the nature and work of the Triune God.

Bibliography

Primary Sources

Shedd, William G. T. *A Critical and Doctrinal Commentary on the Epistle of St. Paul to The Romans.* Eugene, OR: Wipf and Stock, 2001 [1879].
_ *Calvinism, Pure and Mixed.* Edinburgh: Banner of Truth, 1986 [1893].
_ *Discourses and Essays.* Michigan Historical Reprint Series, University of Michigan, MI (n.d.). Andover, MA: Warren F. Draper, 1870 [1856].
_ *Dogmatic Theology, Third Edition,* ed. Alan W. Gomes. Phillipsburg, NJ: Presbyterian & Reformed, 2003 [1888].
_ *A History of Christian Doctrine Vol. 1.* Eugene, OR: Wipf and Stock, 1999 [1864].
_ *A History of Christian Doctrine Vol. 2.* Eugene, OR: Wipf and Stock, 1999 [1864].
_ *Literary Essays.* Eugene, OR: Wipf and Stock, 1999 [1878].
_ *Orthodoxy and Heterodoxy.* Minneapolis, MIN: Klock & Klock, 1981 [1893].
_ *Proposed Revisions of the Westminster Standards.* New York: Schribner and Sons, 1890.
_ *Sermons to The Natural Man.* Edinburgh: Banner of Truth, 1977 [1876].
_ *Theological Essays.* Eugene, OR: Wipf and Stock, 2001 [1877].

Secondary Sources

St. Anselm of Canterbury, *Anselm of Canterbury, The Major Works*, eds. Brian Davies and Gillian Evans. Oxford: Oxford University Press, 1998.
Aquinas, St. Thomas *Summa Theologica* trans. Brothers of the English Dominican Province. New York: Benzinger Bros., 1948.
Armstrong, Brian *Calvinism and the Amyraut Heresy: Protestant Scholasticism and Humanism in Seventeenth Century France.* Madison, WI: University of Wisconsin Press, 1969.
Augustine, St. Aurelius *City of God,* trans. Henry Bettenson. Harmondsworth: Penguin, 1984.
_ *Enchiridion,* trans. Ernest Evans. London: SPCK, 1953.
Baker, Lynne Rudder 'Death and the Afterlife' in William J. Wainwright ed. *The Oxford Handbook of Philosophy of Religion.* Oxford: Oxford University Press, 2005.

Barth, Karl *Church Dogmatics I/2* eds. G. W. Bromiley and T. F. Torrance. Edinburgh: T&T Clark, 1957-1969.
___ *Evangelical Theology: An Introduction*, trans. Grover Foley. London: Fontana, 1965.
Bavinck, Herman *Reformed Dogmatics Vol. 2, God and Creation*, trans. John Vriend, ed. John Bolt. Grand Rapids, MI: Baker Academic, 2004.
___ *Reformed Dogmatics, Vol. 3, Sin and Salvation in Christ*, trans. John Vriend, ed. John Bolt. Grand Rapids, MI: Baker Academic, 2006.
Baxter, Christina 'The Cursed Beloved: A Reconsideration of Penal Substitution' in John Goldingay, ed. *Atonement Today*. London: SPCK, 1995.
eds. Beilby, James and Eddy, Paul *Divine Foreknowledge: Four Views*. Downers Grove, IL: IVP, 2001.
Berkhof, Louis *Systematic Theology*. Edinburgh: Banner of Truth, 1939.
Berkouwer, Gerrit C. *Man: The Image of God*, trans. Dirk W. Jellema. Grand Rapids, MI: Eerdmans, 1962.
Blacketer, Raymond A. 'Definite Atonement in Historical Perspective' in *The Glory of the Atonement*, eds. Charles E. Hill and Frank A. James III. Downers Grove, IL: IVP, 2004.
Blocher, Henri *Original Sin, Illuminating the Riddle*. Leicester: IVP, 1997.
Boettner, Lorraine *The Reformed Doctrine of Predestination*. Philadelphia, PA: Presbyterian and Reformed, 1963.
Boersma, Hans *Violence, Hospitality, and The Cross. Reappropriating The Atonement Tradition*. Grand Rapids, MI: Eerdmans, 2004.
Braine, David *The Human Person: Animal and Spirit*. Notre Dame, IN: University of Notre Dame Press, 1992.
Brümmer, Vincent *Atonement, Christology and The Trinity. Making Sense of Christian Doctrine*. Aldershot: Ashgate, 2005.
Calvin, John *Calvin's Commentaries, Vol. XIX, Commentary on The Epistle to The Romans*, trans. John Owen. Grand Rapids, MI: Baker, 1979 [reprint].
___ *Institutes of The Christian Religion*, ed. John T. McNeill, trans. Ford Lewis Battles. Philadelphia, PA: Westminster Press, 1960.
Campbell, John McLeod *The Nature of the Atonement*, 6th Edition. London: Macmillan, 1895 [1856].
Chisholm, Roderick 'On the Simplicity of the Soul' in James E. Tomberlin, ed., *Philosophical Perspectives 1: Philosophy of Religion, 1991*. Atarscadero, CA: Ridgeview Press, 1991.
___ *Person and Object*. London: Allen and Unwin, 1975.
Cooper, John *Body, Soul and Life Everlasting, Second Edition*. Grand Rapids, MI: Eerdmans, 2000 [1989].
Crisp, Oliver D., *An Essay on Original Sin*. Oxford: Oxford University Press, forthcoming.
___ 'Augustinian Universalism' in *International Journal for Philosophy of Religion* 53 (2003): 127-145.
___ 'Divine Retribution: A Defence' in *Sophia* 42 (2003): 35-52.

_ *Divinity and Humanity: The Incarnation Reconsidered*. Cambridge: Cambridge University Press, 2007.

_ 'Federalism vs. Realism: Charles Hodge, Augustus Strong and William Shedd on The Imputation of Sin' in *International Journal of Systematic Theology* 8 (2006): 1-17.

_ *Jonathan Edwards and The Metaphysics of Sin*. Aldershot: Ashgate, 2005.

_ 'On the theological pedigree of Jonathan Edwards' doctrine of imputation' in *Scottish Journal of Theology* 56 (2003): 308-327.

_ 'Scholastic Theology, Augustinian Realism and Original Guilt' in the *European Journal of Theology* 13 (2004): 17-28.

_ 'Shedding the theanthropic person of Christ' in *Scottish Journal of Theology* 59 (2006): 327-350.

_ 'Sin, atonement and representation: Why William Shedd was not a thorough-going realist' in *Scottish Bulletin of Evangelical Theology* 24.2 (2006): 155-175.

_ 'William Shedd on Christ's Impeccability' forthcoming in Vol. 9 of *Philosophia Christi* (2007).

Cross, Richard *The Metaphysics of the Incarnation*. Oxford: Oxford University Press, 2002.

Cunningham, William *The Reformers and The Theology of The Reformation*. Edinburgh: Banner of Truth, 1967 [1862].

St. Cyril of Alexandria in *De adoratione et culta in spiritu et veritate,* Vol. 68 of *Patrologia Graeca Concursus Completus*. Paris: Migne, 1857-1866.

Day, J. P. 'Temptation' in *American Philosophical Quarterly* 30 (1993): 175-181.

DeWitt, John 'William Greenough Thayer Shedd, D.D., LL.D.', in *Presbyterian and Reformed Review* 5 (1895): 295-322.

Edwards, Jonathan *Original Sin, The Works of Jonathan Edwards, Volume 3,* ed. Clyde A. Holbrook. New Haven, CN: Yale University Press, 1970.

_ *The Works of Jonathan Edwards, Vol. II,* ed. Edward Hickman. Edinburgh: Banner of Truth, 1974 [1834].

Eusebius of Caesarea *Demonstratio Evangelica X. 1, in The Proof of The Gospel,* ed. and trans. W. J. Ferrar, Vol. 2. Eugene, OR: Wipf & Stock, 2001.

Flint, Thomas P. ' "A Death He Freely Accepted": Molinist Reflections on The Incarnation' in *Faith and Philosophy* 18 (2001): 3-20.

_ *Divine Providence, The Molinist Account*. Ithaca, NY: Cornell University Press, 1992.

Foster, John *The Immaterial Self: A Defence of the Cartesian Dualist Conception of The Mind*. London: Routledge, 1991.

Freddoso, Alfred J. 'Human Nature, Potency and The Incarnation', *Faith and Philosophy* 3 (1986): 27-53.

Gomes, Alan W. '*De Jesu Christo Servatore:* Faustus Socinus on the Satisfaction of Christ', *Westminster Theological Journal* 55 (1993): 209-231.

eds. Grecu, Monica M. and Rathbun, John W. *American Literary Critics and Scholars, 1850-1880*. Detroit, MI: Gale, 1988.

eds. Green, Joel B. and Palmer. Stuart L. *In Search of The Soul, Four Views of The Mind-Body Problem.* Downers Grove, IL: IVP, 2005.

Gunton, Colin E. *The Actuality of Atonement.* Grand Rapids, MI: Eerdmans, 1989.

Handy, Robert T. *A History of Union Theological Seminary In New York.* New York: Columbia University Press, 1987.

_ 'Shedd, William Greenough, Thayer' in *American National Biography,* eds. John A. Garraty and Mark C. Carnes. New York: Oxford University Press, 1999.

eds. Hasker, William et. al., *Philosophy of Religion, Selected Readings.* New York: Oxford University Press, 1998.

Hasker, William *God, Time and Knowledge.* Ithaca, NY: Cornell University Press, 1989.

_ *The Emergent Self.* Ithaca, NY: Cornell University Press, 1999.

Helm, Paul 'Are There Few That Be Saved?' in *Universalism and The Doctrine of Hell,* ed. Nigel Cameron. Carlisle: Paternoster, 1992.

_ *The Providence of God.* Leicester: IVP, 1993.

Heppe, Heinrich *Reformed Dogmatics,* trans. G. T. Thomson. London: Collins, 1950.

Hodge, A. A. *The Confession of Faith.* Edinburgh: Banner of Truth, 1958 [1869].

Hodge, Charles *Systematic Theology.* Grand Rapids, MI: Eerdmans, 1968 [reprint].

_ *Systematic Theology, Vol. III.* London: James Clarke, 1960 [reprint].

Hoekema, Anthony *In God's Image.* Grand Rapids, MI: Eerdmans, 1986.

Holmes, Stephen R. 'Can Punishment Bring Peace? Penal Substitution Revisited' in *Scottish Journal of Theology* 58 (2005): 104-123.

_ *Listening to The Past, The Place of Tradition in Theology.* Carlisle: Paternoster Press, 2003.

Horne, Mark 'Real Union or Legal Fiction? John Williamson Nevin's Controversy with Charles Hodge Over the Imputation of Adam's Sin (with a Comparison to Robert L. Dabney' located at: <http://www.hornes.org/theologia/content/mark_horne/real_union-or-legal-fiction.htm>.

Irving, Edward *The Orthodox and Catholic Doctrine of Our Lord's Human Nature.* London: Baldwin and Cradock, 1830.

Jenson, Robert W. *America's Theologian: A Recommendation of Jonathan Edwards.* New York: Oxford University Press, 1988.

_ *Systematic Theology Volume 1, The Triune God.* New York: Oxford University Press, 1997.

ed. Johnson, Rossiter *Notable Americans, A Biographical Dictionary,* Vol. IX. Boston, MA: The Biographical Society, 1904.

Jones, David Albert *The Soul of The Embryo.* London: Continuum, 2004.

Kearney, John 'Jonathan Edwards' Account of Adam's First Sin' in *Scottish Bulletin of Evangelical Theology* 15 (1997): 135-136.

Kripke, Saul in *Naming and Necessity.* Oxford: Blackwell, 1980.

Kuklick, Bruce *Churchmen and Philosophers, From Jonathan Edwards to John*

Dewey. New Haven, CN: Yale University Press, 1985.
___ 'The Place of Charles Hodge in The History of Ideas in America' in John W. Stewart and James H. Moorhead, eds, *Charles Hodge Revisited, A Critical Appraisal of His Life and Work.* Grand Rapids, MI: Eerdmans, 2002.
Kvanvig, Jonathan L. *The Problem of Hell.* New York: Oxford University Press, 1993.
Leftow, Brian 'A Timeless God Incarnate', in Stephen T. Davis, Daniel Kendall and Gerald O'Collins, eds, *The Incarnation.* Oxford: Oxford University Press, 2002.
___ 'Souls Dipped in Dust' in Kevin Corcoran ed., *Soul, Body and Survival.* Ithaca, NY: Cornell University Press, 2001.
Lewis, David 'Do We Believe in Penal Substitution?', *Philosophical Papers* 26 (1997): 203-209.
Locke, John *Essay Concerning Human Understanding,* ed. Peter Nidditch. Oxford: Oxford University Press, 1975.
Lombard, Peter *Sententiarum in IV Libris Distinctae,* ed. Ignatius Brady OFM, 2 Vols. Spicilegium Bonaventurianum 4-5. Grottaferrata: Editions Collegii S. Bonaventurae Ad Claras Aquas, 1971-1981.
Lowe, E. J. *A Survey of Metaphysics.* Oxford: Oxford University Press, 2002.
MacDonald, Gregory *The Evangelical Universalist.* Eugene, OR: Cascade Books, 2006.
Menand, Louis *The Metaphysical Club.* London: Harpercollins, 2002.
Migliore, Daniel *Faith Seeking Understanding, Second Edition.* Grand Rapids: Eerdmans, 2004 [1991].
Minkema, Kenneth P. 'Jonathan Edwards in the Twentieth Century' in *Journal of the Evangelical Theological Society* 47 (2004): 659-687.
Moreland, J. P. and Rae, Scott B. *Body and Soul, Human Nature and The Crisis in Ethics.* Downers Grove, IL: IVP, 2000.
Morimoto, Anri *Jonathan Edwards and The Catholic Vision of Salvation.* Pittsburgh, PA: Penn State University Press, 1995.
Morris, Thomas V. *The Logic of God Incarnate.* Ithaca, NY: Cornell University Press, 1986.
Muller, Richard A. *After Calvin.* Oxford: Oxford University Press, 2003.
___ *Dictionary of Latin and Greek Theological Terms.* Grand Rapids, MI: Baker Books, 1985.
___ *Post-Reformation Reformed Dogmatics, Vol. 1, Prolegomena to Theology, Second Edition.* Grand Rapids, MI: Baker Academic, 2003.
___ *Post-Reformation Reformed Dogmatics Vol. 3, The Divine Essence and Attributes.* Grand Rapids, MI: Baker Academic, 2003.
Murray, John *The Imputation of Adam's Sin.* Grand Rapids, MI: Eerdmans, 1959.
Noll, Mark *America's God: From Jonathan Edwards to Abraham Lincoln.* New York: Oxford University Press, 2004.
Odo of Tournai, *On Original Sin and A Disputation With The Jew, Leo, Concerning The Advent of Christ, The Son of God, Two Theological Treatises,*

trans. Irven M. Resnick. Philadelphia, PA: University of Pennsylvania Press, 1994.
Owen, John *The Works of John Owen, Vol. X*, ed. William H. Goold. Edinburgh: Banner of Truth, 1967 [1850-1853].
eds. Parry, Robin and Partridge, Chris *Universal Salvation? The Current Debate*. Carlisle: Paternoster, 2003.
Packer, James I. 'What Did The Cross Achieve? The Logic of Penal Substitution' *Tyndale Bulletin* 25 (1974): 3-46.
Pannenberg, Wolfhart *Jesus – God and Man, Second Edition*, trans. Lewis L. Wilkins and Duane A. Priebe. Philadelphia, PA: Westminster Press, 1968.
_ *Systematic Theology, Vol. I*, trans. Geoffrey W. Bromiley. Grand Rapids, MI: Eerdmans, 1991.
ed. Park, Edwards Amasa *The Atonement*. Boston, MA: Congregational Board of Publication, 1859.
Plantinga, Alvin 'On Heresy, Mind, and Truth' *Faith and Philosophy* 16 (1999): 182-193.
_ 'Supralapsarianism, Or 'O Felix Culpa'' in *Christian Faith and the Problem of Evil*, ed. Peter van Inwagen. Grand Rapids, MI: Eerdmans, 2004.
_ *The Nature of Necessity*. Oxford: Oxford University Press, 1974.
Porter, Steven L. 'Rethinking The Logic of Penal Substitution' in *Philosophy of Religion, A Reader and Guide*, ed. William Lane Craig. Edinburgh: Edinburgh University Press, 2002.
Prentiss, George L. *The Union Theological Seminary, in The City of New York; Historical and Biographical Sketches of its First Fifty Years.* (n.p.) 1899.
Prestige, G. L. *God in Patristic Thought*. London: SPCK, 1952.
Quinn, Philip L. 'Tiny Selves: Chisholm on the Simplicity of the Soul' in Lewis Hahn, ed., *The Philosophy of Roderick Chisholm*. LaSalle, IL: Open Court, 1997.
Rohls, Jan *Reformed Confessions, Theology from Zurich to Barmen*, trans. John Hoffmeyer. Louisville, KT: Westminster John Knox Press, 1998.
Spence, Alan 'Christ's Humanity and Ours: John Owen' in Christoph Schwöbel and Colin Gunton, eds., *Persons, Divine and Human: King's College Essays in Theological Anthropology*. Edinburgh: T&T Clark, 1991.
eds. Stewart John W. and Moorhead, James H. *Charles Hodge Revisited: A Critical Appraisal of His Life and Work*. Grand Rapids, MI: Eerdmans, 2002.
Strange, Daniel *The Possibility of Salvation Amongst the Unevangelised, An Analysis of Inclusivism in Recent Evangelical Theology*. Carlisle: Paternoster, 2002.
Strong, Augustus *Systematic Theology, Vol. II*. Philadelphia, PA: The Griffith and Rowland Press, 1907.
Strout, Cushing 'Faith and History: The Mind of William G. T. Shedd' in *Journal of the History of Ideas 15* (1954): 153-162.
Stump, Eleonore 'Non-Cartesian Substance Dualism and Materialism without Reductionism' in *Faith and Philosophy* 12 (1995): 505-531.

Sturch, Richard *The Word and The Christ, An Essay in Analytic Christology*. Oxford: Oxford University Press, 1991.
eds. Sweeney, Douglas A. and Guelzo, Alan C. *The New England Theology, From Jonathan Edwards to Edwards Amasa Park*. Grand Rapids, MI: Baker Academic, 2006.
Swinburne, Richard 'Personal Identity: The Dualist Theory' in Michael J. Loux, ed., *Metaphysics: Contemporary Readings*. London: Routledge, 2001.
_ *Responsibility and Atonement*. Oxford: Oxford University Press, 1989.
_ *The Christian God*. Oxford: Oxford University Press, 1994.
_ *The Evolution of the Soul*. Oxford: Oxford University Press, 1986.
Talbot, Thomas *"The Doctrine of Everlasting Punishment"* in, *Faith and Philosophy* 7 (1) 1990: 19-40.
Taliaferro, Charles *Consciousness and The Mind of God*. Cambridge: Cambridge University Press, 1994.
Tertullian, *On The Soul*, § 25 in *Latin Christianity: Its Founder, Tertullian, Ante-Nicene Fathers Vol. III*, trans. P. Holmes, eds. A. Roberts and J. Donaldson. Grand Rapids, MI: Eerdmans, 1981 [1885].
Thomas, G. Michael *The Extent of the Atonement, A Dilemma for Reformed Theology from Calvin to the Consensus*. Carlisle: Paternoster, 1997.
Turretin, Francis *Institutes of Elenctic Theology Vol I*, trans. George Musgrave Giger, ed. James T. Dennison, Jr. Phillipsburg, NJ: Presbyterian and Reformed, 1992.
Van Asselt, Willem 'The Fundamental Meaning of Theology: Archetypal and Ectypal Theology in Seventeenth-Century Reformed Thought' in *Westminster Theological Journal* 64 (2002): 319-335.
Van Inwagen, Peter *Material Beings*. Ithaca, NY: Cornell University Press, 1990.
Walls, Jerry L. *Hell: The Logic of Damnation*. Notre Dame, IN: University of Notre Dame Press, 1994.
Warfield, Benjamin *The Plan of Salvation*. Grand Rapids, MI: Eerdmans, 1975.
Weber, Otto *Foundations of Dogmatics Vol. 2*, trans. Darrell L. Guder. Grand Rapids: Eerdmans, 1983.
Weinandy, Thomas *Does God Suffer?* Edinburgh: T &T Clark, 2000.
Werther, David 'The Temptation of God Incarnate' in *Religious Studies* 29 (1993): 47-50.
Whaling, Thornton 'Review of Shedd's Dogmatic Theology' in *Presbyterian Quarterly* 9 (1895): 323-326.
Wiley, Tatha *Original Sin, Origins, Developments, Contemporary Meanings*. New York: Paulist Press, 2002.
Wolterstorff, Nicholas 'Divine Simplicity' in James E. Tomberlin ed., *Philosophical Perspectives 5: Philosophy of Religion*. Atascadero, CA: Ridgeview Press, 1991.
Zagzebski, Linda Trinkhaus *The Dilemma of Freedom and Foreknowledge*. Oxford: Oxford University Press, 1991.
Zimmerman, Dean 'Material People' in *The Oxford Handbook of Metaphysics*,

eds. Michael J. Loux and Dean Zimmerman. Oxford: Oxford University Press, 2003.

Unpublished Sources

Herzer, Mark A. 'The Influence of Romantic Idealism in the Writings of William Greenough Thayer Shedd', PhD Thesis, Westminster Theological Seminary, 2003.
Schrum, Ethan, 'Evolutionary Metaphysics, Presuppositional Methodology and "Old Calvinist" Theology: The Unusual Blend of William G. T. Shedd's Philosophy of History in the Intellectual Tempests of Nineteenth-Century America' unpublished research paper.
Williams, Garry 'A Critical Exposition of Hugo Grotius' Doctrine of the Atonement in *De Satisfactione Christi*.' DPhil Thesis, University of Oxford, 1999.
_ 'God, The Individual, and Systematic Solipsism: Contemporary Anglo-American Criticism of Penal Substitution' (forthcoming).

Index

Acceptation 115 n. 1, 121-122, 128
Adam 8, 15, 16-18, 24, 33-35, 37, 42, 46, 67, 71-72, 76, 83, 84, 92, 100, 103, 108-109
   Fall of 17, 34 n. 51, 38, 39, 46, 49, 73, 96 n. 41, 145, 148
   Imputed sin of 9, 33, 50, 54, 98, 111
   Progeny of 17, 35, 43, 47, 69, 71, 98, 107
   Two Adams 9, 99-100, 103
   Sin of 14, 44, 45, 51, 77, 90, 105, 111
Adoptionism 65
Angels 82 n. 17
Anhypostasia-enhypostasia distinction (see also Jesus Christ and two natures doctrine) 57-58, 64, 79 n. 12
St. Anselm of Canterbury 28 n. 39, 71, 113, 122, 126, 129, 135, 169
Apollinarianism 59
Aquinas, St. Thomas 11, 12 n. 3, 20 n. 19, 92, 166-167, 169
Arminianism 143, 144, 162
Armstrong, Brian 144 n. 13
Atonement 98-114, 116-137, 138-164
   as expiation 108-109, 122-123
   Extent of 9, 138-164
   as fundamentally objective 117, 125-126
   Nature of 9, 116-137
   Personal or vicarious 120
   Unlimited in nature, limited in application 138, 140-142
St. Augustine, Aurelius 6, 11, 13, 21, 42, 43 n. 15, 46, 158
Augustinian realism 7, 9, 14, 17, 32, 34, 35-36, 37-55, 56, 66-74, 98, 100, 102-103, 108, 112, 149, 168
   Common human nature version of 43-44, 47-48
   Consistent realism 111-114
   Unindividualized whole of humanity version of 47-48, 49, 72

Aulen, Gustav 132 n. 29
Barth, Karl 5, 11, 69, 165, 169
Bavinck, Herman 13 n. 6, 140 n. 4
Baxter, Christina 127 n. 18
Beilby, James 143 n. 12
Berkhof, Louis 40 n. 8, 43 n. 18, 99-100
Bernard of Clairvaux 132
Blacketer, Raymond A. 138 n. 2
Blocher, Henri 49
Boettner, Lorraine 147 n. 17
Boersma, Hans 127 n. 18
Boticelli 50
Braine, David 26 n. 33
Brümmer, Vincent 9, 116, 127-137
Calvin, John 11, 49-50, 116, 164 n. 47
Calvinism 6, 37, 56 n. 1, 144, 149-150, 151
   'Elder' Calvinism 105, 143, 147, 156 n. 35
   'Later' Calvinism 1, 105, 156 n. 35, 169
Campbell, John McLeod 103
Causal and moral responsibility 153-154
Chalcedon, Council of 57, 58, 60, 62
Charnock, Stephen 153
Christ, Jesus 52-53, 61, 63, 71, 98, 111
   Birth of 63
   Divine nature of 65, 81
   Human nature of 7, 21, 57, 59, 62, 64, 72, 75, 79, 82, 87, 90, 94, 123
      As a natural endowment of a human person 60, 91
      Human body as a 'nature' 57, 61
      Human soul as a 'nature' 57, 61
      Ignorance of 89 n. 30
      Peccability of 75, 76, 81, 87-95
      Proleptic justification of 67-70
      as a property 59, 70
      Personalized human nature of 58, 79 n. 12
      Sanctification of 67-69
   Impeccability of 8, 75-97, 167

Immutability of 77
Omnipotence of 77, 78, 82
Omniscience of 77
Righteousness of 104
Sinlessness of 57 n. 2, 66-67, 75-97
Suffering of 122-125
Temptations of 75-76, 80-86, 95-97
Theanthropic person 7, 55, 56-74, 77, 81, 87, 123, 136
Christology 16, 56, 63, 64
  Alexandrian 59 n. 8, 70, 71 n. 30
  Antiochene 60 n. 12, 67, 71
  Dyothelite 60, 80 n. 14, 87-88
  Kenotic 59 n. 10
  'parts' Christology 57-62, 63, 65, 70, 112
Chisholm, Roderick 20 n. 19, 26 n. 34, 29 n. 40, 30 n. 43 and 45, 32
Coleridge, Samuel Taylor 2, 6
Communication of attributes (see also Christology) 65, 79, 80 n. 13
Concrete particulars 25, 70, 87, 96
Constantinople, Council of 57, 59, 61
Creationism 12, 14, 16, 17, 27, 33, 34, 35
  Creationist-representationalism 17
Creel, Richard 124-125 n. 17
Crisp, Claire xiii
Crisp, Oliver D. 22 n. 26, 24 n. 30, 40 n. 7 and 10, 55 n. 36 and 37, 59 n. 11, 113 n. 23 and 24, 114 n. 25, 142 n. 10, 150 n. 21, 153 n. 26
Crisp, Tobias 102 n. 7
Cross, Richard 58 n. 4, 87 n. 26, 121
Cunningham, William 40, 41 n. 12, 151 n. 22
St. Cyril of Alexandria 102 n. 7
Dabney, Robert L. 1 n. 1, 168 n. 5
Damnation 147-148, 151, 161, 164, 168
Day, J. P. 95 n. 38, 96 n. 39
D'Costa, Gavin xiii
Deception 77-78
De Moor-Marck 105 n. 13
Descartes 30
DeWitt, John 4 n. 5
Divine concurrence 151-153
Divine nature 119 n. 9, 124-125, 135, 137, 148, 166
  Absolute and ordained power 118 n. 8, 119, 131-132
  Forgiveness of 127, 130-131
  Goodness of 132
  Immutability of 77
  Impassibility of 124-125
  Infinity of 88
  Justice of 117-119, 120-121, 126, 128, 131, 144 n. 15, 149, 164
  Mercy of 117-118, 126, 144
  Omniscience of (see also Jesus Christ) 77
  Self-glorification of 150
  Simplicity of 63-64, 119 n. 9, 125
  Timelessness of 63
  Will of 117, 135
Eddy, Paul 143 n. 12
Edwards, Jonathan 1, n. 1, 10, 13, 74 n. 31, 77 n. 8, 106 n. 14, 113, 141-142, 158 n. 38, 162, 169
Elect, The 100-101, 107, 112, 136, 140, 142, 145, 148, 154, 165
  Elect infants 156-157
  Elect pagans 158-159, 164
Ens successiva argument 30 n. 45, 32
Essences (see also human nature) 23-24, 25 n. 32, 44 n. 19, 48, 70-71, 77 n. 5
Eusebius of Caesarea 102 n. 7
Eve 78
Extra-terrestrial life forms 21 n. 21
Federalism 49-54
Fides ex auditu principle 160, 162-163
Flint, Thomas P. 87, 91-92 n. 32, 143 n. 12
Forensic fiction (see also atonement, penal substitution) 98, 102 n. 6, 105
Foster, John 25 n. 33
Freddoso, Alfred J. 92 n. 33 and 34
Gale, Theophilus 153 n. 27
Gametes 16, 22
Garden of Eden 50
Garden of Gethsemane 95
Gaudi, Antoni 169
Geach, Peter 121 n. 11
Gibson, James xiii
Gomes, Alan W. xiii, 1 n. 1, 2 n. 2, 11, 57, 61-62, 96 n. 41, 115 n. 1, 118 n. 6
Grecu, Monica 1 n. 1, 2 n. 2
Green Joel B. 59 n. 7

Index 181

Grotius, Hugo 121
Gunton, Colin E. 11, 78 n. 9, 120 n. 10
Habitus 158-159, 163, 165
Handy, Robert 2 n. 2
Hasker, William 20 n. 19, 26, n. 33, 143 n. 12, 159 n. 40
Hawley, Katherine 35 n. 53
Heller, Mark 35 n. 53
Helm, Paul xiii, 138 n. 3, 143 n. 12, 152, 153 n. 27, 159 n. 41, 164 n. 47
Heppe, Heinrich 13 n. 6, 39 n. 6, 134 n. 32, 141 n. 5, 148 n. 19
Herzer, Mark xiii, 6 n. 10
Hill, Charles E. 127 n. 18
Hill, Daniel xiii
Hodge, Archibald Alexander 151 n. 22, 153 n. 29
Hodge, Charles 6 n. 10, 7, 22, 37-55, 56, 138 n. 3
Hoekema, Anthony 48 n. 24
Holmes, Stephen R. xiii, 5 n. 7, 127 n. 18
Holy Spirit 18, 66, 67-68, 70, 72, 73, 79 n. 9 and 12, 100 n. 4, 142 n. 8, 143, 145, 146, 155, 156, 158, 163-164
Hooker, Richard 64
Horne, Mark 168 n. 5
Human nature 15, 22, 24, 44, 46, 67, 70, 87, 91
  Body and soul 22-23, 59 n. 7
  Common human nature 18
  Individual nature 15
  Materialism about 23, 27, 58 n. 7
  Property of 23-24
  Species nature 15-16 n. 11, 19, 24-25, 34 n. 51
  Substance 22, 28, 62, 67, 70
  Suppositum 87, 90, 94
Hypostatic union (see also Jesus Christ and two natures doctrine) 56-57, 61, 62, 6-66, 78-80, 87, 89-91, 93-94, 123
Identity 35
Incarnation 30 n. 42, 58, 60 n. 14, 62, 63-65, 67, 69, 72, 73, 78, 93, 123, 127
Infralapsarianism 147, 148
Irving, Edward 69
James III, Frank A. 127 n. 18
Jenson, Robert W. 10, 80 n. 14
St. John of Damascus 11, 166, 167

Kearney, John 39 n. 5
Kripke, Saul 51 n. 30
Kuklick, Bruce 2 n. 3, 6 n. 10
Kvanvig, Jonathan L. 142 n. 9, 155 n. 32
'Larger hope', The 138, 146-165, 169
Leftow, Brian 60, 64 n. 22, 87 n. 26, 112 n. 21
Lewis, David 128-129, 137
Locke, John 31 n. 46
Lombard, Peter 9, 140 n. 4, 141 n. 5, 162
Lowe E. J. 71 n. 30
Luther, Martin 11
Lutheran Orthodox 66
MacDonald, Gregory 155 n. 32
Marsh, James 2 n. 3, 6 n. 9
Mary *Theotokos* 7, 66-69, 72-73, 79, 167
Magician, The 3
McGinn, Colin 154 n. 301
Menand, Louis 2 n. 3
Mereological essentialism 29, 30 n. 43
Migliore, Daniel L. 59 n. 8
Minkema, Kenneth P. 11 n. 16
Moreland, J. P. 19 n. 15, 22, n. 25, 27 n. 36
Morimoto, Anri 158 n. 38
Morris, Thomas V. 25, 70 n. 29, 75, 88-91, 93, 94, 97
Muller, Richard 38 n. 2, 144 n. 13, 148 n. 19, 166 n. 1
Murray, John 41 n. 12, 42 n. 15, 52-53
Mystery 154
Nestorianism 60, 63 n. 19, 65
Nevin, John Williamson 168 n. 5
Niebuhr, Reinhold 54 n. 34
Noll, Mark xiii, 156 n. 33
Nominalism 71 n. 30
Occam, William 92
Odo of Tournai 6, 19-22
Original sin (see also sin) 17, 33, 45, 72, 161
  Imputation of 37-55, 100, 167
  Original corruption 38, 39, 50 n. 28
  Original guilt 17, 33, 39-40, 52-53, 69, 108
Owen, John 13, 78 n. 9, 102-103, 105, 118, 119, 121, 131, 141 n. 5, 160-164, 169
Pelagius 100 n. 2

Packer, James I. 102 n. 6, 116 n. 2, 127 n. 18
Pactum salutis 133-135
Palmer, Stuart L. 59 n. 7
Pannenberg, Wolfhart 80 n. 14, 166
Park, Edwards Amasa 3
Parry, Robin xiii, 155 n. 32
Partridge, Chris 155 n.32
Penal substitution (see also atonement) 9, 98-99, 103, 108-110, 115, 116, 120-122, 127-137
  Pecuniary and non-pecuniary 129
Perichoresis 79 n. 10, 133
Personal identity 30-31, 33, 36
Plantinga, Alvin 25 n. 32, 59 n. 9, 150 n. 21
Porter, Steven L. 127 n. 18
Possible worlds 91, 93, 94
Prentiss, George L. 2 n. 2
Prestige, Leonard 124 n. 16
Preterition 147-149, 155, 158, 164
Rae, Scott B. 19 n. 15, 22 n. 25, 27 n. 36
Rahner, Karl 159
Rea, Michael C. xiii, 68 n. 26
Reformed theology 8, 13, 37, 51 n. 31, 106, 147
  Reformed Orthodoxy 38 n. 2, 39-40, 49-50, 54, 65, 67, 134, 146, 156
  Reformed Scholasticism 38 n. 2, 54
Representationalism (see also Adam) 13, 17, 32, 37 n. 1, 41, 50-51, 98, 102 n. 5, 105, 106, 111
  and atonement 99, 102, 104-107, 167
  and imputed sin 99, 105, 115
  Representationalist fallacy 110
Reprobate 146, 148, 149, 154, 165
Restrictivism 160
Rohls, Jan 39 n. 5
Salmurian theology 144-146
Salvation 10, 69, 100, 130, 146, 159, 166
Scandal of particularity, The 149, 164
Schleiermacher, Friedrich D. 142 n. 10, 155
Schoonenberg, Piet 54 n. 34
Schrum, Ethan xiii, 2 n. 3
Scotus, John Duns 92, 121-122
Shedd, William G. T. 101, 102
  Biographical sketch of 1-4
  Calvinism: Pure and Mixed 138, 146-157
  Dogmatic Theology 3, 4, 11, 13, 16, 56, 57, 62, 63, 75, 103, 124, 138, 139-146, 169
  Herculean physique of 250
  Problems with interpretation of 4-7
Sider, Theodore 35 n. 53
Sin 10, 36, 38 n. 4, 39, 41, 44, 47, 67, 78, 89, 98, 117, 123 n. 14, 157, 166
  Transmission of 16, 36, 37-55, 47, 69, 108
Soul (see also traducianism) 7, 12, 16-20, 22-24, 30-31, 34, 58 n. 7, 72, 104
  Cartesian 26, 30-31, 32-33
  Hylomorphism 19, 26, 32-33
  Immaterial substance 18, 23, 124
  Incorruptible 27-28
  Origin of 14, 16, 35
  Parturience of 26, 32
  Pre-existence of 12 n. 2
  Propagation of 18, 19, 24
  Simplicity of 26, 27, 32, 35
  Soul-Fission 17, 18, 21, 25, 26, 29, 30-31
  Transmission of 22
Spence, Alan 78 n. 9
Strange, Daniel 158 n. 38, 160 n. 42
Strout, Cushing 2 n. 3
Sturch, Richard 83-84 n. 21
Superman 84
Supralapsarianism 147
Susbtance dualism (see also soul and human nature) 23, 26, 30, 32, 62, 70
Strong, Augustus 7, 37-55, 56, 168
Stump Eleonore 20, n. 19
Swinburne, Richard 25 n. 33, 27, 30, n. 44, 31 n. 46, 40, 86, 94 n. 36, 115 n. 1, 127 n. 18, 136
Talbot, Thomas 155 n. 32
Taliaferro, Charles 26 n. 33
Temporal parts, doctrine of 34 n. 51, 35, 114 n. 25
Tertullian 18 n. 13, 21
Thomas, G. Michael 144 n. 13
Tibbles the cat 114 n. 25
Toplady, Augustus 138 n. 3
Traducianism 7, 8, 12, 14, 16-22, 24-25,

27, 30, 32, 35, 46, 55, 56, 66-73, 111, 112 n. 19, 167-168
Traducian-realism (see also Augustinian realism) 14, 16, 17, 25
Transitivity relation 112 n. 20
Trinity, The 65 n. 25, 78, 91, 92, 93, 133-134, 169
and union of will or wills 133-134
Turretin, Francis 13, 14, 16, 28, n. 38, 50-51, 105, 110
Twisse, William 119, 131
Two-natures doctrine 57, 65, 80
'Two unions' (see also representationalism, Augustinian realism) 106-111
Universalism 140, 142-143, 144, 146, 149, 164, 165
Universals 70-71
Van Asselt, Willem 166 n. 1
Van Inwagen, Peter 58 n. 7, 154 n. 30
Virgin birth 65, 72
Voluntarism 34
Walls, Jerry L. 155 n. 32
Warfield, Benjamin 3, 138 n. 3, 144-145, 160
Westminster Confession of Faith 147, 149-150, 156, 157 n. 36
Westminster Shorter Catechism 38 n. 4
Weber, Otto 59 n. 8
Webster, John xiii
Weinandy, Thomas 124 n. 15
Werther, David 93 n. 35
Whaling, Thornton 1 n. 1
Wiley, Tatha 38 n. 3, 54 n. 34
Williams, Garry xiii, 102 n. 7, 121 n. 12
Wisse, Maartin xiii
Witsius, Hermannus 105 n. 13
Woods, Leonard 3
Wolterstorff, Nicholas 23 n. 29
Word, The 58-67, 70, 72, 78, 79, 87, 89-91
Wyn, Mark xiii
Zanchius, Jerome 158
Zagzebski, Linda Trinkhaus 143 n. 12
Zimmerman, Dean 30-31 n. 45, 32 n. 47
Zwingli, Huldrych 169

Paternoster Biblical Monographs

(All titles uniform with this volume)
Dates in bold are of projected publication

Joseph Abraham
Eve: Accused or Acquitted?
A Reconsideration of Feminist Readings of the Creation Narrative Texts in Genesis 1–3

Two contrary views dominate contemporary feminist biblical scholarship. One finds in the Bible an unequivocal equality between the sexes from the very creation of humanity, whilst the other sees the biblical text as irredeemably patriarchal and androcentric. Dr Abraham enters into dialogue with both camps as well as introducing his own method of approach. An invaluable tool for any one who is interested in this contemporary debate.

2002 / 0-85364-971-5 / xxiv + 272pp

Octavian D. Baban
Mimesis and Luke's on the Road Encounters in Luke-Acts
Luke's Theology of the Way and its Literary Representation

The book argues on theological and literary (mimetic) grounds that Luke's on-the-road encounters, especially those belonging to the post-Easter period, are part of his complex theology of the Way. Jesus' teaching and that of the apostles is presented by Luke as a challenging answer to the Hellenistic reader's thirst for adventure, good literature, and existential paradigms.

2005 */ 1-84227-253-5 / approx. 374pp*

Paul Barker
The Triumph of Grace in Deuteronomy

This book is a textual and theological analysis of the interaction between the sin and faithlessness of Israel and the grace of Yahweh in response, looking especially at Deuteronomy chapters 1–3, 8–10 and 29–30. The author argues that the grace of Yahweh is determinative for the ongoing relationship between Yahweh and Israel and that Deuteronomy anticipates and fully expects Israel to be faithless.

2004 / 1-84227-226-8 / xxii + 270pp

Jonathan F. Bayes
The Weakness of the Law
God's Law and the Christian in New Testament Perspective

A study of the four New Testament books which refer to the law as weak (Acts, Romans, Galatians, Hebrews) leads to a defence of the third use in the Reformed debate about the law in the life of the believer.

2000 / 0-85364-957-X / xii + 244pp

Paternoster Theological Monographs

(All titles uniform with this volume)
Dates in bold are of projected publication

Emil Bartos
Deification in Eastern Orthodox Theology
An Evaluation and Critique of the Theology of Dumitru Staniloae
Bartos studies a fundamental yet neglected aspect of Orthodox theology: deification. By examining the doctrines of anthropology, christology, soteriology and ecclesiology as they relate to deification, he provides an important contribution to contemporary dialogue between Eastern and Western theologians.

1999 / 0-85364-956-1 / xii + 370pp

Graham Buxton
The Trinity, Creation and Pastoral Ministry
Imaging the Perichoretic God
In this book the author proposes a three-way conversation between theology, science and pastoral ministry. His approach draws on a Trinitarian understanding of God as a relational being of love, whose life 'spills over' into all created reality, human and non-human. By locating human meaning and purpose within God's 'creation-community' this book offers the possibility of a transforming engagement between those in pastoral ministry and the scientific community.

2005 */ 1-84227-369-8 / approx. 380 pp*

Iain D. Campbell
Fixing the Indemnity
The Life and Work of George Adam Smith
When Old Testament scholar George Adam Smith (1856–1942) delivered the Lyman Beecher lectures at Yale University in 1899, he confidently declared that 'modern criticism has won its war against traditional theories. It only remains to fix the amount of the indemnity.' In this biography, Iain D. Campbell assesses Smith's critical approach to the Old Testament and evaluates its consequences, showing that Smith's life and work still raises questions about the relationship between biblical scholarship and evangelical faith.

2004 / 1-84227-228-4 / xx + 256pp

Tim Chester
Mission and the Coming of God
Eschatology, the Trinity and Mission in the Theology of Jürgen Moltmann
This book explores the theology and missiology of the influential contemporary theologian, Jürgen Moltmann. It highlights the important contribution Moltmann has made while offering a critique of his thought from an evangelical perspective. In so doing, it touches on pertinent issues for evangelical missiology. The conclusion takes Calvin as a starting point, proposing 'an eschatology of the cross' which offers a critique of the over-realised eschatologies in liberation theology and certain forms of evangelicalism.
2006 / 1-84227-320-5 / approx. 224pp

Sylvia Wilkey Collinson
Making Disciples
The Significance of Jesus' Educational Strategy for Today's Church
This study examines the biblical practice of discipling, formulates a definition, and makes comparisons with modern models of education. A recommendation is made for greater attention to its practice today.
2004 / 1-84227-116-4 / xiv + 278pp

Darrell Cosden
A Theology of Work
Work and the New Creation
Through dialogue with Moltmann, Pope John Paul II and others, this book develops a genitive 'theology of work', presenting a theological definition of work and a model for a theological ethics of work that shows work's nature, value and meaning now and eschatologically. Work is shown to be a transformative activity consisting of three dynamically inter-related dimensions: the instrumental, relational and ontological.
2005 / 1-84227-332-9 / xvi + 208pp

Stephen M. Dunning
The Crisis and the Quest
A Kierkegaardian Reading of Charles Williams
Employing Kierkegaardian categories and analysis, this study investigates both the central crisis in Charles Williams's authorship between hermetism and Christianity (Kierkegaard's Religions A and B), and the quest to resolve this crisis, a quest that ultimately presses the bounds of orthodoxy.
2000 / 0-85364-985-5 / xxiv + 254pp

Keith Ferdinando
The Triumph of Christ in African Perspective
A Study of Demonology and Redemption in the African Context
The book explores the implications of the gospel for traditional African fears of occult aggression. It analyses such traditional approaches to suffering and biblical responses to fears of demonic evil, concluding with an evaluation of African beliefs from the perspective of the gospel.
1999 / 0-85364-830-1 / xviii + 450pp

Andrew Goddard
Living the Word, Resisting the World
The Life and Thought of Jacques Ellul
This work offers a definitive study of both the life and thought of the French Reformed thinker Jacques Ellul (1912-1994). It will prove an indispensable resource for those interested in this influential theologian and sociologist and for Christian ethics and political thought generally.
2002 / 1-84227-053-2 / xxiv + 378pp

David Hilborn
The Words of our Lips
Language-Use in Free Church Worship
Studies of liturgical language have tended to focus on the written canons of Roman Catholic and Anglican communities. By contrast, David Hilborn analyses the more extemporary approach of English Nonconformity. Drawing on recent developments in linguistic pragmatics, he explores similarities and differences between 'fixed' and 'free' worship, and argues for the interdependence of each.
2006 / 0-85364-977-4 / approx. 350pp

Roger Hitching
The Church and Deaf People
A Study of Identity, Communication and Relationships with Special Reference to the Ecclesiology of Jürgen Moltmann
In *The Church and Deaf People* Roger Hitching sensitively examines the history and present experience of deaf people and finds similarities between aspects of sign language and Moltmann's theological method that 'open up' new ways of understanding theological concepts.
2003 / 1-84227-222-5 / xxii + 236pp

John G. Kelly
One God, One People
The Differentiated Unity of the People of God in the Theology of Jürgen Moltmann

The author expounds and critiques Moltmann's doctrine of God and highlights the systematic connections between it and Moltmann's influential discussion of Israel. He then proposes a fresh approach to Jewish–Christian relations building on Moltmann's work using insights from Habermas and Rawls.

2005 / 0-85346-969-3 / approx. 350pp

Mark F.W. Lovatt
Confronting the Will-to-Power
A Reconsideration of the Theology of Reinhold Niebuhr

Confronting the Will-to-Power is an analysis of the theology of Reinhold Niebuhr, arguing that his work is an attempt to identify, and provide a practical theological answer to, the existence and nature of human evil.

2001 / 1-84227-054-0 / xviii + 216pp

Neil B. MacDonald
Karl Barth and the Strange New World within the Bible
Barth, Wittgenstein, and the Metadilemmas of the Enlightenment

Barth's discovery of the strange new world within the Bible is examined in the context of Kant, Hume, Overbeck, and, most importantly, Wittgenstein. MacDonald covers some fundamental issues in theology today: epistemology, the final form of the text and biblical truth-claims.

2000 / 0-85364-970-7 / xxvi + 374pp

Keith A. Mascord
Alvin Plantinga and Christian Apologetics

This book draws together the contributions of the philosopher Alvin Plantinga to the major contemporary challenges to Christian belief, highlighting in particular his ground-breaking work in epistemology and the problem of evil. Plantinga's theory that both theistic and Christian belief is warrantedly basic is explored and critiqued, and an assessment offered as to the significance of his work for apologetic theory and practice.

2005 / 1-84227-256-X / approx. 304pp

Gillian McCulloch
The Deconstruction of Dualism in Theology
With Reference to Ecofeminist Theology and New Age Spirituality
This book challenges eco-theological anti-dualism in Christian theology, arguing that dualism has a twofold function in Christian religious discourse. Firstly, it enables us to express the discontinuities and divisions that are part of the process of reality. Secondly, dualistic language allows us to express the mysteries of divine transcendence/immanence and the survival of the soul without collapsing into monism and materialism, both of which are problematic for Christian epistemology.

2002 / 1-84227-044-3 / xii + 282pp

Leslie McCurdy
Attributes and Atonement
The Holy Love of God in the Theology of P.T. Forsyth
Attributes and Atonement is an intriguing full-length study of P.T. Forsyth's doctrine of the cross as it relates particularly to God's holy love. It includes an unparalleled bibliography of both primary and secondary material relating to Forsyth.

1999 / 0-85364-833-6 / xiv + 328pp

Nozomu Miyahira
Towards a Theology of the Concord of God
A Japanese Perspective on the Trinity
This book introduces a new Japanese theology and a unique Trinitarian formula based on the Japanese intellectual climate: three betweennesses and one concord. It also presents a new interpretation of the Trinity, a co-subordinationism, which is in line with orthodox Trinitarianism; each single person of the Trinity is eternally and equally subordinate (or serviceable) to the other persons, so that they retain the mutual dynamic equality.

2000 / 0-85364-863-8 / xiv + 256pp

Eddy José Muskus
The Origins and Early Development of Liberation Theology in Latin America
With Particular Reference to Gustavo Gutiérrez
This work challenges the fundamental premise of Liberation Theology, 'opting for the poor', and its claim that Christ is found in them. It also argues that Liberation Theology emerged as a direct result of the failure of the Roman Catholic Church in Latin America.

2002 / 0-85364-974-X / xiv + 296pp

Jim Purves
The Triune God and the Charismatic Movement
A Critical Appraisal from a Scottish Perspective

All emotion and no theology? Or a fundamental challenge to reappraise and realign our trinitarian theology in the light of Christian experience? This study of charismatic renewal as it found expression within Scotland at the end of the twentieth century evaluates the use of Patristic, Reformed and contemporary models of the Trinity in explaining the workings of the Holy Spirit.

2004 / 1-84227-321-3 / xxiv + 246pp

Anna Robbins
Methods in the Madness
Diversity in Twentieth-Century Christian Social Ethics

The author compares the ethical methods of Walter Rauschenbusch, Reinhold Niebuhr and others. She argues that unless Christians are clear about the ways that theology and philosophy are expressed practically they may lose the ability to discuss social ethics across contexts, let alone reach effective agreements.

2004 / 1-84227-211-X / xx + 294pp

Ed Rybarczyk
Beyond Salvation
Eastern Orthodoxy and Classical Pentecostalism on Becoming Like Christ

At first glance eastern Orthodoxy and classical Pentecostalism seem quite distinct. This ground-breaking study shows they share much in common, especially as it concerns the experiential elements of following Christ. Both traditions assert that authentic Christianity transcends the wooden categories of modernism.

2004 / 1-84227-144-X / xii + 356pp

Signe Sandsmark
Is World View Neutral Education Possible and Desirable?
A Christian Response to Liberal Arguments
(Published jointly with The Stapleford Centre)

This book discusses reasons for belief in world view neutrality, and argues that 'neutral' education will have a hidden, but strong world view influence. It discusses the place for Christian education in the common school.

2000 / 0-85364-973-1 / xiv + 182pp

Hazel Sherman
Reading Zechariah
The Allegorical Tradition of Biblical Interpretation through the Commentary of Didymus the Blind and Theodore of Mopsuestia
A close reading of the commentary on Zechariah by Didymus the Blind alongside that of Theodore of Mopsuestia suggests that popular categorising of Antiochene and Alexandrian biblical exegesis as 'historical' or 'allegorical' is inadequate and misleading.
2005 / 1-84227-213-6 / approx. 280pp

Andrew Sloane
On Being a Christian in the Academy
Nicholas Wolterstorff and the Practice of Christian Scholarship
An exposition and critical appraisal of Nicholas Wolterstorff's epistemology in the light of the philosophy of science, and an application of his thought to the practice of Christian scholarship.
2003 / 1-84227-058-3 / xvi + 274pp

Damon W.K. So
Jesus' Revelation of His Father
A Narrative-Conceptual Study of the Trinity with Special Reference to Karl Barth
This book explores the trinitarian dynamics in the context of Jesus' revelation of his Father in his earthly ministry with references to key passages in Matthew's Gospel. It develops from the exegeses of these passages a non-linear concept of revelation which links Jesus' communion with his Father to his revelatory words and actions through a nuanced understanding of the Holy Spirit, with references to K. Barth, G.W.H. Lampe, J.D.G. Dunn and E. Irving.
2005 / 1-84227-323-X / approx. 380pp

Daniel Strange
The Possibility of Salvation Among the Unevangelised
An Analysis of Inclusivism in Recent Evangelical Theology
For evangelical theologians the 'fate of the unevangelised' impinges upon fundamental tenets of evangelical identity. The position known as 'inclusivism', defined by the belief that the unevangelised can be ontologically saved by Christ whilst being epistemologically unaware of him, has been defended most vigorously by the Canadian evangelical Clark H. Pinnock. Through a detailed analysis and critique of Pinnock's work, this book examines a cluster of issues surrounding the unevangelised and its implications for christology, soteriology and the doctrine of revelation.
2002 / 1-84227-047-8 / xviii + 362pp

Scott Swain
God According to the Gospel
Biblical Narrative and the Identity of God in the Theology of Robert W. Jenson
Robert W. Jenson is one of the leading voices in contemporary Trinitarian theology. His boldest contribution in this area concerns his use of biblical narrative both to ground and explicate the Christian doctrine of God. *God According to the Gospel* critically examines Jenson's proposal and suggests an alternative way of reading the biblical portrayal of the triune God.
2006 / 1-84227-258-6 / approx. 180pp

Justyn Terry
The Justifying Judgement of God
A Reassessment of the Place of Judgement in the Saving Work of Christ
The argument of this book is that judgement, understood as the whole process of bringing justice, is the primary metaphor of atonement, with others, such as victory, redemption and sacrifice, subordinate to it. Judgement also provides the proper context for understanding penal substitution and the call to repentance, baptism, eucharist and holiness.
2005 / 1-84227-370-1 / approx. 274 pp

Graham Tomlin
The Power of the Cross
Theology and the Death of Christ in Paul, Luther and Pascal
This book explores the theology of the cross in St Paul, Luther and Pascal. It offers new perspectives on the theology of each, and some implications for the nature of power, apologetics, theology and church life in a postmodern context.
1999 / 0-85364-984-7 / xiv + 344pp

Adonis Vidu
Postliberal Theological Method
A Critical Study
The postliberal theology of Hans Frei, George Lindbeck, Ronald Thiemann, John Milbank and others is one of the more influential contemporary options. This book focuses on several aspects pertaining to its theological method, specifically its understanding of background, hermeneutics, epistemic justification, ontology, the nature of doctrine and, finally, Christological method.
2005 / 1-84227-395-7 / approx. 324pp

Graham J. Watts
Revelation and the Spirit
A Comparative Study of the Relationship between the Doctrine of Revelation and Pneumatology in the Theology of Eberhard Jüngel and of Wolfhart Pannenberg
The relationship between revelation and pneumatology is relatively unexplored. This approach offers a fresh angle on two important twentieth century theologians and raises pneumatological questions which are theologically crucial and relevant to mission in a postmodern culture.
2005 / 1-84227-104-0 / xxii + 232pp

Nigel G. Wright
Disavowing Constantine
Mission, Church and the Social Order in the Theologies of John Howard Yoder and Jürgen Moltmann
This book is a timely restatement of a radical theology of church and state in the Anabaptist and Baptist tradition. Dr Wright constructs his argument in dialogue and debate with Yoder and Moltmann, major contributors to a free church perspective.
2000 / 0-85364-978-2 / xvi + 252pp

Paternoster
9 Holdom Avenue,
Bletchley,
Milton Keynes MK1 1QR,
United Kingdom
Web: www.authenticmedia.co.uk/paternoster

Mark Bonnington
The Antioch Episode of Galatians 2:11-14 in Historical and Cultural Context

The Galatians 2 'incident' in Antioch over table-fellowship suggests significant disagreement between the leading apostles. This book analyses the background to the disagreement by locating the incident within the dynamics of social interaction between Jews and Gentiles. It proposes a new way of understanding the relationship between the individuals and issues involved.

2005 / 1-84227-050-8 / approx. 350pp

David Bostock
A Portrayal of Trust
The Theme of Faith in the Hezekiah Narratives

This study provides detailed and sensitive readings of the Hezekiah narratives (2 Kings 18–20 and Isaiah 36–39) from a theological perspective. It concentrates on the theme of faith, using narrative criticism as its methodology. Attention is paid especially to setting, plot, point of view and characterization within the narratives. A largely positive portrayal of Hezekiah emerges that underlines the importance and relevance of scripture.

2005 / 1-84227-314-0 / approx. 300pp

Mark Bredin
Jesus, Revolutionary of Peace
A Non-violent Christology in the Book of Revelation

This book aims to demonstrate that the figure of Jesus in the Book of Revelation can best be understood as an active non-violent revolutionary.

2003 / 1-84227-153-9 / xviii + 262pp

Robinson Butarbutar
Paul and Conflict Resolution
An Exegetical Study of Paul's Apostolic Paradigm in 1 Corinthians 9

The author sees the apostolic paradigm in 1 Corinthians 9 as part of Paul's unified arguments in 1 Corinthians 8–10 in which he seeks to mediate in the dispute over the issue of food offered to idols. The book also sees its relevance for dispute-resolution today, taking the conflict within the author's church as an example.

2006 / 1-84227-315-9 / approx. 280pp

Daniel J-S Chae
Paul as Apostle to the Gentiles
His Apostolic Self-awareness and its Influence on the Soteriological Argument in Romans
Opposing 'the post-Holocaust interpretation of Romans', Daniel Chae competently demonstrates that Paul argues for the equality of Jew and Gentile in Romans. Chae's fresh exegetical interpretation is academically outstanding and spiritually encouraging.
1997 / 0-85364-829-8 / xiv + 378pp

Luke L. Cheung
The Genre, Composition and Hermeneutics of the Epistle of James
The present work examines the employment of the wisdom genre with a certain compositional structure and the interpretation of the law through the Jesus tradition of the double love command by the author of the Epistle of James to serve his purpose in promoting perfection and warning against doubleness among the eschatologically renewed people of God in the Diaspora.
2003 / 1-84227-062-1 / xvi + 372pp

Youngmo Cho
Spirit and Kingdom in the Writings of Luke and Paul
The relationship between Spirit and Kingdom is a relatively unexplored area in Lukan and Pauline studies. This book offers a fresh perspective of two biblical writers on the subject. It explores the difference between Luke's and Paul's understanding of the Spirit by examining the specific question of the relationship of the concept of the Spirit to the concept of the Kingdom of God in each writer.
2005 / 1-84227-316-7 / approx. 270pp

Andrew C. Clark
Parallel Lives
The Relation of Paul to the Apostles in the Lucan Perspective
This study of the Peter-Paul parallels in Acts argues that their purpose was to emphasize the themes of continuity in salvation history and the unity of the Jewish and Gentile missions. New light is shed on Luke's literary techniques, partly through a comparison with Plutarch.
2001 / 1-84227-035-4 / xviii + 386pp

Andrew D. Clarke
Secular and Christian Leadership in Corinth
A Socio-Historical and Exegetical Study of 1 Corinthians 1–6
This volume is an investigation into the leadership structures and dynamics of first-century Roman Corinth. These are compared with the practice of leadership in the Corinthian Christian community which are reflected in 1 Corinthians 1–6, and contrasted with Paul's own principles of Christian leadership.
2005 / 1-84227-229-2 / 200pp

Stephen Finamore
God, Order and Chaos
René Girard and the Apocalypse
Readers are often disturbed by the images of destruction in the book of Revelation and unsure why they are unleashed after the exaltation of Jesus. This book examines past approaches to these texts and uses René Girard's theories to revive some old ideas and propose some new ones.
2005 / 1-84227-197-0 / approx. 344pp

David G. Firth
Surrendering Retribution in the Psalms
Responses to Violence in the Individual Complaints
In *Surrendering Retribution in the Psalms*, David Firth examines the ways in which the book of Psalms inculcates a model response to violence through the repetition of standard patterns of prayer. Rather than seeking justification for retributive violence, Psalms encourages not only a surrender of the right of retribution to Yahweh, but also sets limits on the retribution that can be sought in imprecations. Arising initially from the author's experience in South Africa, the possibilities of this model to a particular context of violence is then briefly explored.
2005 / 1-84227-337-X / xviii + 154pp

Scott J. Hafemann
Suffering and Ministry in the Spirit
Paul's Defence of His Ministry in II Corinthians 2:14–3:3
Shedding new light on the way Paul defended his apostleship, the author offers a careful, detailed study of 2 Corinthians 2:14–3:3 linked with other key passages throughout 1 and 2 Corinthians. Demonstrating the unity and coherence of Paul's argument in this passage, the author shows that Paul's suffering served as the vehicle for revealing God's power and glory through the Spirit.
2000 / 0-85364-967-7 / xiv + 262pp

Scott J. Hafemann
Paul, Moses and the History of Israel
The Letter/Spirit Contrast and the Argument from Scripture in 2 Corinthians 3
An exegetical study of the call of Moses, the second giving of the Law (Exodus 32–34), the new covenant, and the prophetic understanding of the history of Israel in 2 Corinthians 3. Hafemann's work demonstrates Paul's contextual use of the Old Testament and the essential unity between the Law and the Gospel within the context of the distinctive ministries of Moses and Paul.
2005 / 1-84227-317-5 / xii + 498pp

Douglas S. McComiskey
Lukan Theology in the Light of the Gospel's Literary Structure
Luke's Gospel was purposefully written with theology embedded in its patterned literary structure. A critical analysis of this cyclical structure provides new windows into Luke's interpretation of the individual pericopes comprising the Gospel and illuminates several of his theological interests.
2004 / 1-84227-148-2 / xviii + 388pp

Stephen Motyer
Your Father the Devil?
A New Approach to John and 'The Jews'
Who are 'the Jews' in John's Gospel? Defending John against the charge of antisemitism, Motyer argues that, far from demonising the Jews, the Gospel seeks to present Jesus as 'Good News for Jews' in a late first century setting.
1997 / 0-85364-832-8 / xiv + 260pp

Esther Ng
Reconstructing Christian Origins?
The Feminist Theology of Elizabeth Schüssler Fiorenza: An Evaluation
In a detailed evaluation, the author challenges Elizabeth Schüssler Fiorenza's reconstruction of early Christian origins and her underlying presuppositions. The author also presents her own views on women's roles both then and now.
2002 / 1-84227-055-9 / xxiv + 468pp

Robin Parry
Old Testament Story and Christian Ethics
The Rape of Dinah as a Case Study

What is the role of story in ethics and, more particularly, what is the role of Old Testament story in Christian ethics? This book, drawing on the work of contemporary philosophers, argues that narrative is crucial in the ethical shaping of people and, drawing on the work of contemporary Old Testament scholars, that story plays a key role in Old Testament ethics. Parry then argues that when situated in canonical context Old Testament stories can be reappropriated by Christian readers in their own ethical formation. The shocking story of the rape of Dinah and the massacre of the Shechemites provides a fascinating case study for exploring the parameters within which Christian ethical appropriations of Old Testament stories can live.

2004 / 1-84227-210-1 / xx + 350pp

Ian Paul
Power to See the World Anew
The Value of Paul Ricoeur's Hermeneutic of Metaphor in Interpreting the Symbolism of Revelation 12 and 13

This book is a study of the hermeneutics of metaphor of Paul Ricoeur, one of the most important writers on hermeneutics and metaphor of the last century. It sets out the key points of his theory, important criticisms of his work, and how his approach, modified in the light of these criticisms, offers a methodological framework for reading apocalyptic texts.

***2006** / 1-84227-056-7 / approx. 350pp*

Robert L. Plummer
Paul's Understanding of the Church's Mission
Did the Apostle Paul Expect the Early Christian Communities to Evangelize?
This book engages in a careful study of Paul's letters to determine if the apostle expected the communities to which he wrote to engage in missionary activity. It helpfully summarizes the discussion on this debated issue, judiciously handling contested texts, and provides a way forward in addressing this critical question. While admitting that Paul rarely explicitly commands the communities he founded to evangelize, Plummer amasses significant incidental data to provide a convincing case that Paul did indeed expect his churches to engage in mission activity. Throughout the study, Plummer progressively builds a theological basis for the church's mission that is both distinctively Pauline and compelling.

***2006** / 1-84227-333-7 / approx. 324pp*

David Powys
'Hell': A Hard Look at a Hard Question
The Fate of the Unrighteous in New Testament Thought
This comprehensive treatment seeks to unlock the original meaning of terms and phrases long thought to support the traditional doctrine of hell. It concludes that there is an alternative—one which is more biblical, and which can positively revive the rationale for Christian mission.

1997 / 0-85364-831-X / xxii + 478pp

Sorin Sabou
Between Horror and Hope
Paul's Metaphorical Language of Death in Romans 6.1-11
This book argues that Paul's metaphorical language of death in Romans 6.1-11 conveys two aspects: horror and hope. The 'horror' aspect is conveyed by the 'crucifixion' language, and the 'hope' aspect by 'burial' language. The life of the Christian believer is understood, as relationship with sin is concerned ('death to sin'), between these two realities: horror and hope.

2005 / 1-84227-322-1 / approx. 224pp

Rosalind Selby
The Comical Doctrine
The Epistemology of New Testament Hermeneutics
This book argues that the gospel breaks through postmodernity's critique of truth and the referential possibilities of textuality with its gift of grace. With a rigorous, philosophical challenge to modernist and postmodernist assumptions, Selby offers an alternative epistemology to all who would still read with faith *and* with academic credibility.

2005 / 1-84227-212-8 / approx. 350pp

Kiwoong Son
Zion Symbolism in Hebrews
Hebrews 12.18-24 as a Hermeneutical Key to the Epistle
This book challenges the general tendency of understanding the Epistle to the Hebrews against a Hellenistic background and suggests that the Epistle should be understood in the light of the Jewish apocalyptic tradition. The author especially argues for the importance of the theological symbolism of Sinai and Zion (Heb. 12:18-24) as it provides the Epistle's theological background as well as the rhetorical basis of the superiority motif of Jesus throughout the Epistle.

2005 / 1-84227-368-X / approx. 280pp

Kevin Walton
Thou Traveller Unknown
The Presence and Absence of God in the Jacob Narrative
The author offers a fresh reading of the story of Jacob in the book of Genesis through the paradox of divine presence and absence. The work also seeks to make a contribution to Pentateuchal studies by bringing together a close reading of the final text with historical critical insights, doing justice to the text's historical depth, final form and canonical status.
2003 / 1-84227-059-1 / xvi + 238pp

George M. Wieland
The Significance of Salvation
A Study of Salvation Language in the Pastoral Epistles
The language and ideas of salvation pervade the three Pastoral Epistles. This study offers a close examination of their soteriological statements. In all three letters the idea of salvation is found to play a vital paraenetic role, but each also exhibits distinctive soteriological emphases. The results challenge common assumptions about the Pastoral Epistles as a corpus.
2005 / 1-84227-257-8 / approx. 324pp

Alistair Wilson
When Will These Things Happen?
A Study of Jesus as Judge in Matthew 21–25
This study seeks to allow Matthew's carefully constructed presentation of Jesus to be given full weight in the modern evaluation of Jesus' eschatology. Careful analysis of the text of Matthew 21–25 reveals Jesus to be standing firmly in the Jewish prophetic and wisdom traditions as he proclaims and enacts imminent judgement on the Jewish authorities then boldly claims the central role in the final and universal judgement.
2004 / 1-84227-146-6 / xxii + 272pp

Lindsay Wilson
Joseph Wise and Otherwise
The Intersection of Covenant and Wisdom in Genesis 37–50
This book offers a careful literary reading of Genesis 37–50 that argues that the Joseph story contains both strong covenant themes and many wisdom-like elements. The connections between the two helps to explore how covenant and wisdom might intersect in an integrated biblical theology.
2004 / 1-84227-140-7 / xvi + 340pp

Stephen I. Wright
The Voice of Jesus
Studies in the Interpretation of Six Gospel Parables
This literary study considers how the 'voice' of Jesus has been heard in different periods of parable interpretation, and how the categories of figure and trope may help us towards a sensitive reading of the parables today.
2000 / 0-85364-975-8 / xiv + 280pp

Paternoster
9 Holdom Avenue,
Bletchley,
Milton Keynes MK1 1QR,
United Kingdom
Web: www.authenticmedia.co.uk/paternoster

July 2005

www.ingramcontent.com/pod-product-compliance
Lightning Source LLC
Chambersburg PA
CBHW060605230426
43670CB00011B/1986